ULTIMATE Island Escapes

AUSTRALIA

EMMA SHAW

Hardie Grant
EXPLORE

Above Sunset from Fitzroy Island

Map of Australia	iv
Region maps	vi
Welcome to island life	ix
Island hopping around Australia	x
The ultimate island packing guide	xii
A seasonal island travel planner	xiv
Wildlife on the islands	xvi
Booking your island getaway	xviii
Island sustainability	xviii
The best of the best	xx

Luxury getaways	**1**
Lizard Island/Dyiigurra, Qld	2
Hayman Island, Qld	9
Orpheus Island/Goolboddi, Qld	16
Island Hopping: Long Island, Qld	25
Bedarra Island/Biagurra, Qld	26
Tiwi Islands, NT	33
Family fun	**39**
Hamilton Island, Qld	40
Rottnest Island/Wadjemup, WA	49
Magnetic Island/Yunbenun, Qld	56
Moreton Island/Mulgumpin, Qld	63
Island Hopping: Granite Island, SA	68
Great Keppel Island/Wop-pa, Qld	71
North Stradbroke Island/Minjerribah, Qld	76
Adventure awaits	**83**
Dirk Hartog Island/Wirruwana, WA	84
Christmas Island, Indian Ocean Territories	91
Island Hopping: Abrolhos Islands, WA	98

K'gari, Qld	101
Kangaroo Island, SA	109
Hinchinbrook Island/Munamudanamy, Qld	116
Island Hopping: Dunk Island/Coonanglebah, Qld	122

Best of the Great Barrier Reef — 125

Heron Island, Qld	126
Lady Elliot Island, Qld	132
Island Hopping: Frankland Islands, Qld	140
Lady Musgrave Island, Qld	142
Fitzroy Island/Koba, Qld	148
Island Hopping: Whitsunday Island, Qld	157

Off-the-beaten track — 159

Cocos (Keeling) Islands, Indian Ocean Territories	160
Mackerel Islands, WA	168
Pumpkin Island, Qld	174
Island Hopping: Crab Claw Island, NT	180
Torres Strait Islands, Qld	182
Maria Island, Tas	189
Island Hopping: Picnic Island, Tas	195

Island towns — 197

Lord Howe Island, NSW	198
Norfolk Island, Independent Territory	205
Flinders Island, Tas	210
Island Hopping: Cockatoo Island/Wareamah, NSW	217
King Island, Tas	218
Phillip Island/Millowl, Vic	227
Bruny Island/Lunawanna-alonnah, Tas	232

Index	238
Acknowledgments	246
About the author	246

Map of Australia

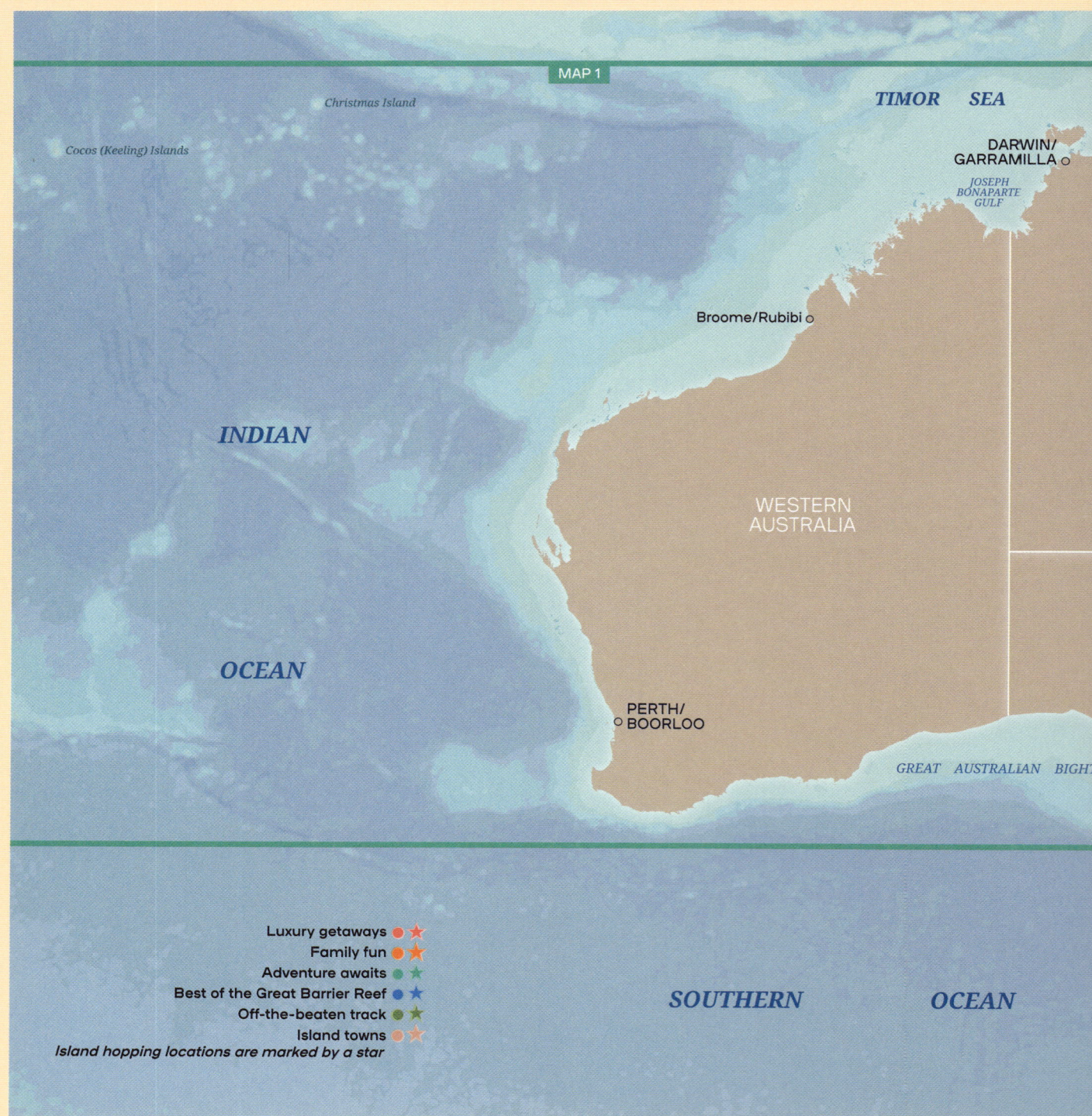

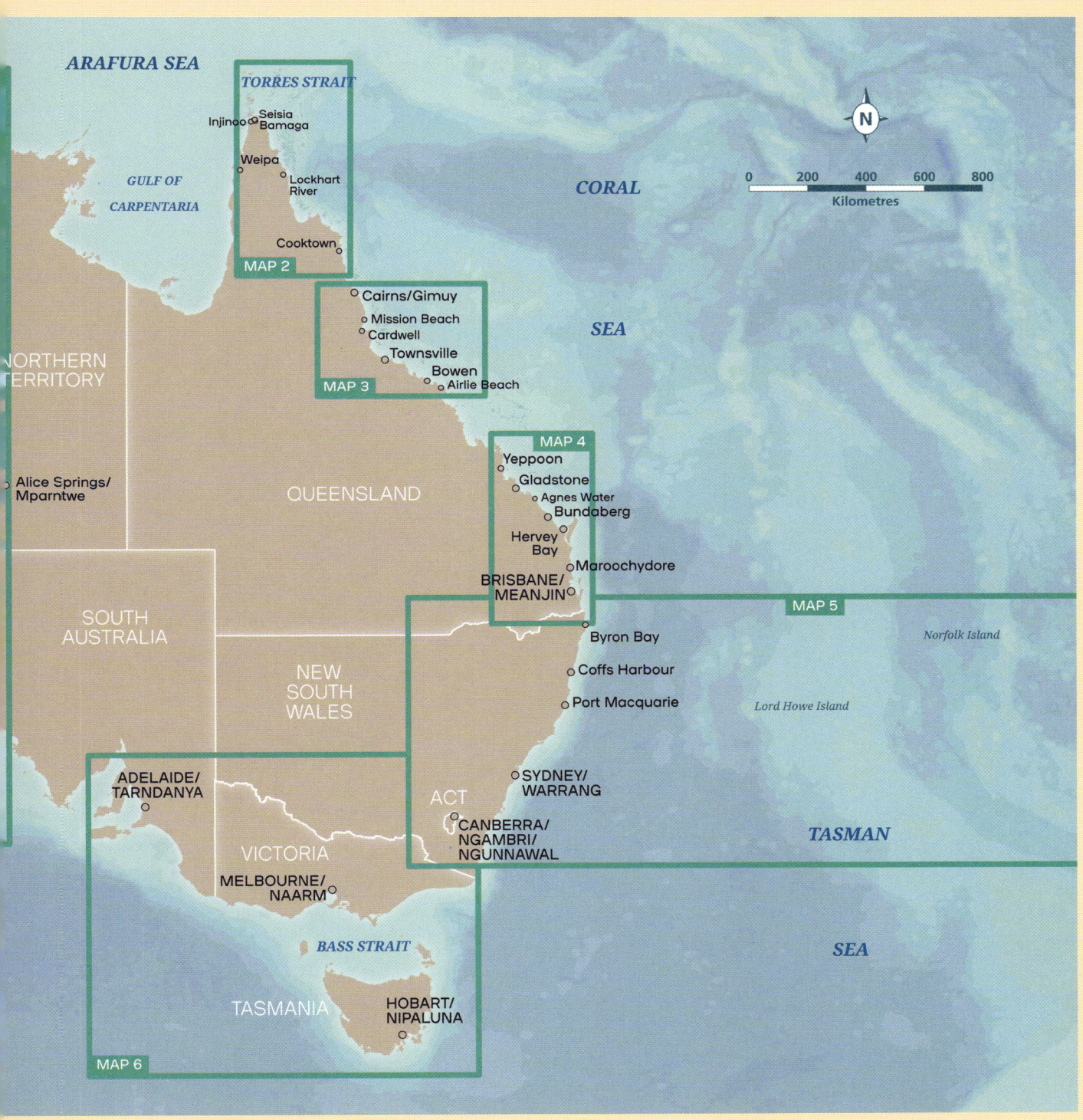

Map of Australia

Region maps

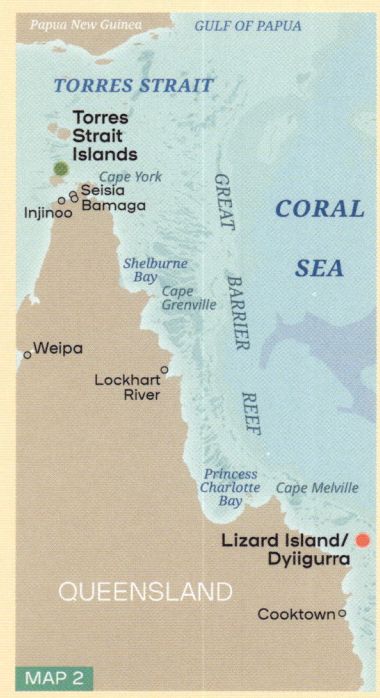

MAP 1
Christmas Island
Cocos (Keeling) Islands
TIMOR SEA
Tiwi Islands
Melville Island
Bathurst Island
DARWIN/GARRAMILLA
Crab Claw Island
Broome/Rubibi
INDIAN
OCEAN
NINGALOO REEF
Mackerel Islands
WESTERN AUSTRALIA
NT
SA
Dirk Hartog Island/Wirruwana
Abrolhos Islands
HOUTMAN ABROLHOS
PERTH/BOORLOO
Rottnest Island/Wadjemup
GREAT AUSTRALIAN BIGHT
ARCHIPELAGO OF THE RECHERCHE

Byron Bay
Norfolk Island
Coffs Harbour
NEW SOUTH WALES
Port Macquarie
Lord Howe Island
SYDNEY/ WARRANG
Cockatoo Island/Wareamah
ACT
CANBERRA/ NGAMBRI/NGUNNAWAL
TASMAN
SEA
MAP 5

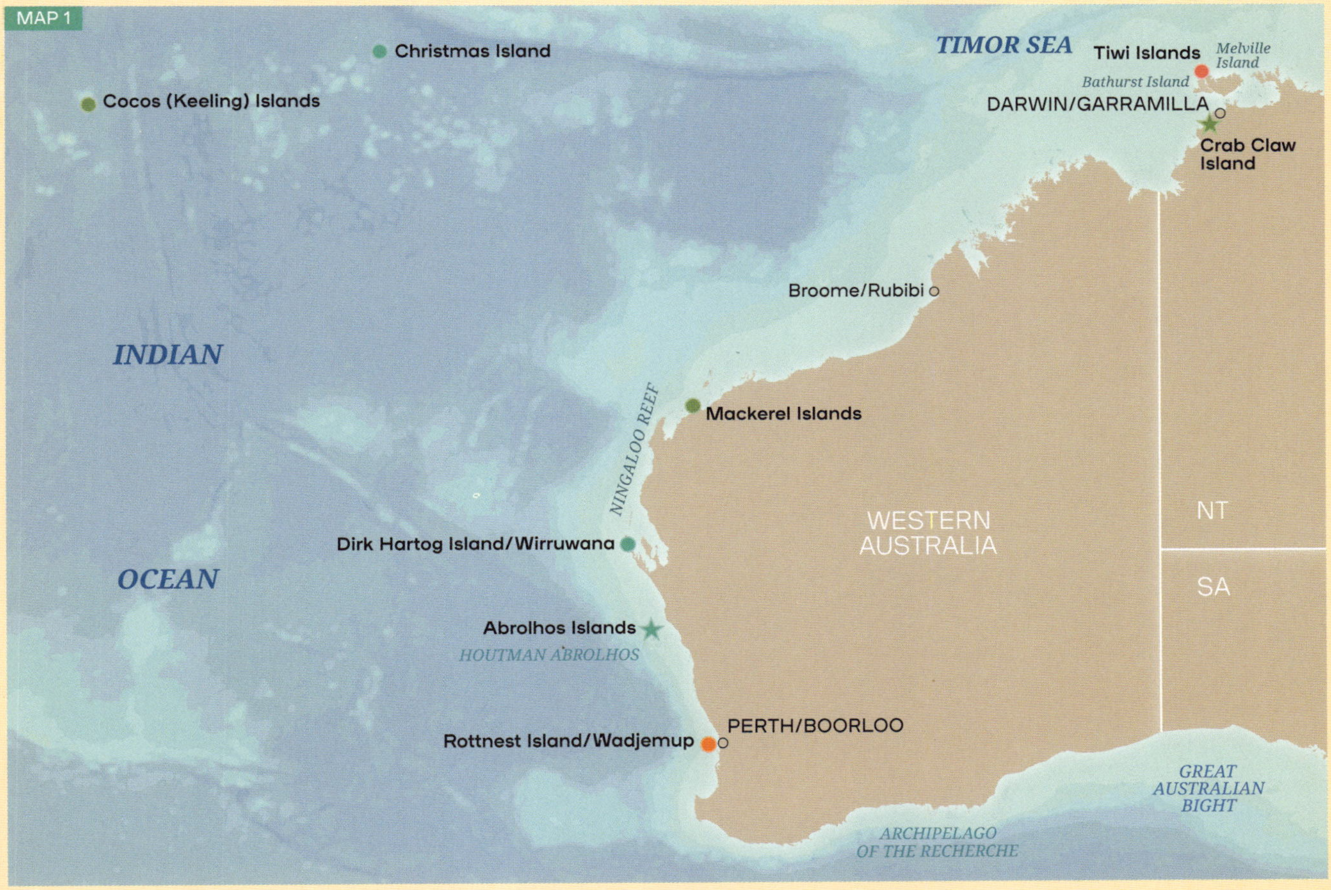

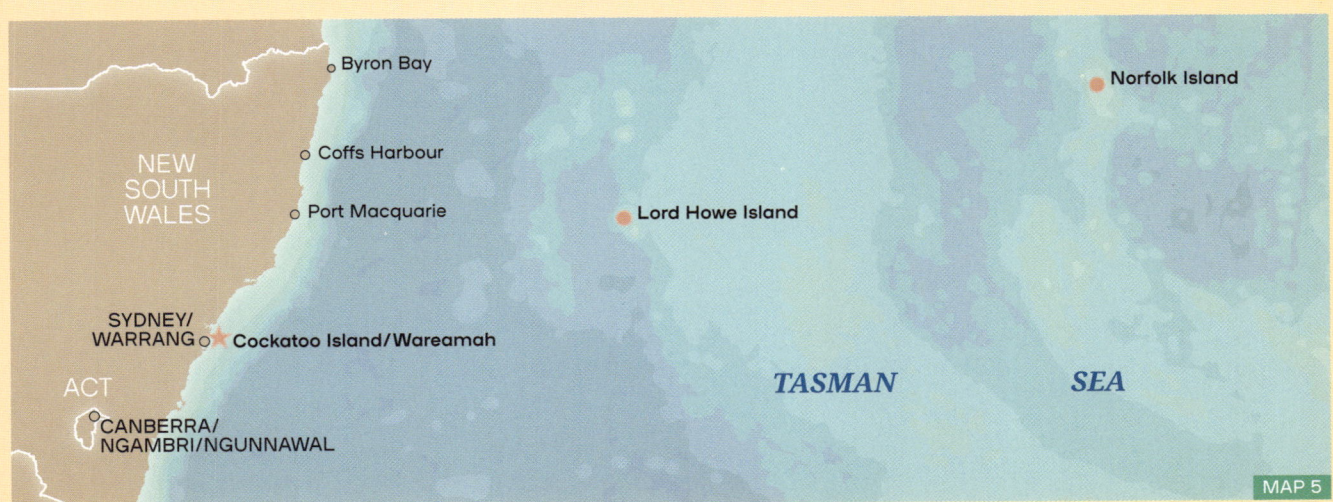

Welcome to island life

ISLAND HOPPING AROUND AUSTRALIA

It's been a big year of travel for our little family. After criss-crossing Australia on land in our vintage caravan (and sharing those adventures in *Ultimate Weekends: Australia*), we thought it might be time to spend a little time offshore, island hopping our way across the many beautiful islands that lie off the coast of Australia's mainland.

From the Tiwi Islands (*see* p.33) in the north, to Bruny Island/Lunawanna-alonnah (*see* p.232) in the south, we island hopped around the country for a year, experiencing turtles nesting and hatching on the beach, whale season during the migration, snorkelling in the largest coral reef in the world, World Heritage–listed Sites, beach driving, cultural workshops, epic landscapes and the incredible local food and drinks the Aussie islands are famous for.

Most of us think of bright white sand, palm tree–lined shores and sparkling turquoise water when we picture an island, and although Australia boasts these aplenty, there are also lots of different types of island experiences around the country. From off-the-beaten track adventures, wildlife experiences, and completely private islands, to fun for the whole family, adults-only islands, fishing meccas, and cultural trips.

Every island offers something completely new and unique. From beach camping under the stars to the epitome of luxury stays and everything in between, you can find every type of holiday on the islands surrounding Australia. You don't need to necessarily have a big budget for an island holiday either – some, like Magnetic Island/Yunbenun (*see* p.56) in Queensland and Rottnest Island/Wadjemup (*see* p.49) in WA, are accessible by a short ferry trip from a city as a daytrip, or require nothing more than campsite fees. It's choosing which island you want to visit that's the hardest part.

Whilst Australia is often considered an island itself to international visitors, as it doesn't share any land borders with other countries, we also have 8222 separate islands sitting off the coastline of the country. Australia is home to two different types of islands – continental islands that were once connected to the mainland, breaking off and creating distance after the most recent ice age thousands of years ago, such as Great Keppel Island/Wop-pa (*see* p.71) and Kangaroo Island (*see* p.109), whilst oceanic islands are created in the ocean, from rising volcanoes, moving sand masses or mountains of coral initially held together by bird poop, like Heron Island (*see* p.126), Lady Elliot Island (*see* p.132) and Christmas Island (*see* p.91).

The logistics of trying to visit so many of Australia's islands in a single year to create this book was no easy feat. Especially for our daughter Macey, who in her short little two-year-old life has been on 60 flights, including 12 small planes, 25 ferry transfers, four helicopters, a seaplane and a train, as well as countless boating excursions, to accomplish this mission. After all that travel and adventure, we present to you 40 of the best islands around Australia to add to your bucket-list. Which one will you visit first?

Emma & Thom Shaw

@exploreshaw | exploreshaw.com

Acknowledgement of Country

We acknowledge the Traditional Owners of Country throughout Australia, and recognise their continuing connection to land, waters and culture. We pay our respects to Elders past and present, and are thankful for the opportunity to travel through so many lands and waters during our travels.

As you embark on your travels around Australia, we encourage you to always be mindful and respectful of the lands and waters, and their Traditional Custodians, as well as ensure you always respect places of spiritual significance you visit along the way.

Previous Aerial views over Lizard Island/Dyiigurra and Anchor Bay *Opposite* You can always find a quiet beach on an island

THE ULTIMATE ISLAND PACKING GUIDE

When you think of packing for an island getaway it's normally all the fun things, right? Your swimwear, a pair of thongs (flip-flops), cute sunglasses and a big sun hat. We've included some other island essentials that are always good to throw in your bag as well. This isn't a definitive packing list but no matter which island you're exploring around Australia, you're going to be happy you thought of packing these things.

Reef-safe sunscreen

Obviously the first thing you throw into your bag when packing for an island getaway is your sunscreen – but is your sunscreen safe for the reef? Chances are you're planning to spend a lot of your island time swimming, snorkelling, maybe even diving to explore a reef, so it's important that your sunscreen is free from chemicals that may be damaging to the corals and marine life that you're visiting. Some tips to choosing a 'reef-safe' or 'reef-friendly' sunscreen is to choose one free from oxybenzone and octinoxate, two ingredients that have been proven to hurt reefs, but also try to ensure your sunscreen is free from cinnamates and parabens. Rub-on lotions with good water resistance are also a good choice, as they stay on the body longer than spray-on options.

Underwater camera

With so many of Australia's islands offering incredible coral reefs, marine life and all kinds of underwater worlds to explore, you're definitely going to want something to capture your travels. A handy GoPro is always a great go-to for underwater photos and videos, or you can even just buy a protective case for your phone. Just make sure you have something, as you'll definitely want a photo swimming with that beautiful turtle!

Travel calm tablets

Between ferries across the ocean, small planes and helicopters, you're often travelling across some pretty bumpy conditions to get to an island. It's always a good idea to bring along something to help with motion sickness, because you never know when it might hit for the first time. There's plenty of options to choose from these days, from traditional travel calm tablets and ginger tablets to calming travel bands. Have a chat with your GP or pharmacist to choose the right option for you.

Mosquito repellent

Islands are often notorious for mozzies, midges and sandflies, and lots of little itchy bites is definitely not what you want when you're living your best life on an island. It's always a great idea to have repellent in your bag, just in case. We have found that Mozzie Patches by Natural Patch Co. are a great option for babies and young kids too.

Travel insurance

Due to their remote ocean locations, travel to islands can often be disrupted by weather, including strong winds, torrential rain, storms and even cyclones in northern Australia – in fact, a cyclone got in our way while we were on Cocos (Keeling) Islands, and we ended up spending an extra, unplanned couple of days there. Purchase travel insurance before travelling to cover you in case of cancellation or delays that impact your other plans. Domestic travel insurance policies can be quite cheap and will give you peace of mind, just in case.

Insulated water bottle

In an effort to take care of the environment, many islands are free of single-use plastic including plastic water bottles. It's a good idea to always travel with your own drink bottle, which you can keep topping up in your room or at drinking water refill stations, depending on the island's water situation. To keep your water cool in warm island temperatures, an insulated water bottle works the best.

Reef shoes

If you're visiting an island that is predominately made up of coral (such as Fitzroy Island/Koba, see p.148, or Lady Elliot Island, see p.132), or you're planning to do lots of reef walking or snorkelling, it's a good idea to bring your own reef shoes. The Crocs brand is a great option, and when you bring your own it'll save you having to use communal reef shoes.

Beach towels

Many island accommodations actually don't include beach towels to use during your stay, so it's always a good idea to pack one. If your luggage space is limited, you can get small quick-dry towels or Turkish-style cotton towels that are more lightweight than traditional beach towels.

Overlooking Turtle Bay on East Wallabi Island in the Abrolhos Islands

A SEASONAL ISLAND TRAVEL PLANNER

Not sure which island to visit when? With so many incredible islands to travel to around Australia, you could easily go to a different one every month of the year. Here's your guide to island planning, with the best time to visit each of them.

JANUARY

Kangaroo Island, SA (see p.109)

Phillip Island/Millowl, Victoria (see p.227)

Flinders Island, Tasmania (see p.210)

FEBRUARY

Heron Island, Queensland (see p.126)

Lady Elliot Island, Queensland (see p.132)

Lady Musgrave Island, Queensland (see p.142)

MARCH

Maria Island, Tasmania (see p.189)

Picnic Island, Tasmania (see p.195)

King Island, Tasmania (see p.218)

Bruny Island/Lunawanna-alonnah, Tasmania (see p.232)

APRIL

Rottnest Island/Wadjemup, WA (see p.49)

Abrolhos Islands, WA (see p.98)

Hinchinbrook Island/Munamudanamy, Queensland (see p.116)

MAY

Dirk Hartog Island/Wirruwana, WA (see p.84)

Lizard Island/Dyiigurra, Queensland (see p.2)

Frankland Islands, Queensland (see p.140)

JUNE

Tiwi Islands, NT (see p.33)

Bedarra Island/Biagurra, Queensland (see p.26)

Mackerel Islands, WA (see p.168)

Torres Strait Islands, Queensland (see p.182)

JULY

K'gari, Queensland (see p.101)

Fitzroy Island/Koba, Queensland (see p.148)

Magnetic Island/Yunbenun, Queensland (see p.56)

Crab Claw Island, NT (see p.180)

AUGUST

Cocos (Keeling) Islands, Indian Ocean Territories (see p.160)

Christmas Island, Indian Ocean Territories (see p.91)

North Stradbroke Island/Minjerribah, Queensland (see p.76)

SEPTEMBER

Hamilton Island, Queensland (*see* p.40)

Hayman Island, Queensland (*see* p.9)

Dunk Island/Coonanglebah, Queensland (*see* p.122)

Whitsunday Island, Queensland (*see* p.157)

OCTOBER

Orpheus Island/Goolboddi, Queensland (*see* p.16)

Moreton Island/Mulgumpin, Queensland (*see* p.63)

Long Island, Queensland (*see* p.25)

NOVEMBER

Pumpkin Island, Queensland (*see* p.174)

Great Keppel Island/Wop-pa, Queensland (*see* p.71)

Cockatoo Island/Wareamah, NSW (*see* p.217)

DECEMBER

Norfolk Island, Independent Territory (*see* p.205)

Lord Howe Island, NSW (*see* p.198)

Granite Island, SA (*see* p.68)

Top Nudey Beach on Fitzroy Island *Bottom* Aerial view over Fitzroy Island jetty

A seasonal island travel planner   xv

WILDLIFE ON THE ISLANDS

If you're planning your island escape in the hopes of having a particular wildlife experience, here's a quick guide to where to go and when so that you have the best chance of the most incredible animal encounters.

Turtles

Swimming with a sea turtle is high on every island hopper's bucket-list, and can be achieved year-round from most islands on the Great Barrier Reef. However, for an extra special experience, the islands of the Southern Great Barrier Reef, predominantly Heron Island (see p.126), Wilson Island (see p.129) and Lady Elliot Island (see p.132), have female turtles coming to the shore to lay their eggs from November to March, and then hundreds of tiny hatchlings emerging from their nests and making the run for the water from January until May. February is a great time to plan your visit, when you have a good chance of experiencing both nesting turtles and the baby hatchlings.

Whales

Humpback whales migrate north to breed early in the season, and then head back south with their new calves, passing by many islands on both the eastern and western sides of Australia. Whale season is generally from June to October, with mesmerising whale watching experiences from both the land and boating excursions found on K'gari (see p.101), North Stradbroke Island/Minjerribah (see p.76) and Moreton Island/Mulgumpin (see p.63) along the East Coast and the Mackerel Islands (see p.168) and Dirk Hartog Island/Wirruwana (see p.84) on the West Coast. The waters surrounding K'gari are an exceptionally good place to see whale calves, as whales often stop here to let their new babies play and feed before heading south. You can also see Southern right whales migrating past Kangaroo Island (see p.109) in SA.

Sea Lions

Get up close and personal with a colony of Australian sea lions at Seal Bay on Kangaroo Island (see p.109) in SA. On a guided walk down to the beach you can watch as these cheeky animals play, swim and eat together, with the older sea lions lazing in the sun and the younger pups chasing each other in and out of the water. Phillip Island/Millowl (see p.227) in Victoria offers a cruise to see its huge population of sea lions, who aren't afraid to swim up to the boat and show you their tricks.

Quokkas

If you're in search of the world's happiest animal, head straight to Rottnest Island/Wadjemup (see p.49) in WA. The country's largest population of the smiling marsupial, quokkas can be found all over Rotto, especially around the main little town and the football field, as well as all around the glamping tents of Discovery Rottnest Island. Quokkas are most active in the late afternoon, however you can also spot them snoozing in the shade throughout the day.

Koalas

If you're looking for koalas, there are plenty of islands to spot them on, mainly on the southern and East Coast islands. Head to the Koala Conservation Reserve on Phillip Island/Millowl (see p.227) in Victoria; Hanson Bay on Kangaroo Island (see p.109) in SA; the Forts Walk on Magnetic Island/Yunbenun (see p.56), or pretty much anywhere around North Stradbroke Island/Minjerribah (see p.76), both in Queensland. All of these islands have large populations of wild koalas that can be spotted year-round high up in the trees.

Top Green turtle swimming around Lady Musgrave Island
Middle Australian sea lion on Seal Bay, Kangaroo Island
Bottom Smiley quokka at Pinky's, Rottnest Island/Wadjemup

Red Crabs

The red crab migration on Christmas Island (*see* p.91) is an unbelievable sight to see. Starting when the first rains of the summer begin to fall (generally in December) and lasting for 18 days, more than 50 million red crabs come out of the rainforest and make their way to the ocean where they mate for the season. Whole parts of the island are completely covered in a sea of red, so much so that island authorities have set up specific crab bridges to help them cross the roads safely. It's a remarkable experience if you can time your visit just right. Even the locals find it amazing how the crabs just know when it's time to migrate.

Wombats

Often not an island animal, but wombats can be found on the islands surrounding Tasmania, most famously on Maria Island (*see* p.189), where they often come out in the early morning or late afternoon for a grassy snack. It's a great place for wombat sightings year-round, as well as for spotting little baby wombats – called joeys. Wombats can also be spotted on Flinders Island (*see* p.210), snoozing in their burrows along the road on the way to Palana Beach.

Crocodiles

Although most islands are free from crocodiles and their waters are safe for swimming, there are a few exceptions, the main ones being the Tiwi Islands (*see* p.33) and Crab Claw Island (*see* p.180) in the NT (and some Queensland islands too). There is a definite 'do not swim' policy in the waters of both of these islands, as crocodile sightings can be a regular occurrence, especially around Tiwi Island Retreat where their resident crocodile Claudia hangs out during the day, coming into shore at night to see if she can snatch any leftover fish. Follow all crocodile warning signs and local advice and check information before you travel.

Wildlife on the islands

BOOKING YOUR ISLAND GETAWAY

With small capacities and limited availability on many islands, it's always a good idea to book your island adventure well in advance. Everything from accommodation and campsites to island transfers, ferries, car rental, tours and restaurant reservations can often be booked out well in advance, especially if you're hoping to travel during school holidays or across public holiday long weekends. Check the availability for every part of your trip before booking any of it, so as to make sure there's availability across the board.

It's important to note that some islands featured in this book also require you to BYO food and drinks for the duration of your visit, but we've shared the details in the relevant island entries.

Island hopping might require a little more forethought and planning than a quick city escape, but it will all be worth it once you get there!

ISLAND SUSTAINABILITY

Most islands have a strong focus on sustainability. With unique and fragile ecosystems, as well as limited options for waste management and water conservation, it's important to do your part to protect the island environments you're travelling on.

Some small ways that can make a massive difference include wearing reef-safe sunscreen, never touching or standing on any reefs, coral or wildlife you encounter, taking reusable water bottles to avoid single-use plastic, hanging up your towels to use again the next day, and always taking all your rubbish with you.

Many islands provide walks and talks that share their approach to sustainability, so check out the tours and presentations available to find out more.

Opposite The golden hour over Orpheus Island/Goolboddi

THE BEST OF THE BEST

Best islands for families
Hamilton Island, Queensland (see p.40)

Rottnest Island/Wadjemup, WA (see p.49)

Moreton Island/Mulgumpin, Queensland (see p.63)

Best islands for couples
Hayman Island, Queensland (see p.9)

Lizard Island/Dyiigurra, Queensland (see p.2)

Cocos (Keeling) Islands, Indian Ocean Territories (see p.160)

Orpheus Island/Goolboddi, Queensland (see p.16)

Best islands for camping
K'gari, Queensland (see p.101)

North Stradbroke Island/Minjerribah, Queensland (see p.76)

Moreton Island/Mulgumpin, Queensland (see p.63)

Best adventure islands
Christmas Island, Indian Ocean Territories (see p.91)

Dirk Hartog Island/Wirruwana, WA (see p.84)

Hinchinbrook Island/Munamudanamy, Queensland (see p.116)

Kangaroo Island, SA (see p.109)

Best islands for First Nations culture
Tiwi Islands, NT (see p.33)

Torres Strait Islands, Queensland (see p.182)

Rottnest Island/Wadjemup, WA (see p.49)

Best islands for wildlife encounters
Turtles, Heron Island, Queensland (see p.126)

Quokkas, Rottnest Island/Wadjemup, WA (see p.49)

Whale watching, North Stradbroke Island/Minjerribah, Queensland (see p.76)

Best all-inclusive luxury islands
Lizard Island/Dyiigurra, Queensland (see p.2)

Orpheus Island/Goolboddi, Queensland (see p.16)

Bedarra Island/Biagurra, Queensland (see p.26)

Easiest islands to get to
Magnetic Island/Yunbenun, Queensland (see p.56)

Rottnest Island/Wadjemup, WA (see p.49)

Great Keppel Island/Wop-pa, Queensland (see p.71)

Cockatoo Island/Wareamah, NSW (see p.217)

Best islands for beach driving
K'gari, Queensland (see p.101)

Moreton Island/Mulgumpin, Queensland (see p.63)

Kangaroo Island, SA (see p.109)

Off-the-beaten track islands
Cocos (Keeling) Islands, Indian Ocean Territories (see p.160)

Mackerel Islands, WA (see p.168)

Norfolk Island, Independent Territory (see p.205)

Best islands for embracing winter

Flinders Island, Tasmania (*see* p.210)

Bruny Island/Lunawanna-alonnah, Tasmania (*see* p.232)

Phillip Island/Millowl, Victoria (*see* p.227)

Best islands for foodies

King Island, Tasmania (*see* p.218)

Lizard Island/Dyiigurra, Queensland (*see* p.2)

Bruny Island/Lunawanna-alonnah, Tasmania (*see* p.232)

Left The beach on Hayman Island *Right* Sunset on Orpheus Island/Goolboddi

Luxury getaways

Lizard Island/Dyiigurra, Queensland................. 2
Hayman Island, Queensland....... 9
Orpheus Island/Goolboddi, Queensland................ 16
Island Hopping: Long Island, Queensland........... 25
Bedarra Island/Biagurra, Queensland................. 26
Tiwi Islands, NT................ 33

Lizard Island/Dyiigurra

An incredible all-inclusive luxury island experience

TROPICAL NORTH QUEENSLAND, QUEENSLAND

If you're looking for luxury island experiences in Australia, Lizard Island/Dyiigurra is the one to beat. A tiny little island, only about 10sqkm in size, surrounded by a lagoon of incredible blue water, it floats at the top of the Great Barrier Reef, and is the northernmost island on the reef. A national park since 1939, Lizard Island is one of the most unique and special little islands found off the coast of Tropical North Queensland. Home to its namesake luxury resort, you'll be blown away by not only the beauty of the island, but also the experience of staying at Lizard Island Resort.

Lizard Island immerses you in luxury from the minute you land. As you step off the plane a golf cart transfer is waiting, which takes you directly to the resort entrance, where you'll be greeted by your own personal waiter, champagne and cheese plate in hand, to welcome you to the resort and answer any questions you may have about your stay. A worthy member of the prestigious Luxury Lodges of Australia, every detail of your experience has been considered and executed perfectly on Lizard Island, making it the ultimate place of indulgence, relaxation and tranquility.

Known as Dyiigurra to the Dingaal Traditional Owners, which means stingray, the Lizard group of islands are believed to have been created in the Dreaming and were used for the initiation of young males, as well as for the harvesting of shellfish, turtles, dugongs and fish. Lizard Island was given its English name by Captain Cook, due to the abundance of yellow-spotted monitor lizards that run across the island. They're still living on the island today, and you're likely to spot a few during your stay.

Luxury getaways

TIME ZONE: AEST (GMT +10)
BEST TIME TO VISIT: May to Oct
ACCESSIBLE FROM: Cairns
GETTING THERE: Charter flight
PHONE RECEPTION: No
WI-FI: Yes
DAYTRIPS: No
KID FRIENDLY: Kids over 10 years old are welcome
SOCIALS: @lizardisland
MORE INFO: lizardisland.com.au

THE BEST BITS

Immerse yourself in total luxury on Lizard Island/Dyiigurra, where everything is included and taken care of for you. With stunning spacious rooms that look out to the turquoise waters of the lagoon, an ever-changing menu of gourmet meals, and nothing but peace, calm and tranquility, it's sure to be an exceptional experience.

Previous The Hayman Island infinity pool overlooking Hayman Beach and Lagoon Bay *Opposite* Aerial view over Lizard Island/Dyiigurra

Luxury getaways

4

➔ GETTING HERE

Located 240km north of Cairns/Gimuy, and 27km off the coast of Tropical North Queensland, **East Air** connects Lizard Island with the mainland. Departing from a private hangar at Cairns Airport, the Lizard Island experience begins with a stunning 1hr scenic flight, flying over about 200km of the Great Barrier Reef. There's always something to see below as you fly over Batt Reef, Tongue Reef, Cairns Reef, Ribbons Reefs and Lark Reef, just to name a few, as well as plenty of sand cays and reef bommies that can be seen from the sky. There are two flights each way per day, departing from Cairns at 11am and 2pm, and then returning from Lizard Island at 12.25pm and 3.25pm.

Once you're at the resort everything is just a short walk away. However, if you do want to explore a little further you can request a golf cart ride to further points of the island.

💤 STAY

There's a range of different accommodation options to choose from at **Lizard Island Resort**, with rooms, suites and villas all on offer. The rooms are beautifully designed and decorated, with plenty of space, views of the ocean or the rainforest, wi-fi in all rooms and some even have their own private plunge pool. To be right near the water you can't go past the Beachfront Suites, which are set along the arc of Anchor Bay, offering ocean views from your balcony, and only a few steps to the water. For larger groups there's also the option of booking **The House** for upto eight guests, a three-storey, three-bedroom property, perched on the point and surrounded by the most impressive blue waters you could imagine. For complete privacy, the Villa or the Pavilion are both completely secluded cliff-top properties, with panoramic views of the ocean. Mini bars are restocked throughout the day and beach towels, beach bags and robes are included in the rooms for you to use during your stay. No matter what type of accommodation you choose, you're sure to be impressed with the elegance of your Lizard Island home.

🍽 FOOD & DRINK

As an all-inclusive resort, you don't have to worry about a thing during your stay at Lizard Island/Dyiigurra. Every meal you have is sure to be absolutely remarkable, as is the exceptional service and attention to detail. Absolutely everything is included: gourmet meals, a selection of wine, beer and spirits, a menu of cocktails, even your own packed picnics for beach adventures. The **Salt Water Restaurant** offers a daily changing menu, with seasonal produce and meals inspired by the local environment. The team works with local farmers, growers and producers from around Queensland to ensure everything is of the freshest quality, as well as supporting the locals. There are normally a couple of options for you to choose from, with several courses for each meal. You can also pop over to the **Driftwood Bar & Wine Cellar** if you feel like a pre- or post-dinner drink, with some of the most comfortable couches I have personally ever sat on in my whole life. On Tuesdays and Fridays you can also head down to the **Marlin Bar** at the end of the boardwalk. The only public bar on the island, and a favourite of the island staff, the Marlin Bar offers a laid-back vibe, with cocktails and casual meals on the lawn from 5pm. For the ultimate Lizard Island dining experience, be sure to book a **degustation beachside dining experience**, held in a private gazebo right on the shore of Anchor Bay. The island's Executive Chef will meet with you personally to design the seven-course menu to suit your occasion and tastes. There are only two gazebos each night, so definitely book this experience in advance, as it's one of the most popular experiences on the island.

Above Beachfront Suites *Opposite top left* Location for the degustation beachside dining *Opposite top right* The blues of Anchor Bay *Opposite bottom* Beachfront suites overlooking the beach

⊘ THINGS TO DO

There is no shortage of things to do to keep you busy during your stay on Lizard Island/Dyiigurra. In your room you will find an activity guide, with everything that's on offer over the next week.

Begin your day with an hour of **yoga** on the beach as the sun rises, before heading out on an **inner or outer reef tour** to spend the day underwater at some of the incredible snorkelling and diving spots in this northern part of the Great Barrier Reef. Or jump on a unique **Aqua Darts snorkelling tour**, for one of the most exciting ways to experience undersea life.

For a day of exploring at your own pace, book a **motorised dinghy**, packed with an esky of morning or afternoon tea, to find your very own private beach. **Watson's Bay** is a wonderful spot for snorkelling, home to the epic **clam gardens** and a great place to spot turtles snacking on seagrass. Or venture a little further around to **Turtle Beach** and **Mermaid Cove** for great snorkelling right off your dinghy. There are also kayaks and stand-up paddleboards available to use from the beach club.

Hike up to the highest point, the iconic **Cook's Look**, where Captain Cook himself hiked to see how best to navigate his ship. The 4km walk can be a bit of a tough one, but the views are unrivalled on the island, looking over the resort and the bright blue waters of the lagoon.

There are plenty of guided activities across the island, from the Blue Lagoon walk to the Historic Nature walk and the Chinaman's Ridge hike in Watson's Bay, as well as birdwatching tours, sunset bat walks, native Aussie animals chats and nature talks to teach you about the island and its unique environment. Throughout the week there's also a rotating roster of immersive activities to keep you entertained, including paint and sip, gin masterclasses, mixology masterclasses, astrophotography, or a twilight cruise.

You can also take a tour of the **Lizard Island Research Station**, which supports more than 100 research projects each year. It's one of the largest research stations on the Great Barrier Reef, and has been operating since 1973. Many tours and activities only run on certain days of the week, so it's a good idea to have a chat with your booking specialist about what you would like to experience during your stay before locking in any dates.

Or if you've come for rest and relaxation, grab your towel and head straight for a beach lounger to watch the waves come in.

ON THE MAINLAND

Give yourself a little extra time on your trip to explore the wonderful world of Tropical North Queensland before or after your visit to Lizard Island/Dyiigurra. The only place in Australia where two UNESCO World Heritage Sites are located side by side, Cairns/Gimuy is the gateway to both the Great Barrier Reef and the Daintree and Wet Tropics Rainforest. There's an endless bucket-list of things to do from Cairns, from waterfall hopping through the **Atherton Tablelands**, to the **SkyRail** up to Kuranda, or hopping through the beachside towns of **Palm Cove** and **Port Douglas**. It's a wonderful region to explore that will keep you coming back again and again.

⊙ WHEN TO GO

Following the climate of Tropical North Queensland, generally the dry season (May-Oct) is the best time to visit Lizard Island/Dyiigurra, and the second half of the dry season (August-Oct) is considered the perfect time of year, as the winds also drop off during these months providing optimal boating conditions. September is Marlin season and one of the busiest times on the island. June and July sees the humpback whales beginning their northern migration, and minke whales can often be spotted during this time too.

⊙ NEED TO KNOW

As an all-inclusive resort, almost everything is included in the room rate for your stay at Lizard Island Resort. The few exclusions include the flights to and from the island, and some of the larger tours, including inner and outer reef snorkelling tours, scuba diving and the sea-darts snorkelling tours. Have a chat with your booking specialist as you create your itinerary for the most up-to-date information on activities and extra charges during your stay.

Opposite Sunset at Anchor Bay

Luxury getaways

Hayman Island

Australia's most iconic private island resort

THE WHITSUNDAYS, QUEENSLAND

From the time you arrive for your luxury launch ferry transfer, everything screams HAYMAN. You are immersed in a luxury island getaway from the very first minute of your stay. Welcomed on board with a glass of sparkling champagne, greeted at the dock and taken to the resort by golf buggy, shown around and to your room by a personal guide, ready to answer any questions you might have. Everything is luxurious, grand and with exceptional attention to detail. Hayman Island is, quite simply, spectacular.

Sitting at the northernmost point of the Whitsunday archipelago, Hayman Island is renowned for its location, bucket-list experiences and supreme beauty. The resort reopened as part of the Intercontinental family in 2019 after being closed for a couple of years due to the devastating effects of Cyclone Debbie in 2017. Nestled amongst the rainforest-covered hills of the island, along 2km of palm-lined golden sand and facing towards the Coral Sea, it really sets the standard for an island paradise.

Hayman Island is the perfect base from which to explore the Whitsundays in style. With its close proximity to the Great Barrier Reef and Whitehaven Beach, there are plenty of options to go a little further, and there are unique experiences found only on Hayman. From sunset picnics on deserted islands nearby to private helicopter tours and guided jetski adventures, there's always something new to try. A stay on Hayman is absolutely a bucket-list experience that will exceed your expectations. And, if you need even more island vibes, a trip to Hayman can be paired with a night or two at Hamilton Island (*see* p.40) pre or post your Hayman Island visit. That's if you ever want to leave …

TIME ZONE: AEST (GMT +10)
BEST TIME TO VISIT: Year-round
ACCESSIBLE FROM: Hamilton Island or Airlie Beach
GETTING THERE: Luxury ferry or private helicopter transfer
PHONE RECEPTION: Yes
WI-FI: Yes
DAYTRIPS: Yes
KID FRIENDLY: Yes
SOCIALS: @intercontinentalhaymanisland
MORE INFO: haymanisland.intercontinental.com

THE BEST BITS

Grab a sun lounge and park yourself beside one of Hayman Island's two exquisite pools, for a relaxing day by the water in paradise.

Opposite The iconic Hayman Pool

➔ GETTING HERE

The easiest way to get to Hayman Island is via the resort's **Luxury Launch** ferry transfer, which connects to most flights arriving into Hamilton Island Airport (HTI). Taking about an hour to make the journey between Hamilton and Hayman Island, you can enjoy drinks and a platter of refreshments on board, as you travel amongst the islands of the Whitsundays to your destination. There are also options to catch the Luxury Launch transfer from Airlie Beach if needed.

Alternatively, you can also organise a private helicopter transfer from Hamilton Island airport, getting you to Hayman in only 15min.

💤 STAY

The **Intercontinental Hayman Island Resort** offers a collection of different room types, including suites and villas, as well as four incredible Hayman Residences sitting on the island's hilltop.

The resort rooms and suites are spread between four distinct wings, the Pool, Lagoon, Pavilion and Beach, offering stunning views across the island and the resort grounds, and ultra-luxurious rooms with plenty of extra special little details. For larger families and groups, the resort also includes the stunning three-bedroom **Hayman Beach House**, the ultimate beach house of your dreams. The resort is actually quite large, so it's a good idea to choose a room type in the part of the resort you want to spend the most time in. All room types include complimentary breakfast each day at the Pacific restaurant, free wi-fi and non-motorised island watersports activities.

🍸 FOOD & DRINK

There are five restaurants scattered around the grounds of the Hayman Island Resort, each with their own distinct menus and flavours. **Pacific** is the resort's signature restaurant and bar, where you will have breakfast in the morning overlooking the ocean. Open for dinner in the

Above Bam Bam restaurant *Opposite* Aeriel view of Hayman Beach

evenings, as well as cocktails in the bar, it has a range of dishes to choose from and its iconic seafood buffet on Friday evenings. **Amici** offers a delicious Mediterranean-style dinner menu of tapas, wood-fire pizzas and handmade pastas. **Aqua** is located in the iconic Hayman Pool and offers laid-back lunches, with options including burgers, fish and chips, tacos and nachos, as well as fresh juices and tasty cocktails. Next to the Infinity Pool, **Bam Bam** offers lunch and dinner menus with Asian fusion cuisine with an Australian twist. They also have a small ice-cream bar inside, perfect for an afternoon treat lazing by the pool. The **Grove Boutique and Cafe** offers sandwiches, muffins, little cheeseboards, ice-creams and snacks if you're not looking for a full meal. There's also plenty of salads, snacks and light meals available for in-room dining.

It's highly recommended that you make reservations for dinner seating times.

✓ THINGS TO DO

Jump on the **Whitehaven Beach Experience** to visit one of the most iconic spots in the Whitsundays - Whitehaven Beach. Wander along the 7km coastline of one of the most spectacular beaches in the world, with a picnic lunch included, as well as stand-up paddleboards (SUPs) and beach games. Or upgrade to the **Whitehaven Indulgence Helicopter Experience** and arrive in style in your very own private helicopter.

Explore more of the Whitsundays with a boat transfer to one of Hayman Island's nearby islands or beaches - **Langford Island**, **Bali Hai Reef**, **Hook Island** or **Blue Pearl Bay North**. The exclusive **Island Escapades** packages include return boat transfers, snorkelling equipment, picnic hampers and light refreshments to make the most of your time on a deserted island.

Lean into luxury island life with a **private boat charter** for the day, taking you anywhere you would like within the Whitsundays. You can completely customise your itinerary with options including Whitehaven Beach tours, Great Barrier Reef snorkelling and gourmet seafood lunches, or really anything else you would like.

Hit the water on the **Guided Jet Ski Adventure**, driving your own jetski around the waters of Hayman Island. You're likely to spot turtles and plenty of marine life. During our visit, we even spotted some big manta rays swimming round, which was an incredible experience! **Sea Kayak Adventures** are also available, to take in the waters at a slower pace. The tours generally take you out to Blue Pearl Bay, Langford Island or Bali Hai, where you can explore the reefs, and jump in for a snorkel with the curious turtles and stingrays in the region. Or just take advantage of the complimentary

Above Hayman Island Marina *Opposite* Aerial view of the Hayman Pool

equipment right off the beachfront, with kayaks, SUPs, snorkelling equipment and sailing catamarans all available to use.

Stay dry while exploring underwater on the **Semi-submersible Coral Reef Viewing** tour. Just a short journey away on the *Reef Dancer*, there is plenty of reef to explore with stunning visibility under the water.

See the Whitsundays from above with a **Scenic Discovery Flight** over the Great Barrier Reef. With several different options to choose from, including Whitehaven Beach and Heart Reef, there's no better way to see this region than from the sky. Heli flights are available on demand, so they're ready whenever you are.

Luxury getaways

Jump on a **fishing charter** and try your luck catching some of the region's big game fish. Starting off with a scenic tour in Hayman Island's all-new fishing vessel, you'll be taken out to some of the fishing hot spots around Hayman, as well as throughout the Whitsundays.

Explore the island on foot with a hike across to **Blue Pearl Bay**. Bring some snorkelling equipment with you for a refreshing jump in the water at the end of the walking trail; there's often turtles and plenty of colourful fish to check out in the water here. Or test your limits with a climb to the top of Hayman Island's peak on the **Sunset Peak Hike**, a high-intensity climb that offers breathtaking views across the Whitsunday Islands. Hikes to Dolphin Point Lookout and Whitsundays Lookout also offer stunning views over the water.

Watch the sun go down from a **Sunset Cruise**, the ultimate way to experience the sun setting over the Whitsunday coastline. With a complimentary beer or sparkling wine and antipasto platter, it's a beautiful way to enjoy the golden hour.

It's also worth checking out the activities schedule on the HAYMAN app for additional activities, including nocturnal tours, trivia nights, fish feeding, champagne and oyster pop-ups, meet the bartender happy hours and wine cellar discovery and guided tasting hours.

ⓘ WHEN TO GO

A great destination to visit year-round, Hayman Island has average temperatures of 31°C between November and April and 25°C between May and October, with sunny days all throughout the year. There is sometimes a little rainfall during the summer months, however it's normally just a passing shower.

ⓘ NEED TO KNOW

When you arrive, download the HAYMAN app, in which you can pair your phone to your room. Through the app you can make restaurant bookings, spa appointments, order room service, find out about island experiences, see the activity schedule, request services, and even chat with a customer service representative. It's super helpful, and your go-to for any information during your visit.

Below Aqua restaurant *Opposite* The Hayman Island infinity pool

Orpheus Island/ Goolboddi

Indulge in all-inclusive island luxury

TOWNSVILLE, QUEENSLAND

Luxury getaways

TIME ZONE: AEST (GMT +10)
BEST TIME TO VISIT: May to Oct
ACCESSIBLE FROM: Townsville
GETTING THERE: Helicopter
PHONE RECEPTION: Yes
WI-FI: Yes
DAYTRIPS: No
KID FRIENDLY: Yes
SOCIALS: @orpheusisland
MORE INFO: orpheus.com.au

For an island experience you will never forget, head to Orpheus Island/Goolboddi, immersed in the Great Barrier Reef, just off the coast of Townsville. Orpheus Island Lodge offers an all-inclusive luxury experience unlike any other island in Australia. It has carved out a little pocket for itself around the middle of the 11km island, with Orpheus Island National Park covering more than 1000 hectares.

Catering to only 28 guests at a time, Orpheus Island Lodge makes it easy to feel like you have this island paradise all to yourself, and your days can be as full or as laid-back as you would like, with candlelight dinners over the water, an incredible infinity pool overlooking the Coral Sea, a schedule of complimentary activities to choose from, walking trails to explore, watercraft waiting for you on the beach or daytrips to secluded close-by islands and beaches. Or if you're not really in the mood for much at all, grab yourself a lounge alongside the infinity pool or make yourself comfy in a hammock between the palm trees and simply enjoy island life.

Known to the Traditional Owners, the Manbarra People as Goolboddi Island, the island was part of the Palm Island Group, linked together with surrounding smaller islands and the mainland through the creation story of the carpet snake, and was used for hunting, fishing and recreation. These days, neighbouring Palm Island is still home to the largest First Nations community in Queensland.

Orpheus is the ultimate island on which to relax and unwind and enjoy luxury island life.

THE BEST BITS

Grab a cocktail and watch the golden sunset over the infinity pool before dinner. It just might be one of the most beautiful sunset locations on the East Coast of Australia.

Opposite Sunset over the Orpheus Island jetty

Luxury getaways

➔ GETTING HERE

Orpheus Island is accessed from Townsville, with a picturesque 30min helicopter flight over the sea with **Nautilus Aviation**. There is one scheduled helicopter flight between Townsville Airport (TSV) and Orpheus Island Lodge each day, or you can also arrange a private helicopter for your arrival. It's important to lock in your transfers with the reservations team as a first step when confirming your stay, as there are only eight seats and they can often be full. Helicopter transfers to and from the island are an additional charge to the resort accommodation.

💤 STAY

Orpheus Island Lodge offers the only accommodation on the island, with only 14 suites for guests. All suites face the beachfront, most have ocean views from their own patio, and all are immaculately decorated, with so much attention to detail and beautiful little touches. Beachfront rooms and villas sit within the northern part of the lodge, all opening to pristine green grass, palm trees and the beach only steps from your door. The south rooms and suites are set within the tropical jungle of the island, with their own short pathway to the beachfront. Your stay includes all meals and drinks, an all-inclusive mini bar, use of water equipment, daily Orpheus experiences, your own insulated drink bottles and so much more. Every suite is super comfy and relaxing, giving you the perfect base to unwind after a beautiful day.

🍴 FOOD & DRINK

As an all-inclusive resort, breakfast, lunch and dinner are all taken care of, with exceptional menus and delicious food on offer for every meal, with stunning views over the Coral Sea right from your table. Breakfast at Orpheus offers a selection from an à la carte menu, with options including avocado toast, smoothie bowls and buttermilk pancakes, paired with fresh fruit, juice and pastries. Lunch is a changing tapas or small plates menu, featuring different cuisines, including Asian, Italian, Spanish, Mexican and Australian dishes. If you're planning on island hopping or spending the day out on the water, you can also collect a picnic hamper with a packed lunch to take with you. Dinner is a four-course degustation menu, with dishes focused on locally-sourced fresh produce and complementary wine pairings, topped off with a sweet dessert. The menu changes daily with much of the fresh produce sourced from the island's very own veggie patch. The island's executive chef is also very accommodating with dietary requirements and requests,

Right Orpheus Island infinity pool and bar *Opposite* Aerial view over Orpheus Island jetty

ISLAND HOPPER: PELORUS ISLAND

Just north of Orpheus Island/Goolboddi is **Pelorus Island** (pelorusprivateisland.au), a tiny private island that you can rent out and have all to yourself. With a beautiful beach house for up to eight guests set on the sandy shores, a private pool and an on-site team to take care of all your meals and anything else you might need, it's truly a private island experience like no other. Get your family or a group of friends together for an island trip of a lifetime.

Luxury getaways

especially if you're travelling with children who might require something a little more basic. Every meal we had on Orpheus was absolutely delicious and the team does an exceptional job.

If you're celebrating a special occasion or looking for something a little extra, you can also book the signature **Dining with the Tides** experience, where you'll be treated to a starlit dinner in the beautiful little gazebo at the end of the pier, dining over the water. The six-course degustation menu is designed by you and the executive chef, to ensure this is a meal and experience you never forget.

⊘ THINGS TO DO

With the Great Barrier Reef right at your doorstep, there are endless options for how to spend your days on Orpheus Island/Goolboddi. You can start exploring the water from the minute you wake up, with stand-up paddleboards, catamarans, kayaks and motorised dinghies available to use at the pier, as well as snorkelling equipment and fishing gear. Explore the mangroves and the bommies around the bay or head out a little further to check out some of the nearby private beaches, or Yanks Jetty, which was built during World War II. Snorkel right off the beach or from your dinghy, to explore some of the incredible underwater life that surrounds Orpheus Island. You can often spot reef sharks, stingrays, and plenty of colourful fish swimming close to the shore.

Grab a chef-prepared picnic lunch and head to your own private beach on a **picnic adventure**. With plenty of deserted beaches to choose from, you can either take your own dinghy or opt for a beach drop-off to enjoy your own private island beach for the day.

Orpheus Island Lodge also offers a rotating schedule of **daily guided tours and activities**, with something new on offer everyday. These include guided snorkelling tours, guided nature walks through the island, kayaking through the mangroves, a lesson in mixology and cocktail making, whisky tastings and cocktails by the fire. Check the blackboard near the bar to see what's on offer each day.

Check yourself in for a luxurious treatment at the **Gwandalan Spa**. You will be treated to its menu of facial therapies, massages, body rituals, body scrubs and indulgent relaxation treatments.

To explore a little further, Orpheus also offers a collection of **bespoke experiences**, allowing you to explore more of this beautiful region. With options to visit the **Museum of Underwater Art** or **Hinchinbrook Island/Munamudanamy**

Opposite The perfect place to relax on Orpheus Island/Goolboddi

(*see* p.116) on a day tour, as well as private **scuba diving charters** to epic Great Barrier Reef dive sites and outer reef **fishing charters** to catch your own dinner, the perfect adventure waits for you.

There is also a handful of unique **Great Barrier Reef eco-tours** on offer, including a visit to the **Research Station** within Pioneer Bay, a marine research facility operated by James Cook University, a beach clean-up at Picnic Bay, and DIY research volunteering, where you can collect data to help protect the reef.

In the evening, watch the sun go down on a pre-dinner **sunset cruise**, with delicious canapés and iconic Australian wine and beer. The sunset on Orpheus Island is so impressive, and what better way to soak it in than a cruise to immerse yourself in the golden hour.

WHEN TO GO

September and October might be the very best months to visit Orpheus Island/Goolboddi, when the weather is starting to heat up but the days are still sunny and dry. Orpheus Lodge is closed in February, as it's the wettest month of the year, re-opening on 1 March. Generally, November to April is considered the wet season, however with Townsville boasting 300 sunny days each year, you're likely to find nice weather year-round.

NEED TO KNOW

Due to the limited capacity both on the island and on the heli transfers, it's a good idea to book your visit to Orpheus Island/Goolboddi as early as possible to avoid missing out on your preferred dates.

ON THE MAINLAND

A stay in Townsville the night before and after your trip is recommended, to avoid any issues with delayed flights or helicopters. **The Ville** (the-ville.com.au) is the ideal location to base yourself in Townsville, owned by the same team as Orpheus Island Lodge. In a stunning location, overlooking the ocean and with views out to Magnetic Island/Yunbenun (*see* p.56) in the distance, The Ville offers award-winning restaurants, an epic infinity pool and a luxurious day spa with a menu of treatments to choose from. There's always exciting special events happening, so check their 'What's On' calendar before you go.

Above left Exploring the water on a motorised dinghy *Above right* Golden hour at the pool bar *Opposite* The tropical palms of Orpheus Island/Goolboddi

ISLAND HOPPING
Long Island

THE WHITSUNDAYS, QUEENSLAND

Offering a Whitsunday experience without the crowds, Long Island's Elysian Luxury Eco Island Retreat is the ultimate adult's-only, inclusive, super sustainable experience on the Great Barrier Reef. Sitting at the southern end of Long Island, Elysian offers a blissful escape from regular life. It's open to only 20 guests at a time, with an exquisite dining menu, bucket-list experiences and whales swimming by and spotted right from the beach during whale season.

Passionate about environmental sustainability and reducing their carbon footprint, Elysian became the first 100 per cent solar powered resort on the Great Barrier Reef in 2019, offsetting 150 per cent of its carbon emissions each calendar year. It has proudly attained Australia's highest ecotourism certification and is committed to protecting the health of the reef, as well as the wider Whitsundays environment. Elysian is also committed to providing guests with a sustainable luxury experience, including offering reef safe sunscreen and focusing on conserving water.

Whilst you can absolutely get out and explore the best of the Whitsundays, Elysian is without a doubt the place to come and relax, soak up the location and surroundings, move slowly and enjoy the little things.

⊙ GETTING HERE
Only a short 10min helicopter ride from either Hamilton Island (*see* p.40) or Airlie Beach, or a 30min boat transfer from Shute Harbour in Airlie Beach, Elysian Retreat is easily accessible within the Whitsundays.

⊙ THINGS TO DO
With the Whitsundays right at your doorstep, there's plenty to do during your stay. Take advantage of the resort's water equipment, with complimentary use of stand-up paddleboards, kayaks and snorkelling equipment ready for you to explore the reef at your leisure. Elysian also offers twice-daily yoga sessions to start and end your day in a peaceful and relaxing way.

Jump on a tour to **Whitehaven Beach**, one of the most beautiful beaches in the Whitsundays and all of Australia, or see the Great Barrier Reef from above with a scenic helicopter flight out to **Heart Reef**, flying over the iconic Hill Inlet and Whitehaven Beach along the way. Take a **Whitsundays Jet Ski Tour**, cruising around the waterways between nearby Daydream and South Molle islands.

Whales can be spotted passing by the island on their annual migration, heading north from July to August to breed, and then back south in September and October, often with their newborn calves in tow.

⊙ STAY
In one of the most beautiful settings on the Great Barrier Reef, **Elysian Luxury Eco Island Retreat** is a beautiful boutique resort, surrounded by the tropical rainforest of Molle Islands National Park on one side, and the pristine waters of the Whitsundays on the other. With only 10 beautiful coastal oceanfront villas, offering both island and mountain views, complete with their own outdoor hammocks, day beds and outdoor showers, Elysian offers relaxation at every turn. Rates include three gourmet meals each day, hot and cold drinks (alcoholic drinks are an additional charge), use of watersports equipment, snorkelling gear and daily yoga classes.

ⓘ MORE INFO
Elysian is an adult's-only resort, catering to guests age 16 years and over. For more information and to book your stay head to elysianretreat.com.au or check out @elysianretreat on Instagram for all the inspo.

Above The pool at Elysian *Opposite top* Aerial view over Elysian Retreat *Opposite bottom* Elysian's coastal oceanfront villas

Bedarra Island/ Biagurra

Your very own secluded island

CASSOWARY COAST, QUEENSLAND

Just off the coast of Mission Beach, about halfway between Cairns/Gimuy and Townsville is Bedarra Island/Biagurra. A small granite island, covered in lush rainforest and surrounded by sparkling green waters, it's part of the Family Group of Islands, a collection of continental islands that was once part of the mainland until sea levels rose around 8000 years ago. Bedarra Island is considered the mother within the family group, the second-largest island after Dunk Island (*see* p.122).

Bedarra Island is known as Biagurra, which means the place of endless water to the Traditional Owners, the Bandjin and Djiru Peoples. Local folklore believes that that the name Bedarra Island came from legendary beachcomber E.J. Banfield who lived on Dunk Island. The story goes that he did not hear the name 'Biagurra' correctly, and named the island Bedarra, thinking he was giving it its correct Traditional name.

There are two completely different ways to stay on Bedarra Island. On the western side of the island is Bedarra Island Resort, an all-inclusive, adult's-only, tropical resort, with private plunge pools overlooking the ocean. Over on the eastern side of the island you will find a handful of holiday homes, catering more to groups and families, where you're completely self-sufficient and bring all your own supplies. Both options offer you quite the private island experience, immersed in the rainforest and right on the water's doorstep.

Bedarra Island is the sort of place that you're likely to go hours without running into another person, have stunning palm-lined beaches all to yourself, and even the best snorkelling spots all to yourself.

TIME ZONE: AEST (GMT +10)
BEST TIME TO VISIT: Sept to Nov
ACCESSIBLE FROM: Mission Beach
GETTING THERE: Boat transfer or helicopter
PHONE RECEPTION: Yes
WI-FI: Check with your accommodation
DAYTRIPS: No
KID FRIENDLY: Only at some holiday homes
SOCIALS: @bedarraisland
MORE INFO: bedarra.com.au or search for individual holiday homes on Airbnb

THE BEST BITS

Keep an eye out for Doorila beach's resident dugong! She can often be spotted during the afternoon, having a snack on the seagrass close to the shore. If you see her while you're snorkelling, make sure to move slowly, with no sudden movements, so you don't scare her away.

Opposite Aerial view over Doorila Bay

Luxury getaways

➔ GETTING HERE

Boat transfers are the easiest way of getting to Bedarra Island. A short 30min scenic journey through the Family Islands, there's plenty to see on the way out to the island. When you stay at Bedarra Island Resort you can choose between boat or helicopter transfers to the island, with boats departing from Mission Beach and helicopter transfer options from both Mission Beach and Cairns.

If you're staying on the eastern side of Bedarra at one of the holiday homes, **Great Barrier Reef Safaris** offers Bedarra Island transfers from Clump Point Boat Ramp. As well as transferring you and your luggage across to the island, they can also provide secure parking for your car on the mainland during your time on the island. Transfer times are dependent on the tides, so have a chat with them about the dates you're thinking of visiting.

Once you're on the island it's barefoot vibes all round, with everything only a very short walk away.

😴 STAY

There are two different accommodation options for your stay on Bedarra Island/Biagurra. The ultra-exclusive **Bedarra Island Resort** prides itself on its uniqueness. Think Pimms on arrival, private plunge pools overlooking the ocean and candlelight dinners on the deck. Comprising of twelve private villas, all hidden amongst the overgrowth of the tropical rainforest, it's a place of seclusion and complete relaxation, where everything is taken care of you. The villas are all unique in their own way, with some being only a couple of steps from the beach, some offering their own private infinity-edge plunge pools, some with outdoor rainforest bathrooms and some with expansive private sundecks and daybeds. All as luxurious as the next, each villa offers its own unique Bedarra Island experience. Most of the villas sit along the stunning curved beach of Hernandia Bay, with only two private villas set looking over Wedgerock Bay, facing the Coral Sea.

On the other side of the island, seven holiday homes sit within the hillside. Think barbecues on the deck, bedrooms overlooking the rainforest and beaches all to yourself. Most offer water views, plenty of space to relax and unwind, outdoor dining and some have their own pools. They all have their own website and rules for visitors, however most of them are listed on **Airbnb**, so that's a great starting place to compare your options. Our personal favourite is **Pavilions of Bedarra**. Spread over three levels and surrounded by

Opposite Aerial view of Bedarra Island

Bedarra Island/Biagurra

luscious rainforest, the Pavilions was the perfect base for our stay. With a top-level deck looking out to the ocean, an outdoor tropical bathroom, plenty of space for kids to play and a super comfy king-sized bed, it was the ultimate island holiday house. Pavilions also includes everything you need to explore the water during your stay, with a three-person kayak, fishing gear, snorkelling equipment, body boards and beach chairs all available to use.

Both the resort and holiday home options offer an exceptional stay, it just depends how you would like to experience the island.

DAYTRIPS

Whilst there are no daytrips to Bedarra Island/Biagurra, **Great Barrier Reef Safaris** (greatbarrierreefsafaris.com) offer snorkel safaris around the Family Islands, often with stops to the reefs that surround Bedarra Island, depending on the weather and sea conditions. You can choose between a three- to five-hour safari with a marine biologist guide, with the five-hour safari offering a delicious seafood lunch on a secluded beach.

FOOD & DRINK

At **Bedarra Island Resort** the ever-changing menu has something for everyone, with the open terrace restaurant, bar and lounge considered the heart and soul of the resort. The open bar is always flowing and the menu is rich with fresh produce and locally sourced foods. The restaurant overlooks the waters of Hernandia Bay, while still being surrounded by the rainforest, as well as a magnificent 300-year-old calophyllum tree. There are also a handful of private dining decks on the beachfront or in the rainforest, for a one-of-a-kind candlelight dinner. You can arrange for a picnic hamper to take on your island hopping adventures, or head to dinner early to catch cocktail hour.

For any of the holiday homes on the eastern side of Bedarra, you will need to bring all your own food and drinks, with enough provisions for the entirety of your stay. **Great Barrier Reef Safaris** offers a pick-up service from both Woolworths and BWS, so you can place your orders online in advance and then not have to worry about anything when you arrive in Mission Beach. It's always a good idea to grab a little extra food than you think you might need, as once you're on the island there is nothing there.

⊘ THINGS TO DO

Whilst the main objective of Bedarra Island/Biagurra is to get you to relax, there are still plenty of things to see and do. However, activities are of course dependent on where you choose to stay on the island.

At the resort there are lots of activities included in your stay, like sea kayaking, stand-up paddleboarding, snorkelling and fishing. For those wanting to explore a little further, there are options for half- and full-day snorkelling and scuba charters to the outer Great Barrier Reef, or you can rent your very own motorised dinghy, packed with a picnic hamper to explore one of the nearby uninhabited tropical islands. For the ultimate in relaxation, book yourself in for an indulgent **massage** in the beachfront massage pavilion, where you can hear the waves lapping the shore. What could be more relaxing than that?! There is also a menu of **spa treatments** to be sure you leave feeling like a whole new person. There are plenty of self-guided rainforest walks to lookout spots across the island, with the **Old Jetty Lookout**, **Turtle Bay Lookout** and **South Lookout** being some of the favourites. Make sure you allow yourself plenty of time to swim and lounge and soak up the sun, to make the most of your island time.

On the other side of the island, a spot called **Five Ways** offers you five different directions to explore the island. There are two beaches to choose from, both of which you're likely to have to yourself. **Doorila** faces the Coral Sea, a small picture-perfect patch of sand surrounded by palm trees of all sizes, granite boulders and a cove of clear blue water. It's a great place for snorkelling and fishing right off the beach, or grab a kayak and take a trip over to the ruined jetty. **Coomol** is on the mainland side of the island, and is where you'll be dropped off when you arrive. Coomol has incredible bommies for snorkelling right off the beach, with an abundance of schools of juvenile fish swimming around here. If you want to get out a little further, at low tide you can follow the **Coomol Ocean Walk**, taking you around the rocks to secluded beaches and mangroves, and then finally out to the sand spit. It's a great place to find rockpools full of starfish, sea life and shells. About a 5km-return walk, it's important you leave as the tide is going out (check tide times ahead) to give yourself enough time to get back. Along the remaining paths of Five Ways, you can find short bushwalks, offering great sunrise and sunset viewing spots around the island.

ⓘ WHEN TO GO

Spring is considered the best time to visit Mission Beach and Bedarra Island/Biagurra, from around September to November when temperatures are warm and the average monthly rainfall is the lowest of the year.

ON THE MAINLAND

Mission Beach is the gateway to Bedarra Island/Biagurra, a beautiful coastal village about a 2hr drive south of Cairns/Gimuy. It's best known for its namesake beach, which stretches for 14km and has palms growing along the sand of the beach, often a little bent over to be the perfect climbing palm. Mission Beach is also the heart of the Cassowary Coast, bordered by both the Wet Tropics Rainforest and the Great Barrier Reef.

ⓘ NEED TO KNOW

With only limited availability on the island, both the resort and the holiday homes can book out quite far in advance, especially during the peak seasons. Make sure you lock in your dates as early as possible to avoid missing out.

Above Sunset over Bedarra Island/Biagurra *Opposite* Climbing the baby palms at Doorila Bay

Tiwi Islands

Where rugged Top End beauty meets ancient culture

TOP END, NORTHERN TERRITORY

Awungana, welcome to the Tiwi Islands.

There are only a handful of islands off the coast of the Northern Territory, and the Tiwi Islands are very special. Affectionately known as the 'island of smiles', the Tiwi Islands are actually an archipelago of 11 islands. The two main islands, Bathurst Island and Melville Island, which are known as Ratuwati Yinjara (Two Islands) to the Traditional Owners are the largest and most used, while the other nine islands are quite small and uninhabited. Surrounded by inviting blue waters that are full of crocodiles, with plenty of natural beauty and incredible cultural experiences, a visit to the Tiwi Islands is simply unforgettable.

Ratuwati Yinjara is home to just under 3000 Tiwi People, separated by the Apsley Straight. The Tiwi People have a very different history to Australian mainland First Nations People, having been isolated from the mainland for thousands of years, and therefore they consider themselves uniquely Tiwi. With a fierce passion for AFL football, art and fishing, the Tiwi People are beautifully welcoming, and happy and excited to share their island home with visitors who want to learn about their culture and traditions.

To make the most of everything the Tiwi Islands have to offer, combine an introduction to art and culture at Tiwi by Design with a stay at the barefoot beach resort Tiwi Island Retreat for the ultimate Tiwi experience. With Top End sunsets, a traditional welcome ceremony, mud crabbing, secluded waterholes, and cultural walking tours around the main settlement, the Tiwi Islands offer a completely unique and memorable adventure.

TIME ZONE: ACST (GMT +9.5)
BEST TIME TO VISIT: May to Aug
ACCESSIBLE FROM: Darwin
GETTING THERE: Ferry or plane
PHONE RECEPTION: No
WI-FI: No
DAYTRIPS: Yes
KID FRIENDLY: Yes
SOCIALS: @sealinknt & @tiwiislandretreat
MORE INFO: sealink.com.au/tiwi-islands & tiwiislandretreat.com.au

THE BEST BITS

A visit to the Tiwi Islands can perfectly combine Traditional local art and culture with the stunning beachfront accommodation of Tiwi Island Retreat.

Opposite Aerial view over Tiwi Island Retreat and the surrounding rainforest

Early mornings at Tiwi Island Retreat

➔ GETTING HERE

Sitting 80km off the coast of Darwin/Garramilla, the Tiwi Islands are accessible via ferry or charter flight. **SeaLink NT** (sealink.com.au/tiwi-islands) operates a ferry service between Cullen Bay Ferry Terminal in Darwin and Wurruminyanga on Bathurst Island several times per week, which takes around 2.5hr one way. Daytrips are available on Thursdays and Fridays, departing from Darwin at 8am and returning from Wurruminyanga at 3.15pm. Charter flights are also able to be organised with **Air Frontier** (airfrontier.com.au) to fly directly to the Port Hurd airstrip for a stay at Tiwi Island Retreat.

💤 STAY

The ultimate place to stay during your visit to the Tiwi Islands is **Tiwi Island Retreat**. An oceanfront, barefoot beach retreat, created by the Northern Territory's very own crocodile wrangler, Matt Wright, Tiwi Island Retreat has a collection of beachfront rooms, larger rooms to accommodate families and groups, and luxury glamping tents complete with their own private spa overlooking the ocean. It is the place to go when you want to get away from it all and escape for a little while. Enjoy ocean-to-plate dining, a pool overlooking the water for a dip, cocktails around the bonfire in the evening, and their resident crocodile Claudia, popping her head up during the golden hour to see if she can steal any discarded fish from the day's haul.

For those focused on fishing, **Tiwi Islands Adventures** offers multi-day, all-inclusive fishing charters from Melville Island Lodge and Johnson River Camp.

⊚ DAYTRIPS

SeaLink NT offers several day tour options to the Tiwi Islands from Darwin/Garramilla. The most immersive is the **Tiwi By Design** day tour, which is a jam-packed daytrip full of culture, art and exploring Wurrumiyanga. The day starts with a traditional Welcome to Country, with a smoking ceremony and dancers. There's a walking tour around the historic mission precinct with a local Tiwi guide, including a guided tour through the old Catholic Church, and a visit to the **Patakijiyali Museum** where you can learn about the Tiwi creation story. You'll get a behind-the-scenes screen-printing workshop, where you can learn how to screen print from

some of the local artists, and even create your own piece to take home with you. It's a great way to learn more about the Tiwi Islands and their people, traditions and culture.

Alternatively, you can choose to jump on the **Tiwi Islands Day Tour** which takes you on a minibus tour of Wurrumiyanga with a local Tiwi guide, as well as taking part in the Traditional Welcome to Country ceremony.

FOOD & DRINK

If you're visiting on a day tour with SeaLink NT, morning tea and lunch are provided. There aren't places to buy food in Wurrumiyanga, so it's best to bring anything specific you may want with you.

When staying at Tiwi Island Retreat, there is an onsite restaurant and bar that serves all your meals, as well as small snacks throughout the day. An ever-changing menu, often centering around whatever fresh fish was caught that day, every meal is prepared by award-winning chefs and is absolutely delicious.

THINGS TO DO

Explore the town of **Wurrumiyanga** and take in everything the Tiwi Islands has to offer.

Whether you're visiting for the day or staying a little longer, you can never go past a visit to the gallery **Tiwi Designs**, one of the oldest and most artistically diverse art centres in Australia. Learn how to screen print with local artists, watch artists creating their next masterpiece, or purchase your own pieces to take back home.

Munupi Art is another great spot to visit, known for its pottery and works by female and emerging artists.

Pop into **Bima Wear**, a women's group sewing shop with locally made designs.

Visit **Patakijiyali Museum** for Traditional art and depictions of Tiwi Dreaming stories.

Explore the **historic mission precinct**, home to the famous wooden Catholic Church which featured in the 2019 movie *Top End Wedding*.

For guests of Tiwi Island Retreat there is a whole menu of once-in-a-lifetime experiences and activities to choose from. Take a **picnic buggy tour** along the beautiful 5 Mile Beach before stopping for a peaceful picnic by the water. Jump onboard an **estuary fishing tour** with a local guide to discover secret fishing spots hidden down the estuaries that wind around the retreat, or opt for a **blue water fishing charter** to head out to the deep sea and target some of the Top End's popular tropical fish, including blue salmon, thread-fin salmon and golden snapper. Take a helicopter scenic flight to the **Ranku swimming hole**, where you can take in the incredible landscapes of the dense forests and winding waterways from the sky before landing at your own private waterhole for a refreshing dip in a natural paradise. Immerse yourself in Traditional culture on the **Jilamara Fine Art Experience**, taking a helicopter to Milikapiti on Melville Island where you'll be treated to an exclusive tour of the **Jilamara Arts & Crafts Association** and **Muluwurri Museum** by a local artist.

WHEN TO GO

During the dry season, from May until September, is generally the best time to visit the Tiwi Islands, when there is little rain or humidity and you can enjoy beautiful sunny days. Day tours operate from April to November. Tiwi Island Retreat is closed between mid-December until the end of March. The biggest event on the Tiwi calendar is the **Footy Grand Final and Art Sale**, which is held during March. SeaLink NT offers extra services for this event and it always sells out, so book your tickets in advance.

NEED TO KNOW

The Tiwi Islands are privately owned. If you are travelling to the Tiwi Islands on the SeaLink NT ferry or staying at Tiwi Island Retreat, permits are taken care of for you. However, if you plan to travel outside the community of Wurrumiyanga without a tour or guide you will need to contact the **Tiwi Land Council** (tiwilandcouncil.com) to apply for the required permits.

Do not swim at any time, as there's always crocs around the Tiwis - even if you can't see them.

ON THE MAINLAND

To make the most of your time in the Top End combine your visit to the Tiwi Islands with a few days exploring Darwin/Garramilla to make the most of your time in the Top End. Head to the **Mindil Beach Sunset Markets** (Thurs and Sun) for dinner and an epic sunset. Take a famous **Darwin Harbour sunset cruise**, complete with seafood buffet and sparkling wine to watch the golden glow from the water. Explore the city's World War II history at the **World War II Darwin Tunnels** and the **Darwin Military Museum**. Get out of the city and experience a **jumping crocodile cruise** on the Adelaide River, or spend a day waterfall hopping through beautiful **Litchfield National Park**.

Left Quiet beaches at Tiwi Island Retreat *Opposite top left* Welcome ceremony at Tiwi by Design *Opposite top right* Arriving on the dirt runway on Tiwi Island *Opposite bottom* Sunset on Tiwi Island

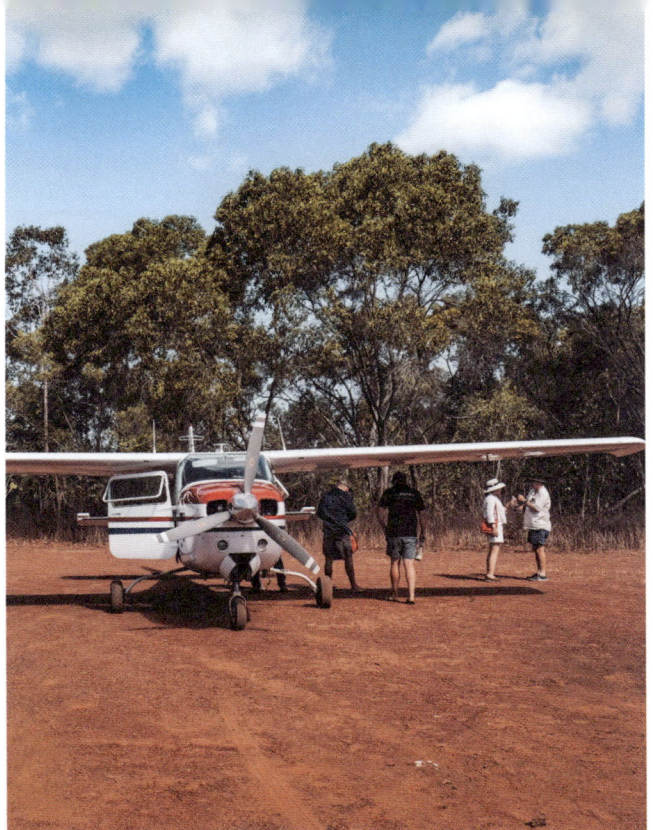

Tiwi Islands

Family fun

Hamilton Island, Queensland......40
Rottnest Island/Wadjemup, WA...49
Magnetic Island/Yunbenun, Queensland.................56
Moreton Island/Mulgumpin, Queensland.................63
Island Hopping: Granite Island, SA..................68
Great Keppel Island/Wop-pa, Queensland..................71
North Stradbroke Island/ Minjerribah, Queensland.......76

Hamilton Island

The ultimate family friendly island getaway

THE WHITSUNDAYS, QUEENSLAND

Family fun

Sitting in the heart of the Whitsundays, surrounded by the most spectacular sparkling blue water and white sand, with palm tree–lined beaches, is Hamilton Island. The ultimate holiday island, Hamilton Island offers near-perfect weather year-round, with daytrips and excursions out to the Great Barrier Reef and iconic bucket-list locations like Whitehaven Beach. There are stunning views over the Whitsundays everywhere you look. Golf buggies are the main form of transport to get you around the island and the vibe is chilled and laid-back, with everyone happy to be on holidays in the sun.

The largest inhabited island of the 74 islands of the Whitsundays, where the Ngaro People have cared for Country for millennia, Hamilton Island is only 4.5km from north to south and 3km from east to west. It's super easy to get around, with restaurants and shops found around the marina and most resorts sitting along the main beach.

There's an endless amount of ways to spend your days, with all the watersports and activities you could imagine, hikes to secret beaches you'll likely have all to yourself, and restaurants offering delicious cuisine and colourful drinks from all around the world.

A holiday destination you'll never want to leave and one that will likely call you back again and again, Hamilton Island is really a one-of-a-kind island.

THE BEST BITS

With perhaps the most fun island transport possible, book yourself a golf buggy to get around during your stay and explore more of the island.

TIME ZONE: AEST (GMT +10)
BEST TIME TO VISIT: Year-round
ACCESSIBLE FROM: Airlie Beach
GETTING THERE: Flight or ferry
PHONE RECEPTION: Yes
WI-FI: Yes
DAYTRIPS: Yes
KID FRIENDLY: Yes
SOCIALS: @hamiltonisland
MORE INFO: hamiltonisland.com.au

Previous Putney Beach on Great Keppel Island/Wop-pa
Opposite Views over Catseye Beach from the Reef View Hotel

Family fun

➔ GETTING HERE

Hamilton Island is the only island in the Great Barrier Reef to have its own airport (HTI), with direct flights from Melbourne, Sydney and Brisbane. Most accommodation offers free airport transfers, so you can be taken straight to your island home on arrival.

From the mainland, you can hop on an island transfer from Airlie Beach with **Cruise Whitsundays**, which will drop you off at the Hamilton Island Marina. The ferry transfer takes about 1hr and is also the best option if you fly into Whitsunday Coast/Proserpine Airport (PPP).

© GETTING AROUND

To make the most of your island getaway, rent a golf buggy to explore. You can hire one from outside the resort centre, with options to hire for as little as 4 hours. There are two free island shuttle bus options, with the Green Shuttle travelling between the Resort Centre and the Marina Village every 15min (Mon-Sun 6.50am-11pm), and the Blue Shuttle covering the entire island on a 20min loop (11am-7pm, 40min loop at other times). No matter where you are though you're never far away from where you need to be, with most of the island within walking distance.

ⓩ STAY

There are accommodation options on Hamilton Island for every type of traveller, from holiday homes and bungalows, to ultra-luxury escapes.

For those iconic Hamilton Island views over Catseye Beach and all the palm trees, book a hotel room at the **Reef View Hotel** or **Whitsunday Apartments**, with plenty of room options for families.

The **Beach Club** offers adult's-only accommodation right on the beach, with its own infinity pool and ground level beach views.

The **Palm Bungalows** offer cute A-frame bungalows set amongst the island's tropical gardens.

And for the utmost luxury, **qualia** offers ultra-private pavilion accommodation, some with infinity pools and private plunge pools, their own restaurants, complimentary golf buggies and chauffeur service, and more.

There are also lots of holiday homes to rent, perfect for groups and large families, set all around the island.

Top Golf buggies are the best method of transport on Hamilton Island *Bottom* Happy hour cocktails at the resort pool *Opposite* The Reef View Hotel

Hamilton Island 43

Family fun

ON THE MAINLAND

Airlie Beach is the mainland gateway to the Whitsundays and an extremely laid-back beach town to wander through. Have a dip in the **beachfront lagoon** overlooking the Coral Sea. **Skydive** over the Great Barrier Reef, what better views for jumping out of a plane?! Explore the rainforest and hidden waterfalls of **Conway National Park**. Jump on a sunset **Sundowner Cruise** and watch the golden hour over the Whitsundays from the water.

DAYTRIPS

It's easy to hop over to Hamilton Island from Airlie Beach for a daytrip with **Cruise Whitsundays** island transfers (cruisewhitsundays.com/island-transfers). For a DIY daytrip, simply book your own island transfers, so that you're free to explore however you please. Alternatively, they also have a range of organised daytrips, which can include add-ons to Whitehaven Beach, the Hamilton Island Golf Course, or lunch on the island.

FOOD & DRINK

There's no shortage of delicious food on Hamilton Island, with cuisine from all around the world to choose from.

Head to **Romano's** for a contemporary Italian menu with views over the marina, **TAKO** for delicious Mexican options, or **coca chu** for flavours from South-East Asia, hidden within the resort pool and sitting over Catseye Beach.

Bommie Restaurant is the island's premier fine-dining restaurant and located in the yacht club. It's *the* place if you're looking to celebrate a special occasion, and make sure you book ahead.

The **Marina Tavern** is your go-to for great pub meals, with plenty of options for everyone. There are also plenty of casual options, including **Bob's Bakery** for fresh sandwiches, pies and pasties, **Popeyes Takeaway** for fish and chips, **Hamilton Island Wildlife Cafe** for the best coffee on the island, **Sails** for snacks at the resort pool, and the **Pizzeria and Gelato Bar** for a casual dinner and dessert by the water.

There's an IGA supermarket where you can grab supplies to cook for yourself if your accommodation has a kitchen.

Opposite Sunset over Hamilton Island marina

Family fun

⊙ THINGS TO DO

Don't miss a daytrip out to iconic **Whitehaven Beach**, made of 98.9 per cent silica sand and regularly voted one of the best beaches in the world; there's nothing like spending a day here. Make sure to choose a tour that also takes you to Hill Inlet, to see the famous white and blue swirl of the Whitsundays. The water here always offers perfect swimming conditions, with crystal-clear water that's so lovely and warm you can jump right in.

Check out some of the hiking trails on the eastern end of the island. There are a number of different bushwalks to choose from, with options for all fitness levels. The ultimate hike is up to **Passage Peak Lookout**, a particularly beautiful spot to watch the sunrise, 200m above sea level at the end of a 5.3km incline trail. Some of the shorter walks take you to secluded beaches, including **Hideaway Bay, Coral Cove** where you can find the giant swing and **South East Head** which has a giant chair.

Head to **Catseye Beach** for some water fun, with kayaks, snorkelling equipment, stand-up paddleboards, catamarans and windsurfers available to hire from the **Hamilton Island Beach Sports Hut**. You can also choose from dinghy hire, jetski tours, wakeboarding and tube riding, with hours of ways to take advantage of the water here.

There is also an endless amount of land activities to choose from, with go-kart racing, offroad adventure tours, quad bikes for kids, mini golf, a bowling alley, the golf driving range, art classes and of course treatments at spa **wumurdaylin** to book into. Head to the Resort Centre and chat to the activities team for all the options available during your stay.

Have breakfast with the koalas at **Hamilton Island Wildlife Park**. The koalas are right out the front, so you can grab a smoothie and say good morning to them. To see more wildlife, the park is also home to kangaroos, crocodiles, dingoes and reptiles. Tickets include unlimited entry for the duration of your stay.

For some of the best views of the Whitsundays, book a helicopter ride over **Heart Reef and Whitehaven Beach**. About 1hr long, the heli will take you over Whitehaven Beach, Hill Inlet, Hardy Reef and out to the iconic Heart Reef, for some of the best views of the Great Barrier Reef. For the ultimate way to experience the reef, **Hamilton Island's Journey to the Heart** lands you on the private Heart Reef pontoon, where you can go swimming around the actual Heart with some of the most active marine life on the Great Barrier Reef. It's such a beautiful spot, and a really unforgettable experience - one to save up for.

Take a trip across to neighbouring **Dent Island**, home to the **Clubhouse** at Hamilton Island Golf Club for an incredible lunch experience. With views across the Whitsundays right from your table and a delicious menu to choose from, this is one of Hamilton Island's foodie experiences you will not want to miss. Make sure to book in advance so you don't miss out. If you want to hit a round of golf, the **golf course** is one of the most unique in the world, covering the whole island and offering ocean views from every hole.

In the evening, head up to **One Tree Hill** for cocktails and a cheese platter as you watch the sun go down. It's a beautiful sunset spot, with panoramic views over the water, but definitely get there early to secure yourself a table.

⊙ WHEN TO GO

Hamilton Island offers great weather year-round, so there's really no bad time to visit. There can be a little more rainfall during the summer months, but it's generally a quick shower passing through. If you can, avoid visiting during the Queensland, NSW or Victorian school holidays, which are all usually extremely busy times on the island.

⊙ NEED TO KNOW

As soon as you arrive, download the Hamilton Island App, your go-to guide for everything about the island. Through the app you can make restaurant reservations and spa appointments, see a live 'What's On' guide for activities and events, order takeaway food, find ferry and shuttle timetables, flight information, maps of the island and more.

During the summer months Irukandji jellyfish can be present in the water around Hamilton Island. Stinger suits are recommended for swimming and can be borrowed from the Beach Sports hut.

Opposite Catseye Beach

Family fun

Rottnest Island/ Wadjemup

Home of beautiful beaches and the happiest animal in the world

WESTERN AUSTRALIA

Only 19km off the coast of Fremantle in WA is the tiny island paradise of Rottnest Island/Wadjemup, affectionately known as 'Rotto'. An island of bicycles and beaches and home to the happiest animal on earth, the quokka. Here, everything you need is a short walk away – there's great food and drinks, 63 stunning beaches and 20 bays to swim in, and plenty of history and Traditional culture to learn about, with guided walking tours taking you all over the island.

Traditionally known as Wadjemup in the Noongar language, meaning 'the place across the water where the spirits are', the island was used by the Whadjuk Noongar People for ceremonies and important meetings, more than 6500 years ago, when it was still connected to the Australian mainland. During your visit, jump on a guided walking tour with a Noongar guide and Traditional Owner to learn more about the history and culture of the island and how to be respectful when visiting sites of significance.

An easy getaway from Fremantle or Perth/Boorloo, Rottnest feels like a whole different world. Stay for as little or as long as you like, with daytrip options and relaxing accommodation available for you to enjoy the island for a little longer. No matter how long you visit for, you're likely to go home with a camera roll full of beautiful blue beaches and smiley quokka snapshots.

TIME ZONE: AWST (GMT +8)

BEST TIME TO VISIT: During the warmer months, from Oct to April

ACCESSIBLE FROM: Perth and Fremantle

GETTING THERE: Ferries leave from Perth City, Fremantle (Victoria Quay), North Fremantle (Rous Head) and Hillarys Boat Harbour. There are also options to arrive by small plane, helicopter or seaplane, or to bring your own boat.

PHONE RECEPTION: Yes

WI-FI: Yes

DAYTRIPS: Yes, and there are lockers available behind the visitor's centre for daytrip visitors

KID FRIENDLY: Yes

SOCIALS: @rottnestislandwa

MORE INFO: rottnestisland.com

THE BEST BITS

Rent a bike or jump on the hop-on, hop-off bus to explore the whole island, with some of the most beautiful bays, beaches, views and swimming spots a little further out of the main town. And don't forget to take an iconic smiling quokka selfie, these little guys are the ultimate posers.

Opposite top left Happy quokka *Opposite top right* Kuld Creamery at the Basin *Opposite bottom* Sunset aerial view over Rottnest Island/Wadjemup

➔ GETTING HERE

Rottnest Island is easily accessible by ferry, plane or even your own boat, with plenty of options for getting to and from the island. The most popular option is by ferry, with several companies making the trip between the island and the mainland daily. Rottnest Island is only a 30min ferry ride from Fremantle (Victoria Quay), or you can hop on a ferry from Perth City (Barrack St Jetty) and enjoy a scenic cruise along the Swan River before making your way to the island.

Alternatively, you can also arrive by air. **Swan River Seaplanes** offer the unique experience of a water landing, either on Thomson Bay on Rotto or the Swan River, offering beautiful views of the city and the island as you fly between the two. There are also several charter planes and the **Rottnest Air-Taxi** that fly between the city and the island.

You can also take your own boat over to the island, and what a beautiful way to spend the day! There are admission fees and specific places to moor, so check the website (rottnestisland.com/visit/getting-here/by-private-boat) for all the information before heading over in your own boat.

© GETTING AROUND

Once you're on the island there are a few different options for getting around, with no cars to be seen. The easiest way to get around is on the **Quokka Coaches Island Explorer** hop-on, hop-off bus. Taking you to 19 stops, it gives you a great opportunity to see as much of the island as possible in a short amount of time. You can choose where you get on and off throughout the day, hopping your way across many of the beautiful beaches and bays. Purchase your tickets at the visitor's centre. The other option is to cycle your way around the island. **Pedal & Flipper Hire** have everything you need, with bikes (electric and regular), helmets, kids' bikes, baby seats, kids' trailers, snorkel gear, stand-up paddleboards, sports equipment and scooters all available to hire. It's about a 22km ride to make your way around the whole island, and with a few hills and often windy weather, we highly recommend choosing the electric bike option.

☾ STAY

Nestled behind the dunes of Pinky's Beach, **Discovery Rottnest Island** is the favourite place to stay. You can stay in one of their unique eco-tents, some of the most epic glamping tents you can imagine, kitted out with their own bathrooms, kitchens and outdoor decks. They are in the perfect location, right on Pinky's Beach and only a couple of

Opposite **Steps down to Parker Point**

minutes' walk to The Basin. There's a pool to dip in during the day, and Pinky's Rottnest Island beach club for an afternoon cocktail as the sun begins to set. There's also a campground here if you want to bring your own camping gear.

Another great option is **Samphire Rottnest**, a luxury hotel in the heart of Thomson Bay. With ocean views and its very own exclusive beach club, you'll start unwinding the minute you step foot here.

There are also self-contained holiday home options on Geordie Bay, with beachfront units, bungalows, cottages and cabins if you prefer a quieter stay, away from the main strip.

DAYTRIPS

Rotto is the perfect destination for an island daytrip. You can literally get around the whole island in one day, jumping into the bright blue water whenever the urge hits. There are all different kinds of daytrips on offer, with bike tours, snorkelling tours, cruises and hop-on, hop-off tours to choose from. **SeaLink Rottnest Island** or **Rottnest Express** are great places to start, where you can choose a daytrip option that suits your plans. Pair your return ferry ride with snorkelling and bike rental or a bus ticket to explore the island a little further on your own, or jump on a cruise or guided tour to be looked after for the whole day.

FOOD & DRINK

With an endless list of great food options, you'll struggle to fit them all in before it's time to leave the island.

Pop into the iconic **Rottnest Bakery**, for all kinds of homemade bakery treats, including pies, sausage rolls, fresh rolls and sandwiches and sweet treats.

Frankie's on Rotto offers delicious takeaway and dine-in sourdough pizzas and a great menu of pastas and salads for lunch and dinner.

The iconic **Hotel Rottnest** has a menu of pub classics in a great location overlooking Thomson Bay, and an outdoor stage and live music and entertainment in the summer months.

Indulge in the taste of Italy at **Isola Bar E Cibo**, with a menu of fresh pasta, spritzers, WA-sourced seafood and a cured meat platter that is highly recommended.

Above Sunset at Pinky's *Opposite* Sunset below the Wadjemup Lighthouse on Pinky Beach

Family fun

After all that walking and cycling, grab a refreshing afternoon ice-cream from **Kuld Creamery** at The Basin.

The Mezz on Rotto is a great place for an afternoon drink and small snacks as the sun begins to set, with fairy lights overhead, quokkas running around and a laid-back vibe overlooking the water.

Pinky's Rottnest Island is also a great sunset spot, offering West Australian wine, a locally inspired menu and a sky swirling with all different shades of pink as the sun goes down.

✓ THINGS TO DO

The best way to spend your time on Rottnest Island/Wadjemup is to either hire a bike or jump on the **Quokka Coaches Island Explorer** hop-on, hop-off bus and explore as many of the beautiful bays and beaches as you can get to. Jump off the bus at **Parker Point** for stunning views that will have you feeling like you're in Europe. From here you can jump on a free guided walking tour with the **Rottnest Island Voluntary Guides** (look out for the yellow T-shirts) and walk around to **Little Salmon Bay**, a perfect little beach sliced out from the rocky coastline, good for kids to play in the sand and great for snorkelling. It's definitely a can't-miss part of the island. **The Basin** is another stunning beach spot, with clear calm water and an ice-cream truck for an afternoon treat after your swim.

Explore the island from the water on a tour, with **snorkelling cruises**, **sunset cruises** or luxury island **seafood cruises** to choose from.

Learn more about the First Nations culture on Wadjemup on a guided walking tour with **Go Cultural** (gocultural.com.au). With a Noongar guide you'll discover the cultural significance of the island, and learn about the culture and traditions of the Whadjuk Noongar People.

Wander through the island's heritage buildings including the **Wadjemup Museum for Children** and the **Pilot Boathouse**.

Check out the views from the iconic **Wadjemup Lighthouse**, or learn more about the working lighthouse on a tour with the Rottnest Island Voluntary Guides.

Enjoy a round of golf or barefoot bowls at the **Rottnest Island Golf Club Clubhouse**.

Jump on the **Captain Hussey Historical Train** for a unique train ride to Oliver Hill, a significant Australian World War II heritage site where there is still a maze of underground tunnels to explore.

For the adrenaline junkies, the ultimate views of the island can be found jumping out of a plane with **Skydive Geronimo Rottnest**, before landing gracefully on the beach below.

ON THE MAINLAND

Only a 30min ferry ride from Fremantle or a 90min ferry ride from Perth/Boorloo's CBD, it's easy to explore either place if you're planning a visit to Rottnest Island/Wadjemup. In Perth, cruise down the Swan River to some of Western Australia's oldest **wineries**, have a picnic in **Kings Park** overlooking the city, and take a photo at the iconic blue **boatshed**. In **Fremantle** wander through the **boutiques and markets**, and stop in for a local beer and a bite on the harbour at **Gage Road Freo Brewery**.

? WHEN TO GO

Rottnest Island/Wadjemup can have good weather year-round, however the summer, spring and autumn months, generally from September to April offer the nicest conditions, when it's a little bit warmer, and there's little to no rain. It can sometimes be a little windy on the island though, so it's always a good idea to bring at least a light jacket regardless of the time of year. The island can be extremely busy during school holidays and on public holiday long weekends, with crowds flocking to the island. To avoid the crowds, it's best to plan your visit outside these times.

! NEED TO KNOW

Rottnest Island/Wadjemup doubled as a prison and labour camp for almost 100 years, for Aboriginal men and boys, who were forcibly removed from Country across Western Australia. To date, hundreds of unmarked Aboriginal graves have been uncovered in burial grounds across the island. It is a stark reminder of the treatment First Nations People were subjected to, with Rottnest's beauty giving no clue as to the atrocities that took place. You can learn more about this history at the **Wadjemup Museum** during your visit, by stopping at the **Koora-Yeye-Boordawan-Kalyakoorl** (Past-Present-Future-Forever) sculpture at the end of the main jetty to listen to a Welcome to Country, or heading online to find out more (rottnestisland.com/learn/history/aboriginal-history).

All visitors to Rottnest Island are required to pay a government admission fee, which is generally included in the fare for your ferry transfer to the island. The fee contributes to the conservation of the island and the upkeep of facilities and is, at the time of writing, $20 per adult for a day visitor and $27 per adult for overnight visitors, with discounts for children and families.

Opposite Glamping tents at Discovery Rottnest Island

Magnetic Island/ Yunbenun

Everything from palm-fringed beaches to granite boulders

TOWNSVILLE, QUEENSLAND

Family fun

TIME ZONE: AEST (GMT +10)
BEST TIME TO VISIT: Year-round
ACCESSIBLE FROM: Townsville
GETTING THERE: SeaLink ferry
PHONE RECEPTION: Yes
WI-FI: Yes
DAYTRIPS: Yes
KID FRIENDLY: Yes
SOCIALS: @thisismagneticisland
MORE INFO: thisismagneticisland.com and sealink.com.au/magnetic-island

Maggie, as it's affectionately called by the locals, is sure to quickly become one of your favourite island escapes. Lying close to the mainland, only 8km off the coast of Townsville, Magnetic Island/Yunbenun is in an ideal location. Easy to get to and explore, in one of the most consistently sunny parts of the country, and with palm-lined beaches and sparkly blue water, large granite boulders creating impressive lookout points, fringing coral reefs and an abundance of both land- and sea-based wildlife, Magnetic Island is a very special place.

Yunbenun, as it's known to its Traditional Owners, the Wulgurukaba People, who are known as the 'canoe people', has been a place of significance for thousands of years. Shell middens, stone tools and art sites across the island demonstrate the Traditional Owners' connection to the island that dates back tens of thousands of years, while stories such as the Big Carpet Snake tell of the creation of this landscape during the Dreaming, encompassing Yunbenun, Palm Islands and the mainland.

Magnetic Island is the only self-contained island within the Great Barrier Reef Marine Park, with two-thirds of the island listed as national park. Only a short 20min ferry ride away from Townsville, Maggie is the perfect spot for any kind of island getaway, from a weekend of sunshine and beach hopping to just a quick afternoon visit. Bursting with great eateries, 23 quiet beaches and bays, epic views and northern Australia's largest colony of wild koalas, there's always something new to see and explore on Maggie.

THE BEST BITS

For one of the most iconic Magnetic Island/Yunbenun views, head to the Arthur Bay Lookout. Found along the Forts Walk, it's the ultimate spot for a postcard shot over beautiful Arthur Bay. For a more off-the-beaten track view of the Maggie coastline, follow the pathway at the end of Olympus Crescent.

Opposite Views from Arthur Bay lookout

➔ GETTING HERE

SeaLink (sealink.com.au/magnetic-island) makes it super easy to explore Magnetic Island/Yunbenun, with passenger ferries running between the island and Townsville on the mainland every hour or so between 5.30am and 11pm. Departing from the Breakwater Terminal in Townsville, you can book your tickets in advance (recommended during peak periods) or at the terminal, making Magnetic Island one of the most accessible islands in Australia. **Magnetic Island Ferries** (magneticislandferries.com.au) operates the only vehicle barge across to the island, if you're planning on taking your car across with you.

© GETTING AROUND

Once you arrive on the island there are plenty of different ways to get around. The **Sunbus Bus Service** meets each ferry at the terminal, connecting you to the four main villages around the island. There are 29 bus stops around the island, so it's sure to get you everywhere you want to explore. Just make sure you bring cash for your ticket. To explore at your own pace you can also hire a car from Nelly Bay. For the ultimate island vibe, there are still a few of the iconic Magnetic Island 'Barbie' cars getting around the island from **Isle Hire**, as well as the super colourful topless jeeps available for hire from **MI Rentals**. Bikes are also available to hire. There are extensive walking trails across the island but it is quite hilly, so factor that into your plans!

🌙 STAY

Magnetic Island/Yunbenun is broken up into four main villages, each with their own places to stay and eat. There are plenty of accommodation options, from camping to beachfront holiday houses, with something for every budget.

Nelly Bay acts as the entrance to the island, as it's where the ferry arrives. Here you can find most of the island's shops and services, including the supermarket, post office and pharmacy. **Peppers Blue on Blue Resort** and **Grand Mercure Apartments** both offer apartment-style accommodation with views over the marina and the Coral Sea, while **Amaroo on Mandalay** is surrounded by the tropical bushland of the national park. **Horseshoe Bay** is a favourite for many visitors to base themselves, with plenty of

Family fun

cafes and restaurants, all the watersports' action and turtles, rays, dugongs and dolphins often spotted from the shore; it is also a lifeguard-patrolled beach. **Sails on Horseshoe** offers beachfront accommodation, only a couple of minutes' walk from the main street in town. There are also plenty of holiday houses to book around Horseshoe Bay, Arcadia and Picnic Bay, with space for groups and large families.

Magnetic Island is also known for its iconic A-frame cabins, which can be found at many of the backpackers' villages across the island. Offering all kinds of accommodation, from backpackers' dorms to private cabins and camping grounds, book a stay in an A-frame at either **Selina Magnetic Island** (formerly Bungalow Bay Koala Village) or **Nomads Magnetic Island**. Or search online for 'Maggie A-frame' on Airbnb for your own private little triangle house.

DAYTRIPS

Daytrips are easy to Magnetic Island/Yunbenun, with such regular ferry times allowing you to customise your own day on Maggie. Create your own itinerary before you go and then hop on the bus or rent a car when you arrive and enjoy your day on the island.

FOOD & DRINK

There's no shortage of excellent places to eat on Magnetic Island/Yunbenun, with plenty of great options in all of the villages.

For breakfast head to the **Early Bird Cafe** or **Cafe Nourish**, both in Horseshoe Bay and with delicious menus full of fresh food, as well as plenty of smoothies and coffees.

On the opposite side of the island, the **Magnetic Island Brewery** serves some of their signature brews alongside a walk-up food van, with a menu from **Straight Down BBQ** that changes weekly. A little way down the road, **Island Burger** serves delicious burgers and small bites on the beachfront, with happy hour and live music.

Great coffee can be found at the **Tiny Palm Coffee Van** at Jungle Club.

Scally Wags Cafe is the island's unique pirate-themed cafe, serving burgers and acai bowls and everything in between.

Mamma Roma offers 'authentic Italian' pizzas and pastas on the Esplanade of Picnic Bay.

Saltwater is the place to go for fine dining and is the ideal venue for celebrating.

Top A-frame bungalows at Selina Magnetic Island *Bottom* Rock wallaby at Geoffrey Bay *Opposite* Radical Bay

There are plenty of options for good old-fashioned pubs, from the **Picnic Bay Hotel** to the **Arcadia Village Pub** and **Marlin Bar Tavern** in Horseshoe Bay.

Other island favourites include **Noodies on the Beach**, **Maggie Island Bubble Tea**, and **Ceylon Curry Corner** - a Sri Lankan street food van in Nelly Bay.

✓ THINGS TO DO

Whether you're planning on getting wet or staying dry, there are endless ways to explore Magnetic Island/Yunbenun. From self-guided snorkelling trails, to granite boulder hikes taking you to incredible viewpoints.

On land, start with the **Forts Walk**, one of the most popular walks on the island. Taking you from Horseshoe Bay to Arcadia, the trail leads you through the bushland of Maggie, home to World War II history, stunning lookouts over the bays and the island, as well as a huge number of wild koalas. The 5km-return walk is best started early in the day to avoid the extreme heat. The **Arthur Bay Lookout** can be found towards the beginning of the Forts Walk (at the Horseshoe Bay end), with one of the best and most iconic views of the island. When you get to Arcadia, stop by **Geoffrey Bay** (also known as Bremner Point) to meet the cute little rock wallabies that live amongst the boulder rocks.

Hawkings Point offers panoramic views over Nelly Bay and Picnic Bay, as well as all the way across to Townsville on a clear day. It's essentially a giant granite boulder, emerging from the native bushland surrounding it, with a rocky hiking trail to the top.

During the winter months the **Butterfly Walk** next to Selina is home to thousands of blue tiger butterflies that migrate to the island. You can see the stunning detail of their wings on the lower branches, or watch as hundreds flutter above.

ON THE MAINLAND

Take some time on your trip to explore Townsville, the sunny gateway to Magnetic Island/Yunbenun. Grab lunch at **The Ville**, the hub of Townsville, with six different restaurants and bars, and views overlooking Magnetic Island. Explore the one-of-a-kind **Museum of Underwater Art (MOUA)**, Australia's first underwater museum - SeaLink actually offers tours out to the underwater installations. Hike to the top of **Castle Hill** or **Mount Sonder** at sunset for stunning views across the city, or waterfall hop your way through nearby **Little Crystal Creek**. Or simply feel like a local and take a walk around the city on Townsville's **street art trail**.

For a complete overview of the island, taking you to the best attractions and hidden gems, jump aboard the **Maggie Comprehensive**, a half-day guided bus tour that shares plenty of history and an insight into local life on the island. It's a great way to see the best of the island, especially if you're short on time.

To get up close and personal with some native Aussie wildlife, stop by **The Koala Park** at Selina. With daily tours, you can cuddle a koala, pat a wombat or even have a python wrapped around your body.

Jump on a private tour with **Pilgrim Adventures**, who will take you to your own remote beach on Maggie, with a gourmet picnic in hand.

Once you've warmed up on the land, take to the water to explore the unique underwater world that surrounds the island. The **Maggie Discovery Tour with Aquascene** gives you a tour of the island through the eyes of the locals, with plenty of fishing, swimming and snorkelling throughout the day. It's a great way to see parts of the island that you can't access from the mainland, as well as hear a little bit about the island's unique history. Hop your way across the beaches on a **self-guided snorkelling tour** to some of Maggie's favourite fringing reefs. Snorkelling trails can be found in Nelly Bay (great for beginners) and Geoffrey Bay (for more advanced snorkellers), winding around to Arthur Bay and Florence Bay, where you can often see hundreds of colourful reef fish, turtles and dolphins. Geoffrey Bay also has a shipwreck, the *Moltke*, that you can snorkel around, which was scuttled here in 1911, and is now home to all kinds of undersea life.

Jump on a **sunset sailing cruise** with **Pilgrim Sailing**, the ultimate luxury sailing experience, on their luxury 58ft yacht. Watch the sun go down while grazing on a local cheese platter and sipping a glass of bubbly. What could be better?!

? WHEN TO GO

With more than 320 sunny days per year, and an average temperature sitting between 27 and 29°C throughout the year, and little rainfall, there's never a bad time for a trip to Maggie.

! NEED TO KNOW

Stingers (stinging jellyfish) can be present in the waters around the island, and are especially frequent when it's warm. Stingers are dangerous but you can protect yourself by wearing stinger suits and following local advice.

Opposite top Looking out over Hawkings Point *Opposite bottom* Aerial views over the bays of Magnetic Island/Yunbenun

Magnetic Island/Yunbenun

Moreton Island/ Mulgumpin

An adventure lover's playground

SOUTHERN QUEENSLAND, QUEENSLAND

TIME ZONE: AEST (GMT +10)

BEST TIME TO VISIT: Year-round

ACCESSIBLE FROM: Brisbane

GETTING THERE: Passenger and vehicle ferries depart from Brisbane

PHONE RECEPTION: Yes - at the resort and sporadically around the island

WI-FI: Yes - at the resort

DAYTRIPS: Yes

KID FRIENDLY: Yes

SOCIALS: @tangaloomaislandresort, @visitmoretonbay & @moretonislandadventures

MORE INFO: tangalooma.com & moretonislandadventures.com.au

Just off the coast of Brisbane/Meanjin is Moreton Island/Mulgumpin, an adventure lover's paradise jam packed with activities and experiences to keep you going for days on end. It sits within Quandamooka Country and is known to the Traditional Owners, the Ngugi People as Mulgumpin, meaning the place of the sandhills. The island is the ultimate 4WD island adventure, with epic sandhills and beach drives to tackle, as well as inland lagoons and Queensland's oldest lighthouse. It's also home to Tangalooma Island Resort, a good base from which to explore the island in a little more luxury, and with more adventure activities on offer than you can count.

The third-largest sand island in the world, Moreton Island is made up of 98 per cent sand, with just 2 per cent of its composition made up of rock at Cape Moreton on the northern tip of the island. Gheebulum Kunungai (Moreton Island) National Park covers 95 per cent of the island, and is home to the highest coastal sand dune in the world, Mount Tempest, which stands at 285m tall and offers incredible 360-degree views of the island. Moreton Island is also iconic for the Tangalooma Wrecks, a cluster of 15 shipwrecks that were intentionally placed here by the Queensland Government between 1963 and 1984 to provide a safe anchorage place for boats. These days it's a great place for snorkelling, with a coral reef growing amongst the shipwreck debris.

There are countless ways to experience Moreton Island, from scenic helicopter flights, ATV tours, desert safaris and snorkelling trips from Tangalooma Island Resort, to pristine deserted beaches, champagne pools, giant sandhills and red rock sand formations to find when exploring with your own 4WD. The calm coastline on the western side of the island is home to sea turtles, dugongs, dolphins and stingrays, with whales passing close to the shore during their migration season.

THE BEST BITS

To make the most of your time on Moreton Island/Mulgumpin, combine a 4WD adventure with a stay at Tangalooma Island Resort, giving you the opportunity to explore the remote side of the island and also access to all the resort's incredible activities.

Opposite The Tangalooma shipwrecks

➔ GETTING HERE

Only 75min from Brisbane, there are two ferries servicing Moreton Island/Mulgumpin. The **Tangalooma Island Resort Passenger Ferry** is for resort guests only (including daytrippers), and is the easiest way to get to the island. The Holt Street Wharf is just 10min by taxi from Brisbane Airport, with four passenger services operating daily in each direction. To bring your 4WD, **Moreton Island Adventures** runs a Micat Ferry from Lytton in Brisbane which takes 90min to get to the island. Car spots can sell out quite far in advance, so book your tickets at least four weeks in advance to secure your spot. The Micat arrives right alongside the Tangalooma Wrecks and also has a passenger saloon and bar on board.

💤 STAY

Tangalooma Island Resort is the main place to stay on Moreton Island/Mulgumpin, offering a range of beachfront accommodation. There are hotel rooms, units, villas and apartments, surrounded by tall palms and overlooking the calm waters of Moreton Bay. If you're visiting as a group or larger family there are also a handful of holiday houses which can be booked through the resort. The resort offers several restaurants and shops, as well as plenty of adventure experiences and free activities that are exclusive to resort guests only. Fun fact: Tangalooma Island Resort was transformed into Spooky Island for the *Scooby-Doo* movie in 2001.

Alternatively, you can experience the wild side of the island on a camping adventure. There are campgrounds and camping zones found all around the island, amongst the sand dunes, often close to main sites such as the Tangalooma Wrecks, the Blue Lagoon, and North Point. Campsites need to be booked in advance via **Mulgumpin Camping** (mulgumpincamping.net.au), along with a vehicle access permit. To make the most of your visit to Moreton Island, combine a camping adventure with a resort stay and experience everything this incredible island has to offer. There is a carpark for resort guests at Tangalooma, so after a few nights exploring life in the wild, you can check in for a more luxe stay at the resort and make the most of its guest-only experiences and facilities.

🎯 DAYTRIPS

Tangalooma Island Resort offers the easiest and most affordable way to experience Moreton Island/Mulgumpin on a daytrip. It has plenty of options to combine a daytrip with some of its signature experiences, including desert safaris, marine discovery cruises, snorkelling the wrecks, ATV quad bike tours and whale watching cruises during the season.

For an even longer day, you can also upgrade to include a sunset cocktail cruise and wild dolphin feeding experience before returning on the last boat of the day.

Moreton Island Adventures also offers its own daytrip experiences, with the DIY Day Tour option allowing you to bring your car over and explore as much of the island as you can in just one day. You'll be dropped off right near the wrecks, with plenty to explore as soon as you arrive.

🍴 FOOD & DRINK

When staying at Tangalooma Island Resort, there are several different restaurants and food outlets open all day long. The **Beach Cafe** has burgers, salads, pizzas and light meals for lunch and dinner, the **Beach BBQ** offers open-air dinners with pub favourites, and the **Coffee Lounge** is open all day for coffees and drinks, sandwiches, snacks and sweet treats. **Fire & Stone** offers traditional Asian dishes, designed to be shared, in a more formal dining setting. Before you head to dinner, make sure to pop in for a cocktail at the **Wheelhouse Deck** during the golden hour - it's the best place at Tangalooma to watch the sunset each night.

For anyone coming to the island on a camping adventure, you'll need to bring all of your own food and supplies for the duration of your visit. There is a small general store called **Castaways** located in Bulwer (around 20min north of the ferry) if you need extra essentials or fuel and it stocks bread, milk, fresh produce, ice, snacks, sunscreen, alcohol, fishing bait and some camping supplies. Castaways is also a cafe, offering a delicious breakfast and lunch and coffee. At the southern end of the island in Kooringal you can find the **Gutter Bar**, a restaurant, bar and general store with fresh seafood, burgers, cold beers and great island vibes.

✓ THINGS TO DO

Moreton Island/Mulgumpin has enough sites and activities to keep you busy from the moment you arrive until you leave. It really is an adventure paradise. For those staying at or visiting Tangalooma Island Resort, there are endless options for activities, including an extensive list of free activities. It's important to mention that activities at Tangalooma Island Resort are only available to resort guests.

On land, explore the Tangalooma Desert on an **ATV quad bike tour** or an exciting **desert safari**, or for a unique tour of the beaches jump on a **segway tour**.

Opposite top left Whale watching at the North Point of Moreton Island/Mulgumpin *Opposite top right* Scenic helicopter ride over the island *Opposite bottom* ATV tour to Tangalooma Desert

Moreton Island/Mulgumpin

Family fun

There are also plenty of activities to get you wet, including clear-bottom kayaks for underwater viewing, banana boats, stand-up paddleboards and motor boats for hire. Tangalooma is famous for its **wild dolphin feeding program**, where you can hand-feed a bottlenose dolphin at around sunset each night.

Explore the **Tangalooma Wrecks** on a snorkelling, scuba diving or sea scooter safari, and there's also an option for an **illuminated night tour** of the shipwrecks.

Stay dry on a **Marine Discovery Cruise**, searching for sea turtles and the resort's resident dugong - named Dougie.

During the winter months jump on a **whale watching cruise** to see gentle humpback whales passing by the northern tip of the island on their migration.

To see the island from the sky, you can jump on a **scenic helicopter flight**, or get your adrenaline pumping by **parasailing** over Moreton Bay.

If you want to explore a little further than the resort, there are **safari bus tours** that take you to either the north or south of the island, getting off-the-beaten track and exploring some of the island's best spots. In the evening, jump on a sunset cruise to enjoy the golden hour from the bay.

If you're exploring with your own 4WD there are plenty of unique sites around the island. **Cape Moreton Lighthouse** is Queensland's oldest lighthouse, standing tall at the northern point of the island since 1857. The **Champagne Pools** and **Blue Lagoon** are great swimming spots to cool down in after a long drive, as well as **Mirapool Lagoon** and **Honeymoon Bay**. Check out some of the island's unique sand dunes, including **Mount Tempest** and **Big and Little Sandhills**. Or hit the waves for a spot of surfing on **Eastern Beach**, stretching 27km along the eastern side of the island.

WHEN TO GO

A great destination to visit year-round, Moreton Island/Mulgumpin has an abundance of sunny days no matter what time of year. Autumn is considered one of the best times to visit, with blue skies throughout most of the season and warm water for swimming and snorkelling. June to September is whale season, when you can see whales migrating past the island either from the northern tip of the island, or on a whale watching cruise.

NEED TO KNOW

If you're planning to drive your 4WD on Moreton Island/Mulgumpin you will need to purchase a 4WD Vehicle Access Permit from **Mulgumpin Camping** (mulgumpincamping.net.au). There are one month or one year permits available depending on how often you visit. Campsites will need to be booked in addition to this permit. Also, always check the tide times if you're driving around the island to make sure you don't get stuck.

ON THE MAINLAND

With ferries leaving from the Brisbane River itself, it's easy to pair your visit to Moreton Island/Mulgumpin with a short city break as well. See the city from above with a spin on the **Wheel of Brisbane**. Take a dip at **Streets Beach**, Australia's only inner-city, built beach overlooking the river. Check out the exhibitions at **QAGOMA**, Australia's largest gallery of modern art, with changing exhibitions from both local and international artists. Take the ferry from Eagle Street Pier to the **Eat Street Markets** for delicious street food on the weekends.

Above Sunset over Tangalooma Resort *Opposite* The pools at Tangalooma Resort

ISLAND HOPPING
Granite Island

FLEURIEU PENINSULA, SOUTH AUSTRALIA

Whilst technically connected to the mainland by a narrow walking path, Granite Island on South Australia's Fleurieu Peninsula is a favourite for holidaymakers and quite a unique island to explore. Accessible via the beautiful beachside town of Victor Harbor, the town and island alike are full of character, history and stunning natural beauty, with a historic horse-drawn tram connecting the two.

The tiny island is home to a colony of little penguins on the land, as well as the mysterious southern right whale in the water (whale watching season is May to Oct). It's around 62 acres in size and is made up predominantly of huge granite boulders, covered in orange lichen, with bright blue water lapping the shore. In fact, it's considered one of the most-recognised ecological attractions in Victor Harbor. Granite Island Recreation Park covers the whole island, and is free to visit.

Give yourself plenty of time to explore the town of Victor Harbor. There are plenty of parks and beaches to explore (Horseshoe Bend just down the road is our favourite), the oldest steel railway in Australia, alpacas to befriend, shops, and the nearby village of Port Elliot with its famous bakery. Or, if you want to indulge in the local wineries, there's plenty to taste test your way through in the nearby Adelaide Hills, and a range of great places to eat offering diverse menus.

Family fun

Opposite top Views along the Kaiki walking trail *Opposite bottom left* Horse-drawn tram from Victor Harbor to Granite Island *Opposite bottom right* Cute sign on Granite Island

➔ GETTING HERE

It's only a short walk along the causeway from Victor Harbor to Granite Island (around 630m), however the best way to get there is on the historic horse-drawn tram. One of the few remaining horse-drawn trams in the world, a team of beautiful Clydesdale horses take visitors to and from the island. Trams depart throughout the day roughly every 40min, between 10.30am (first tram to the island) and 3.40pm (last tram returning).

⊙ THINGS TO DO

Once you're on Granite Island, the **Kaiki Walking Trail** is a favourite for visitors wanting to explore the whole island. The 2.9km walking trail is an easy trail, expected to take just 45min to 1hr, taking you past all the island's points of interest, including art sculptures, the lighthouse, and the jetty. There are a few short trails off the main path as well, offering panoramic views across the island and back to the mainland.

Between May and October is considered whale watching season, when Southern right whales make their way along the coastline of the Fleurieu Peninsula. Often swimming with their calves in tow, these gentle giants move slowly throughout the water and are frequently spotted from the island. Little penguins are also present on the island, although their population is quite small. Best spotted at dusk, guided tours are available at times throughout the year.

For drinks, snacks and refreshments head to **The Island Cafe**. With a wide selection of foods and drinks to choose from and views overlooking the water, it's the ideal location to stop for a refuel before making the walk back along the causeway.

💤 STAY

Base yourself in Victor Harbor, or the pretty villages of Port Elliot or Goolwa nearby, for your visit to Granite Island, with plenty of hotels, holiday houses, caravan parks, farm stays and boutique-style stays to choose from. There are lots of options within walking distance of Victor Harbor, as well as near the causeway to Granite Island. Book ahead over summer and for public holiday weekends, as it's a popular holiday town.

ⓘ MORE INFO

For more information and to plan your visit head to visitvictorharbour.com, or check out @visitvictorharbour on socials.

ISLAND HOPPING: Granite Island

Great Keppel Island/Wop-pa

Fringed by 17 deserted beaches

CAPRICORN COAST, QUEENSLAND

Just a half-hour ferry ride from Yeppoon, Great Keppel Island/Wop-pa is the versatile island that provides the perfect balance between exploration and relaxation. Your days can be as busy or as laid-back as you choose, with 17 pristine deserted beaches to lounge on, bushland hiking trails across and through the island, watersports to keep you busy all day long, and an abundance of marine life to swim alongside.

Great Keppel is the largest of the 18 Keppel Islands, at almost 1500ha in size, and is known as Wop-pa to the Woppaburra People, the Traditional Owners. Many middens have been found on the island, recording the Woppaburra People's presence on the island that dates back many thousands of years. The Woppaburra People have also been formally recognised as Native Title holders for Great Keppel Island/Wop-pa (which also includes North Keppel).

One of the Great Barrier Reef's only continental islands, Great Keppel was historically part of Australia's mainland, until it broke off to become an island of its own about 5 million years ago. These days it floats 18km off the coast of Yeppoon, which you can see from the shore.

Sitting just north of the Tropic of Capricorn, Great Keppel Island has squeaky white sand and beautiful crystal-clear water, is home to more than 100 species of birds including kookaburras and rainbow lorikeets, as well as plenty of turtles, colourful fish, dolphins and even a family of dugongs. Easy to get to, Great Keppel is the perfect daytrip destination, or place to stay a little longer and enjoy life right on the beach.

TIME ZONE: AEST (GMT +10)
BEST TIME TO VISIT: Year-round
ACCESSIBLE FROM: Yeppoon
GETTING THERE: Ferry from Keppel Bay Marina
PHONE RECEPTION: Yes
WI-FI: Yes, but limited and only at the front reception
DAYTRIPS: Yes
KID FRIENDLY: Yes
SOCIALS: @greatkeppelislandhideaway
MORE INFO: visitcapricorn.com.au & greatkeppelislandhideaway.com.au

THE BEST BITS

Home to 17 incredible white sandy beaches, you can always find a beach to yourself on Great Keppel Island/Wop-pa. The water is warm and crystal clear, full of healthy reef, colourful fish and plenty of sea turtles to meet as you snorkel around. The sunsets on Great Keppel can't be beaten, so grab a cocktail from the Hideaway Bar to watch.

Opposite Beautiful views from Putney Beach

GETTING HERE

Great Keppel Island is just 30min from the mainland, with two ferry options for you to choose from. **Keppel Konnections** (keppelkonnections.com.au) takes you to Great Keppel from Keppel Bay Marina. Departing from the 'Red Jetty', Keppel Konnections has three departures a day. Alternatively, **Freedom Fast Cats** (freedomfastcats.com) also offers transfers between the island and Rosslyn Bay Marina seven days a week.

GETTING AROUND

Once you're on the island there are no cars, but there are walking trails connecting you to the various beaches and lookout points from the main hub at Great Keppel Island Hideaway. **Keppel Dive** (greatkeppelwatersports.com.au) also offers beach drop-offs – essentially a boat transfer to any of the beaches around the island so you have more time to swim and enjoy the beach, and they can come back and pick you up when you're ready.

STAY

Great Keppel Island Hideaway is the main hub of the island, and in the perfect location, sitting along Putney Beach and only a few steps away from where the ferries come in, so it's a great place to stay. With beachfront cabins, motel-style rooms, studio apartments, and even a large beach house, there are plenty of options when choosing where to stay.

There are also a number of holiday houses scattered around the island if you're looking for something a little more removed and self-contained.

DAYTRIPS

There are a few different ways to explore Great Keppel Island/Wop-pa on a daytrip. For those wanting to explore the island at their own pace, **Keppel Konnections** offers full daytrips from Keppel Bay Marina, dropping you directly onto the beautiful Fishermans Beach. From there you're free to wander the island at your own leisure and spend the day however you choose. Snorkel equipment and lunch at the **Hideaway Bar & Bistro** is included in your daytrip too.

For more of a guided tour, the **Keppel Explorer** offers small group tours with a local guide, taking you to lots of great snorkelling hotspots, secluded islands and secret spots around the Keppel Islands.

FOOD & DRINK

The main place to eat on Great Keppel/Wop-pa is the **Hideaway Bar & Bistro**, part of the Great Keppel Island Hideaway, which is the only fully licensed restaurant on the island. The Bar & Bistro is open daily for breakfast, lunch and dinner, welcoming both daytrippers and guests staying at the Hideaway. The menu offers a huge variety to choose from, with everything from smashed avo to acai bowls for breakfast, and fresh barramundi to barbecue pork ribs for dinner. It's also the best place to watch the sunset on the island, with one of their signature cocktails in hand and happy hour enjoyed between 4pm and 5pm.

There are also a couple of small shops, including a convenience store and a pizza shop a short walk down the road from the Hideaway.

ISLAND HOPPER: KEPPEL BAY ISLANDS

For an off-the-beaten track experience, seven of the islands within **Keppel Bay Islands National Park** offer camping, including the main islands, **North Keppel Island** and **Humpy Island**. There are basic facilities on some of the islands, including composting toilets and picnic tables, but you will need to bring everything with you (including drinking water) and purchase a camping permit. **Keppel Dive** offers camping transfers to North Keppel Island and Humpy Island from Great Keppel Island/Wop-pa. For details, head to Queensland Parks (parks.des.qld.gov.au/parks/keppel-bay-islands/camping).

THINGS TO DO

Without a doubt, the main way to spend your time on Great Keppel Island/Wop-pa is to explore as many of its 17 incredible beaches as you can. Whether you get a boat transfer to them, or you hike your way across the island to explore them all on foot, each of the beaches are unique and beautiful in their own way. Venture a little further to find some more secluded beaches, that you're likely to have all to yourself as well.

Pick up some snorkel equipment and check out life underneath the water. Sitting in the Great Barrier Reef Marine Park, there is plenty of reef and underwater life to explore off the beaches. The best snorkelling spots can be found at **Monkey Point**, **Clam Bay** and **Shelving Beach**, which are all an easy walk from the Hideaway, where you can often spot turtles swimming around in the shallows.

Opposite top left Take your pick of activities on the island *Opposite bottom left* Afternoon cocktails at Great Keppel Island Hideaway *Opposite far right* Aerial views over Monkey Bay

GUIDED SNORKEL TOURS
STAND UP PADDLE BOARDS
SNORKEL GEAR HIRE
KAYAKS
PADI DIVE CENTR
BEACH DROP OFFS

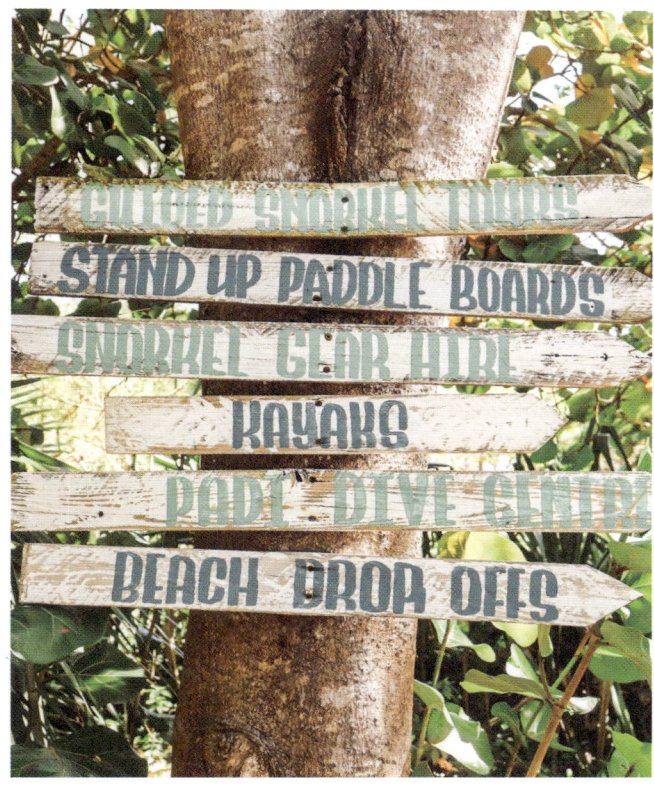

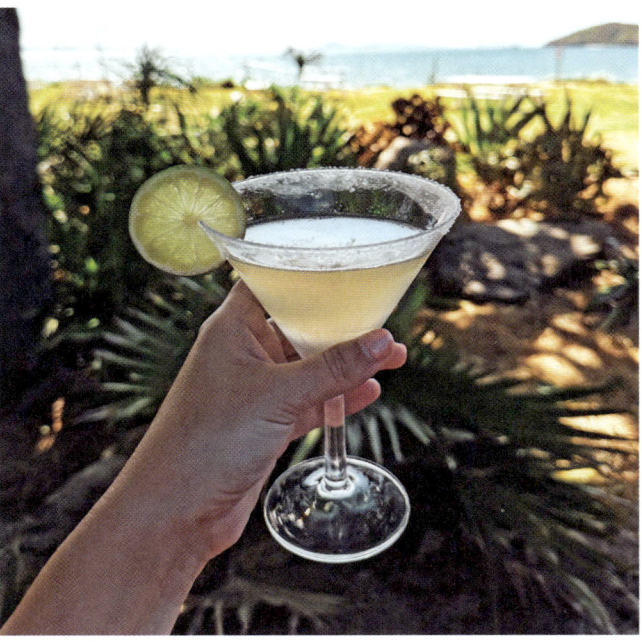

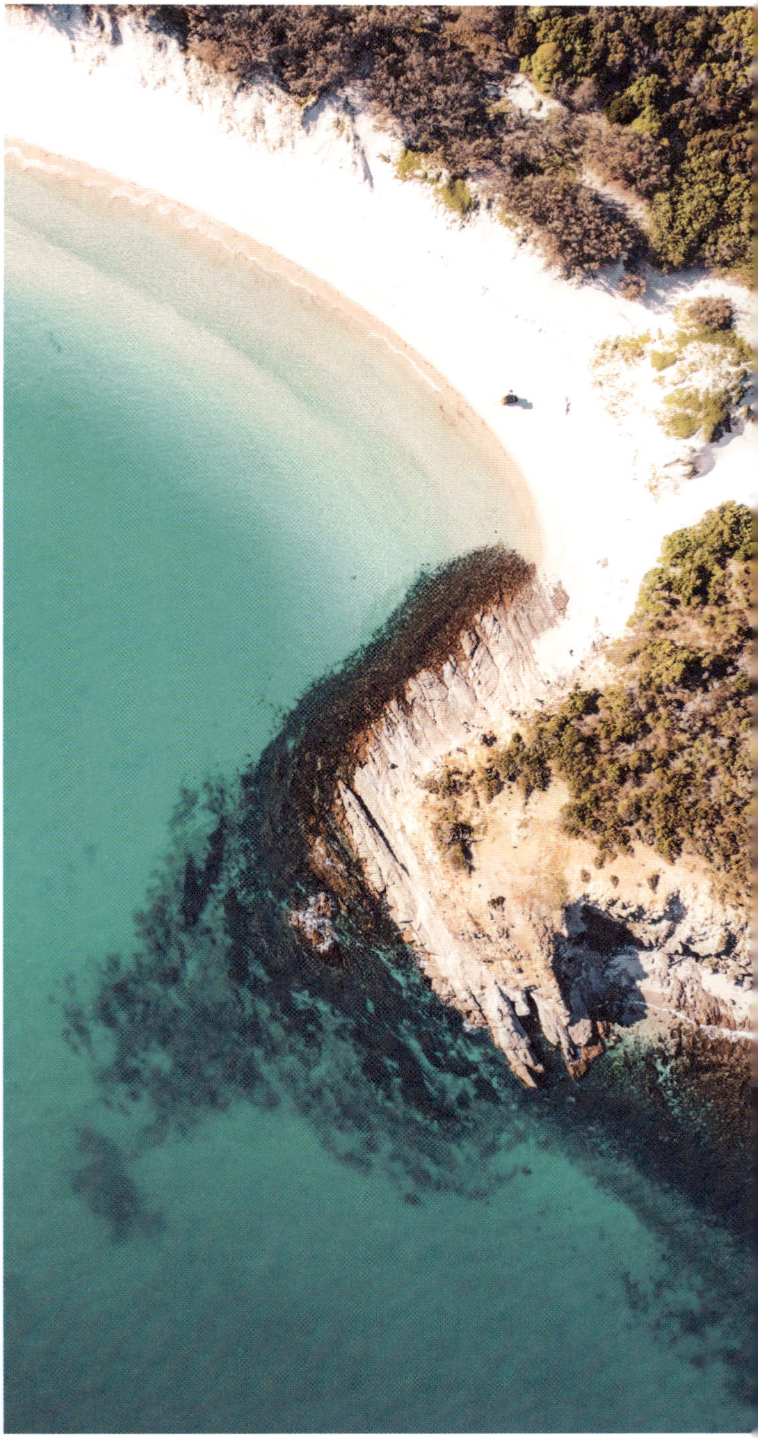

Family fun

Hike your way around the island and check out the views along the way. While some lookout spots are marked, many of the best lookouts can be found by walking along the various trails that take you between the beaches. The **Lighthouse** has some of the best views, where you can see many of the other Keppel Islands.

Learn about the local marine life on the **GKI Sea Way Trail**. The 300m-long boardwalk trail takes you through the grounds of Great Keppel Hideaway and features 15 colourful boards, sharing information and images about the marine life of the Great Barrier Reef, as well as the conservation projects the Turtle Fund program has initiated.

With the water surrounding Great Keppel Island beautifully calm and peaceful, it's an enviable place to jump on a **kayak tour** to explore from the water. **Great Keppel Watersports** offers 2hr kayak tours with a local guide, to show you the best of the island from the water, or you can rent your own kayak for a few hours or a whole day to explore your own way.

WHEN TO GO

Great Keppel Island/Wop-pa is a great year-round destination, with warm, sunny weather and little rainfall throughout the year. The winter months can be a little cooler, especially at night, so it's a good idea to pack some warm layers. At different times throughout the year you can see spectacular wildlife experiences, with humpback whales migrating past the island (July-Sept), manta rays feeding offshore (May-Aug), turtle nesting (Nov-Feb) and turtle hatching (Jan-March). No matter what you're hoping to see and experience, there's never a bad time to visit Great Keppel Island.

ON THE MAINLAND

Venture a little further into the mainland and check out the city of **Rockhampton**. As your arrival and departure point if you're flying to visit Great Keppel Island/Wop-pa, Rockhampton is worth spending a couple of extra nights to explore. Making its name as the beef capital of Australia, Rockhampton is a bustling regional city, teeming with activities that will keep you busy for days! Wander along the Riverside Precinct, say hi to the baby chimpanzees at the free **Rockhampton Zoo**, take a bull statue tour around the city, have a sunset picnic at **Mount Archer**, and immerse yourself in local life at the PBR (Professional Bull Riding) night.

Above Sunset at the lookout seat at Great Keppel Island Hideaway *Opposite* Stroll on Leeke's Beach

North Stradbroke Island/Minjerribah

One of the world's best land-based whale watching sites

SOUTHERN QUEENSLAND, QUEENSLAND

Family fun

North Stradbroke Island/Minjerribah is one of the most accessible islands from Brisbane/Meanjin, but it will have you feeling like you're a whole world away from the city. Known as Minjerribah to the local Quandamooka People, the island has rich culture dating back more than 21,000 years. With spectacular sunsets, an abundance of wildlife, a proud First Nations culture, campsites right on the beach and holiday houses overlooking the ocean, it's an ideal destination in which to unwind and escape to nature for a few days.

Straddie, as it's affectionately known, is an incredible place for wildlife spotting – you're likely to see kangaroos and koalas wandering across the road, turtles and manta rays swimming not too far from the shore, kookaburras and eagles flying overhead, and then of course, there's the whales. Sitting alongside the 'whale highway', the island is considered one of the best land-based whale-watching sites in the world, where thousands of humpback whales migrate, often with their newborn calves in the later part of the season. You can see them right from the land, breaching, tail slapping and blowing water into the air.

North Stradbroke is the second-largest sand island in the world, with three townships spread across it: Dunwich (Goompi), Amity Point (Pulan) and Point Lookout (Mooloomba). With extensive walking trails overlooking the ocean, 4WD tracks to explore inland on the island, beaches you can drive on and plenty of great places to eat, there's always something to do and explore on Straddie.

TIME ZONE: AEST (GMT +10)
BEST TIME TO VISIT: May to Nov
ACCESSIBLE FROM: Cleveland (Brisbane)
GETTING THERE: SeaLink runs passenger and vehicle ferries between Cleveland and North Stradbroke Island
PHONE RECEPTION: Yes
WI-FI: Yes but check with your accommodation
DAYTRIPS: Yes
KID FRIENDLY: Yes
SOCIALS: @northstraddieisland and @discover_stradbroke
MORE INFO: stradbrokeisland.com and sealink.com.au/north-stradbroke-island

THE BEST BITS

Point Lookout on the eastern corner of the island is *the* place to watch the whale migration. Humpback whales pass by the island from May to Sept, often travelling with their calves in the latter half of the season, and are easily spotted from the boardwalks and beaches.

Opposite Humpback whales migrating along the 'Whale Highway'

OYSTERS
COFFIN BAY OYSTERS $19 DOZ OR 1/2 DOZ
PRAWN & AVO ROLLS $14-50 FROM 10.30 AM

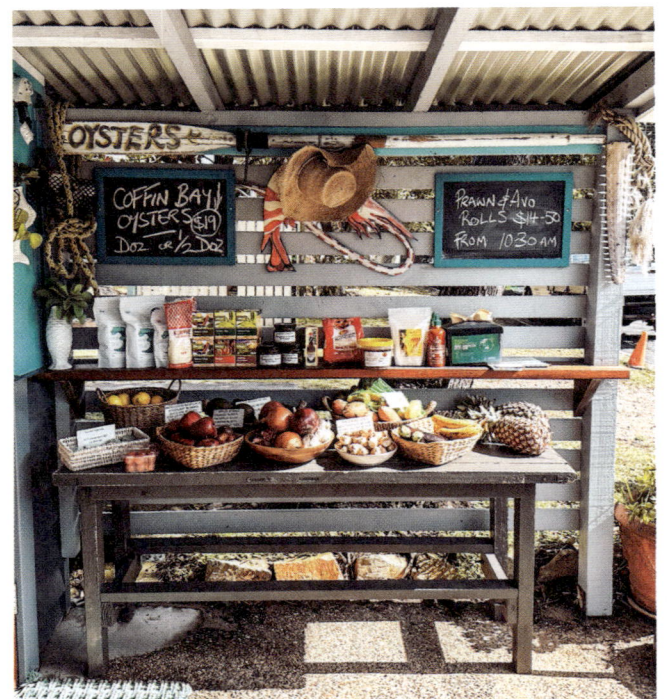

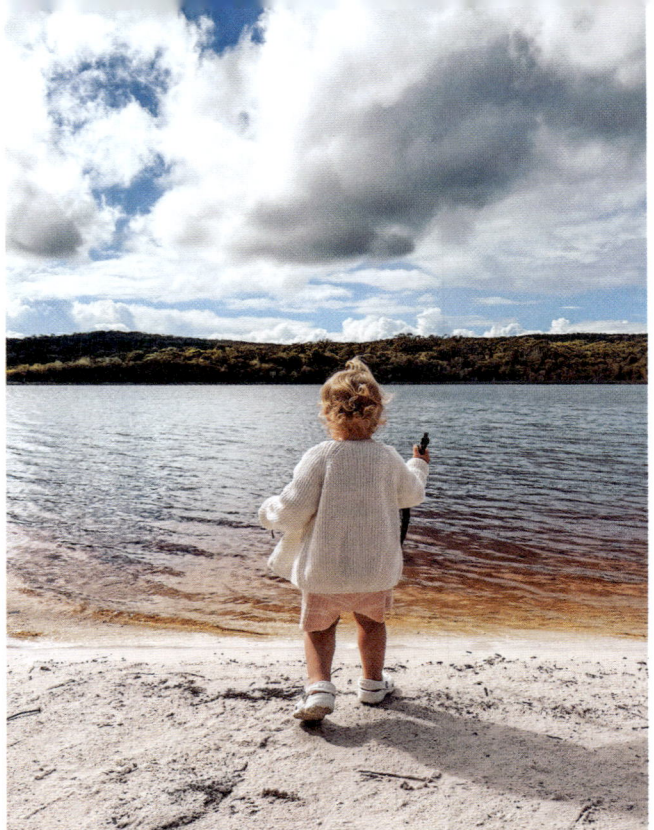

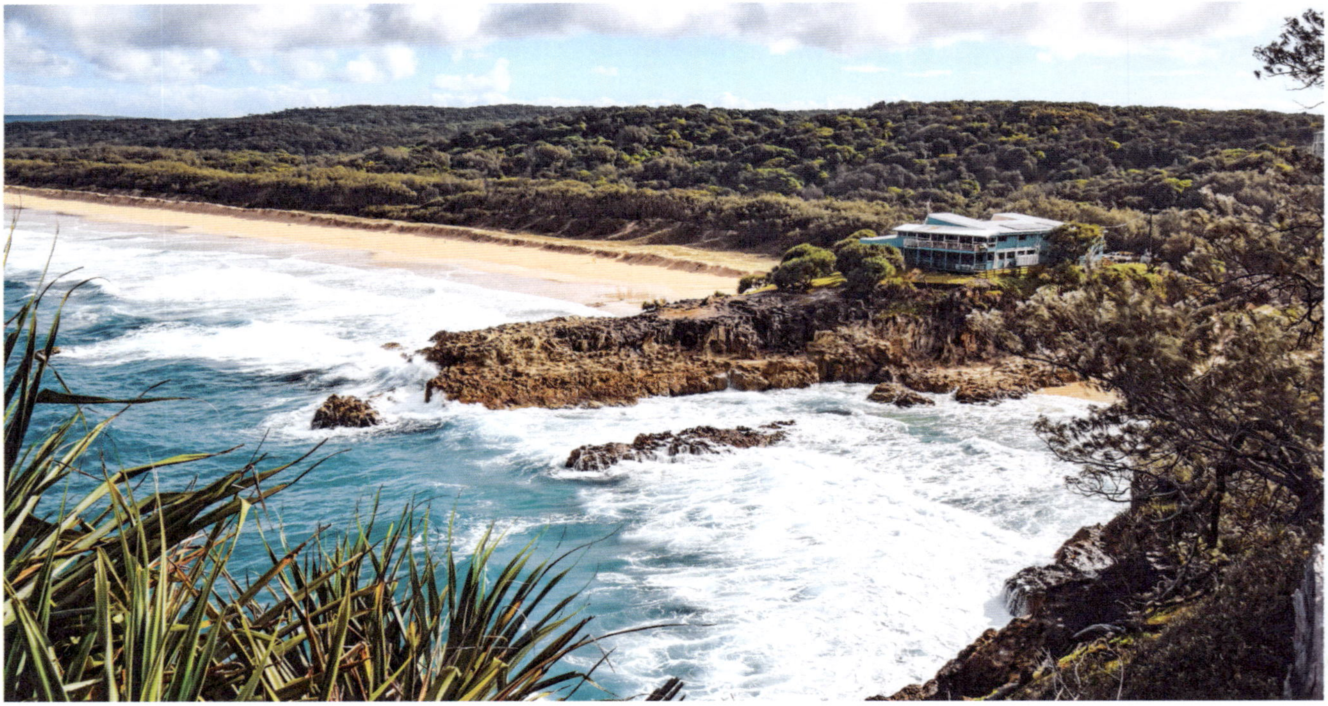

GETTING HERE
SeaLink South East Queensland (sealink.com.au/north-stradbroke-island) offers passenger and vehicle ferries between North Stradbroke Island/Minjerribah and Cleveland on the mainland (about a 45min drive from Brisbane's CBD). It takes about 45min each way, with regular ferry services running every hour to 90min. You're also able to take caravans, camper trailers and boat trailers with you on the vehicle ferry.

GETTING AROUND
By far the easiest way to explore the island is by bringing your own car. However, there is also a bus service that travels between the main towns of Dunwich, Amity Point and Point Lookout. The bus will meet most ferries and water taxi services, so you should be able to jump on as soon as you arrive. There are single trips, daily and weekly tickets available, with tickets starting from as low as $5 a ride.

STAY
Really immerse yourself in nature during your visit to Straddie with campsites right on the beach, where you can wake up to the waves rolling in, kangaroos bouncing by and the most beautiful pastel sunrises. **Minjerribah Camping** (minjerribahcamping.com.au) has six beachfront campgrounds across Dunwich, Amity Point and Point Lookout, as well as 4WD-accessible campsites on Flinders Beach and Main Beach. Camping fees apply and can be booked and paid for at Adder Rock. There are also luxe glamping options at Cylinder Beach, Adder Rock, Amity Point and Bradbury's Beach.

Discover Stradbroke (accommodationstradbroke.com.au) also has a great range of accommodation options across the island, from apartments to beach houses, pet-friendly stays and places to suit every budget. There are excellent beach houses for large families and groups.

To watch whales swimming by right from your balcony, check out **First Point Down**, above the Discover Stradbroke office.

DAYTRIPS
It's easy to visit Straddie on a self-guided daytrip, by simply booking an early ferry over to the island in the morning and heading back on the last ferry of the day in the evening. Take your own car over to explore at your own pace, giving you the flexibility to explore the whole island.

Opposite top left The Prawn Shack *Opposite top right* The Brown Lake *Opposite bottom* View over Main Beach and the Point Lookout Surf Lifesaving Club

FOOD & DRINK
With delicious menus across the island, you're never far away from a great meal.

Straddie has some great spots for coffee, snacks and lunch stops. In Point Lookout start your day at **Blue Room Cafe** (Wed-Mon) with healthy smoothies, acai bowls, homemade sandwiches and great coffee. **Loaves Bakery** is also a great spot for homemade pies, sausage rolls and fresh salad rolls. Pick up fresh local seafood at the **Prawn Shack**, stop at local favourite coffee spot **FEVER on Straddie**, the cute vintage caravan in the Bowls Club carpark, or grab a sweet afternoon treat at **Oceanic Gelati**.

For meals, head to **Oasis Mexican Cantina** for tasty tacos and margaritas, or watch the sunset with a classic pub meal at the **Beach Hotel**. Down at Cylinder Beach, the **Straddie Woodfire Pizza** food truck can be found on the weekend, for a delicious pizza right on the beach. In Amity Point **Sealevel 21** (Wed-Sun) is a favourite, serving lunch and dinner, as well as snacks and cakes throughout the day. **Rufus King Seafood** is another favourite for locals and visitors, with the freshest quality seafood Straddie has to offer. In Dunwich the new favourite hotspot is **Straddie Brewing** (Thurs-Mon), with local beers on tap and a great island menu. It's a great spot to watch the sunset too.

THINGS TO DO
Start your day with the beautiful **Gorge Walk**, an easy 1km wander along the boardwalk with great views of the ocean, Main Beach and North Gorge. It's one of the best places to spot whales during the season, as well as turtles, rays, koalas and kangaroos year-round. The new headland boardwalk extends across many of the beaches around Point Lookout, giving access to the beach as well as great lookout spots all along the coastline. **South Gorge** is a great swimming spot, surrounded by rocky gorge walls, so it feels more like a secret beach than one of the main spots in town. **Cylinder Beach** is another favourite swimming spot, right in front of the campsites. As well as being a great surf beach, there's also a nice lagoon running along the sand, perfect for kids to play or for a lazy soak in the water. Rockpool hop your way along **Deadmans Beach**, best visited at low tide when the rockpools are accessible and out of the water. There's also a giant sandhill here, with incredible views across the island from the top. Take a drive along **Main Beach**, a great place to park up on the sand for a beach barbecue, swim or fish. There's also a patrolled part of Main Beach, the safest place to swim on the island with lifeguards watching over you.

Take a daytrip out to the **Manta Bommie**, known as one of the best diving sites in Australia, where you can swim with turtles, reef sharks, and the elusive manta rays. Head to the

Manta Lodge at Adder Point to book a tour and find out about other diving sites around the island.

Jump on an island adventure tour with **Straddie Kingfisher Tours** with sandboarding, kayaking, 4WD adventures, bushwalking and fishing trips all on offer.

Learn more about the Traditional culture and customs of Minjerribah with a guided walk along the **Goompi Trail** led by a local Quandamooka guide. The walk takes around 1hr along the Dunwich foreshore, and you'll hear stories about Traditional hunting methods, bush-tucker recipes, medicines and traditional ochres.

Stop for a dip at **Brown Lake/Bummiera**, which received its English name and colour from the tea trees that surround it. It's a sacred place for the local Quandamooka women.

Check out some of the local art galleries, to see beautiful works of art created on the island. The main galleries can be found in Dunwich, including **Made on Minjerribah**, **Island Arts Gallery** and **Salt Water Murris**.

Amity Point Jetty is the go-to place to watch the sunset. There's a grassy spot to sit with a fish and chip dinner, and plenty of wildlife coming out to play as the sun goes down. Dolphins can often be spotted swimming around the jetty, as well as koalas in the trees.

ⓘ WHEN TO GO

May to November is considered the best time to visit the island, when there is little rainfall, the days are sunny, and the whales migrate north to breed (in the first half of the season) and south with their calves (in the second half). The **Island Vibe festival** at the end of October is a great time to experience the island, with three days of live music, workshops and island culture on the beach. The **I Am Straddie Arts Trail**, held each August, is a great event, with art installations across the island, markets and tours.

⚠ NEED TO KNOW

If you're bringing your 4WD over to the island and plan to drive on the beach, you will need to purchase a Vehicle Access Permit from **Minjerribah Camping** (minjerribahcamping.com.au/4wd-permits). Permits are valid for one month from the date of issue and can either be purchased online or at the Adder Rock Camping Ground when you arrive. You will need to collect the physical sticker and display the permit on your dashboard whenever you're driving along the beach or in restricted bushland.

ON THE MAINLAND

Only 45min from Brisbane/Meanjin, it's easy to pair your island getaway with a little bit of a city stop as well. Stay in the heart of Brisbane to be within easy walking (or scooting) distance of plenty to see and do. Take in the city from the water on a cruise down the Brisbane River. Stroll through the iconic bright pink bougainvillaea flower walk on South Bank. Head to the **Howard Smith Wharves** under the Story Bridge at sunset for a delicious dinner and colourful cocktail.

Left Aerial view over Amity Point jetty *Opposite* Sunset views from the headland boardwalk at Point Lookout

Adventure awaits

Dirk Hartog Island/Wirruwana, WA	84
Christmas Island, Indian Ocean Territories	91
Island Hopping: Abrolhos Islands, WA	98
K'gari, Queensland	101
Kangaroo Island, SA	109
Hinchinbrook Island, Queensland	116
Island Hopping: Dunk Island, Queensland	122

Dirk Hartog Island/ Wirruwana

A unique desert island experience

CORAL COAST, WESTERN AUSTRALIA

Adventure awaits

TIME ZONE: AWST (GMT +8)
BEST TIME TO VISIT: From March to Nov
ACCESSIBLE FROM: Denham, Shark Bay
GETTING THERE: Catch a passenger ferry or light plane from Denham, or if you're taking your car to the island, hop on the vehicle barge at Steep Point
PHONE RECEPTION: Yes - at the Eco Lodge
WI-FI: No
DAYTRIPS: Yes
KID FRIENDLY: Yes
SOCIALS: @dirkhartogisland
MORE INFO: dirkhartogisland.com.au

At the most westerly point of Australia, you will find Dirk Hartog Island/Wirruwana, the largest island in Western Australia. It's a wild place, overgrown by bushland and scrub, surrounded by calm peaceful bays on one side, and thunderous crashing waves on the other, with enormous sand dunes, rocky landscapes and steep cliff-faces to navigate as you explore the island. The national park is a playground for four-wheel drivers, campers and people coming to fish, while the Eco Lodge is a tranquil place to relax and unwind, overlooking a beautifully calm beach.

The island sits off the coast of Denham on the mainland, within the UNESCO World Heritage Area of Shark Bay. Known as Wirruwana in the local Malgana language, the island is 80km long, and about 14km wide at the widest point, with rough, overgrown 4WD tracks criss-crossing across the island. First Nations People have cared for Country in the Shark Bay region, including Wirruwana, for more than 40,000 years. In 1616 the island was the site of the first European landing in Australia when Dutch sea captain Dirk Hartog arrived.

These days, Dirk Hartog Island is one of Australia's top eco destinations. The Wardle family has run the island for over 50 years. While most of the island is still wild and untouched, Kieran and Tory Wardle have created a unique and special experience at the Eco Lodge. With rustic boutique accommodation built into the old shearing quarters offering ocean views, gourmet home-cooked meals, and adventure tours that take you out to explore the island, every little detail has been thought of to bring you the ultimate island experience.

THE BEST BITS

Stay at the Dirk Hartog Island Eco Lodge (also known as the Homestead) for a completely unforgettable island experience. They've considered everything, from accommodation styling to menu choices, tour options and activities, and have even developed their own gin label. A stay here will absolutely blow your expectations out of the water.

Previous Views across Homestead Bay on Dirk Hartog Island/Wirruwana *Opposite* Wild landscpaes across Sunday Island Bay

➤ GETTING HERE

Denham is the closest mainland point to Dirk Hartog Island, which is about an 8hr, 40min drive from Perth/Boorloo or you can catch a flight with **REX Airlines**, connecting through Carnarvon, to Shark Bay Airport (MJK). From Denham you can catch either a boat transfer (included in your stay at the Eco Lodge, weather permitting), which takes about 1hr to get to the island, or go on a scenic charter flight with Shark Bay Aviation, which takes about 15min.

If you're planning to visit with your own car, the island barge, **Hartog Explorer** transfers 4WD vehicles from Steep Point to Dirk Hartog Island. The barge takes one vehicle and trailer at a time, with a maximum length of 10.6m. The barge operates on demand between 7am and 9am (with a prior booking) and takes about 15min from one side to the other. It is recommended that you camp at Steep Point the night before your barge transfer.

💤 STAY

For the ultimate Dirk Hartog Island/Wirruwana experience, book a stay at the luxury **Eco Lodge**. Every room opens up to sea views, with their own ensuite bathroom and luxury finishes. A stay here includes all meals and snacks, as well as tours to explore the island and return boat transfers to the island. Located right on the beach, you have access to stand-up paddleboards and kayaks, and if you're lucky, you might get to spot their resident horse and sheep roaming around. There is also the option of booking a private **Ocean Villa**, right next to the Eco Lodge. The villa is fully self-contained and self-catering, so you will need to bring all your own food, drinks and snacks. It is great for large families and groups, with three bedrooms, as well as your own kitchen, dining/living area and a large outdoor entertainment area with a barbecue.

Alternatively, if you're planning to camp around Dirk Hartog, there are plenty of options. The **Homestead Camping**

Grounds offers plenty of amenities, with a camp kitchen, private fire-pit, fresh drinking water, hot water showers and flushing toilets. There are two private campsite options to choose from, either **Jed's Beach Camp** or **Buddy's Beach Camp**, both great for larger groups and families. There are also nine national park campsites to choose from around the island. Make sure to check out the Dirk Hartog Island website (dirkhartogisland.com.au/stay/national-park-camping) for a detailed description of each campsite, including what to expect, size, access limitations and facilities before you book. You will need to bring absolutely all of your own supplies when camping in the national park, and leave your campsite exactly as you found it.

DAYTRIPS

Jump on the **A Day at Dirk** tour with **Island Life Adventures** to experience the best Dirk Hartog Island/Wirruwana has to offer. Departing from Denham, the boat ride to the island is a great chance to spot dolphins, manta rays and even whales in season. Start your day with morning tea at The Inscription, before a 4WD tour to the blowholes and Surf Point sanctuary zone within Shark Bay Marine Park, a guided walk to learn about the island's history and the unique Return to 1616 Nature Conservation Program. Plus there's plenty of time to soak up the sunshine, swimming, stand-up paddleboarding, kayaking or just kicking back in a sun bed. You will be treated to a decedent seafood barbecue buffet, as well as a signature island cocktail in the afternoon. The day tour is approximately 9hr long (departing from Denham at 8.30am and returning around 5.30pm), and operates daily, except Mondays, from April to November.

FOOD & DRINK

The Inscription (Mon-Sun 7.30-9.30am for your morning coffee fix, and 5-7.30pm for sunset drinks each evening) is Australia's most remote cafe and bar, and is the only place to buy drinks on the island. With a sandy floor and views across Homestead Bay, it's a great little spot to check out no matter where you're staying on the island. You can try some of Dirk Hartog/Wirruwana's signature Inscription Gin here, or the delicious Dark & Stormy cocktail. If you're staying at the Eco Lodge, all meals and snacks are included in your stay, so you don't have to think about anything. The food here is seasonal, with menus changing daily depending on what's available and what's been caught that day, with plenty of seafood and fresh fish. Every single meal we had here was absolutely delicious.

If you're camping or staying at the Ocean Villa, you will need to bring everything with you - all food, snacks, drinks and supplies. There is nowhere to buy anything once you're on the island, so you will need to be 100 per cent self-catered and self-sufficient.

Top Homestead Bay *Bottom* Eagle rays in the shallow waters of Homestead Bay *Opposite* Views from The Inscription Bar

✓ THINGS TO DO

How you spend your days on Dirk Hartog Island/Wirruwana will depend on where you're staying. If you're bringing your own car and camping around the island, you'll likely spend your day hopping along different beaches and following every dirt track you see, to find an endless number of incredible spots around the island. Some of the favourite spots include Turtle Bay, Cape Inscription, Mystery Beach, Sandy Point, Dampiers Landing, Quoin Head, the Blowholes, Surf Point, Sunday Island Bay and Notch Point.

When you stay at the Eco Resort, many of the tours are tailored to you and included in your stay. Experience **Australia's Last Sunset**, high atop the cliffs on the western side of the island, with panoramic views over the Indian Ocean, a tasting of DHI's Inscription Gin and a grazing platter to enjoy. This is the last place in Australia the sun sets each day, and what a magical sunset it is. On the way to the sunset spot you get a guided tour of the island, passing soaring sand dunes and you may even spot the elusive island wallabies, Shark Bay bandicoots and tiny little desert mice that have been reintroduced to the island as part of the Return to 1616 Conservation project.

Take a **4WD Adventure** to the western side of Dirk Hartog and check out some of the island's most unique spots. The Blowholes will make you feel like you have stepped onto the moon, with a hilly, rocky landscape as far as the eye can see, alongside steep cliffs met by thumping waves at the bottom. Next, the Surf Point sanctuary zone within Shark Bay Marine Park offers incredible views of both the wild west side of the island and the calm bays of the east from one viewpoint. It's a great spot for rockpool hopping on the west and peaceful snorkelling on the east (but only snorkel on a slack tide - check ahead, and be alert for boats), with a nursery of lemon sharks swimming in the shallows. Surf Point is also a great place to spot the unique bright yellow Dirk Hartog Island crabs.

For a full day of exploring, you can choose the **Cape Inscription 4WD Adventure Tour**, which will take you all the way to Cape Inscription, the most northern point of the island where Dirk Hartog landed in 1616. You'll get to check out the lighthouse that's still standing, as well as stop at Turtle Bay, a great place for both swimming with turtles and seeing turtles nesting and hatching in season.

Explore the water with a **Big 5 Marine Safari**, for the chance to get up close and personal with Dirk Hartog's Big 5 - dolphins, turtles, sharks, manta rays and whales. It's a wonderful experience seeing the incredible island coastline from the water as you travel up to Sandy Point, as well as learning more about the unique marine environment in Shark Bay. Bring your own snorkel equipment for this one, if you'd like to jump in the water.

Enjoy a morning coffee or sunset cocktail from **Inscription Bar**, Australia's most remote bar and cafe, overlooking Homestead Bay.

? WHEN TO GO

Dirk Hartog Island/Wirruwana's season runs from 1 March to 30 November. The national park camping will sometimes be open for bookings over the summer, but not always. Weatherwise, the best time to visit is from around April to October, when days are warm and sunny, there is less wind and little rainfall. July and August are a particularly beautiful and exciting time to visit during wildflower and whale season.

! NEED TO KNOW

Whether you're planning a stay at the Homestead or to camp in the national park, advance bookings are absolutely essential for your visit to Dirk Hartog Island/Wirruwana. Availability is extremely limited, with only 20 vehicles allowed to camp on the island at any one time in the national park. If you're planning to bring your own car and explore, it's a good idea to have some experience four-wheel driving in soft sand and consider bringing a satellite phone in case of emergencies.

ON THE MAINLAND

A unique part of Australia, Shark Bay is home to deep red dirt roads that lead right to the azure blue waters of the ocean it meets. Sometimes you might find a strip of bright white sand separating them, sometimes they run right into each other, swirling around together in the shallows. It's a beautiful spot, with incredible beaches to explore and emus wandering down the main roads. Base yourself in either Denham, right in the heart of Shark Bay, or venture out a little further to visit **Monkey Mia**, home to the friendliest dolphins in the world.

Opposite Aerial view over Dirk Hartog Island Eco Resort

Christmas Island

A Jurassic wonderland ready to be explored

INDIAN OCEAN TERRITORIES

TIME ZONE: Christmas Island Time (GMT +7)

BEST TIME TO VISIT: During the dry season, May to Oct

ACCESSIBLE FROM: Perth

GETTING THERE: Virgin Australia flies to Christmas Island (XCH) on Tues and Fri

PHONE RECEPTION: Yes - Telstra reception for calls and texts only in the main Settlement area, no data

WI-FI: Yes

DAYTRIPS: No

KID FRIENDLY: Yes

SOCIALS: @christmasisland

MORE INFO: christmas.net.au

Rising from the Indian Ocean, Christmas Island looks like a Jurassic wonderland as you're coming in to land, covered in a thick blanket of jungle greenery, and surrounded by the sapphire turquoise swirl of the ocean, with waves crashing over the reef and onto the shore. It's rugged and remote and the ideal place for an island adventure. Geographically closer to South-East Asia than Australia, only 400km from Indonesia to be precise, Christmas Island is one of Australia's most remote islands.

The famous red crab migration at the beginning of the wet season is often what draws visitors to the island, where each year millions and millions of red crabs make their way from the jungle to the ocean for mating season, covering roads, bridges, beaches and everything in between in a sea of red as far as the eye can see. Whilst it is definitely a special sight to see, you'll quickly find that there's so much more to Christmas Island, with its dramatic wild landscapes, tall limestone cliffs, and powerful blowholes. Two-thirds of the island is protected by Christmas Island National Park.

Its rich multicultural population creates an island that doesn't feel like anywhere else in the world, and is uniquely its own, with 60 per cent Chinese residents, 30 per cent Malaysian and 10 per cent made up predominantly of people from Australia, Aotearoa New Zealand and the Philippines. Because of this there are lots of different cultural experiences to be had, with Chinese temples dotted around the island, Ramadan observed by the Malaysian population, and delicious cuisines to try.

It's an island that feels like a big country town. Where everyone knows everyone else, where restaurant specials, news and announcements are written on the blackboard in the main roundabout, and where by the time your trip comes to an end, you'll definitely feel like a local.

THE BEST BITS

Rent a car to get out and explore every corner of Christmas Island. With some incredibly dramatic landscapes and millions of red crabs running around the island, this is really a place unlike any other.

Opposite View from Martin Point

➔ GETTING HERE

Virgin Australia makes the round trip to the Indian Ocean Territories twice a week, travelling Perth/Boorloo to Christmas Island to Cocos (Keeling) Islands on Tuesdays, and in the opposite direction on Fridays. When travelling to Christmas Island you will be travelling through the Perth International Terminal and will need to clear customs and immigration at both ends. Travelling with your passport is highly recommended and the easiest way to travel (as well as being the only form accepted for children), however a Photo ID (such as a driver's licence) is also accepted.

Ⓒ GETTING AROUND

Pre-book a rental car in advance (so you don't miss out) to pick up from the airport when you arrive, so you can get around the island at your own pace. Book directly through the Christmas Island website. It's important to note that there are no car seats available to hire on Christmas Island, so you will need to bring your own if you're travelling with a baby or toddler.

💤 STAY

There is a range of different accommodation options on Christmas Island, including boutique hotels, self-contained units and apartments or holiday houses and villas. Most accommodation is located in the Settlement or Kampong area, so you're close to everything during your visit.

We stayed at **Cocos Padang Lodge**, which was in a great central location - walking distance from restaurants, shops, playgrounds and the supermarket, and had fast complimentary wi-fi, air-conditioning, our own kitchen, a washing machine and dryer, and access to a pool on another property. It's perfect for longer stays and larger groups too.

C.I Apartments in Poon San is the most modern, newly renovated accommodation on the island, although it is a drive from the Settlement.

For a complete luxury experience, **Swell Lodge** is an indulgent eco-lodge, offering only two glass-front eco-chalets right on the rocky coastline of Christmas Island National Park. Your stay at Swell includes all meals made by a private chef, drinks, transport and daily guided tours tailored to whatever you want to see while you're on the island.

🍴 FOOD & DRINK

When you arrive on Christmas Island, pick up a 'Taste Guide' from the airport visitor's centre stand (next to where you pick up your rental car), for information about the island's restaurants and cafes and their opening hours, addresses and special menus for the next week. It's immensely helpful in trying to plan meals, so keep it on you at all times.

Head to the **CI Supermarket** (Mon-Fri 9am-5pm, Sat 9am-1pm) if you want to stock up on groceries.

The Golden Bosun is a great dinner option, with good pub food and it's open for dinner most nights.

Tracks Tavern in Drumsite is a local favourite and is open daily, offering pies and salad rolls for lunch and different theme nights throughout the week, including Korean BBQ, Thai night and a Sunday roast.

Seaview Fish & Chips in Poon San has fresh seafood and chicken dinners a few nights a week.

Head to **Le C.L.A** (Chinese Literacy Association) or **Lucky Ho** for great Chinese food.

The **CI Bakery** is always a breakfast favourite with lots of different options.

Left Slow down for crabs on Christmas Island *Opposite top left* Red crabs on Christmas Island *Opposite top right* Island hotspots *Opposite bottom* Views from the Territory Day Park lookout

DOLLY BEACH 20km
GRETA BEACH 18 km
FLYING FISH COVE
10 km LILY BEACH
WEST WHITE BEACH 19km
the GROTTO 3.8km
MERRIAL BEACH 22KM
the DALES 21km

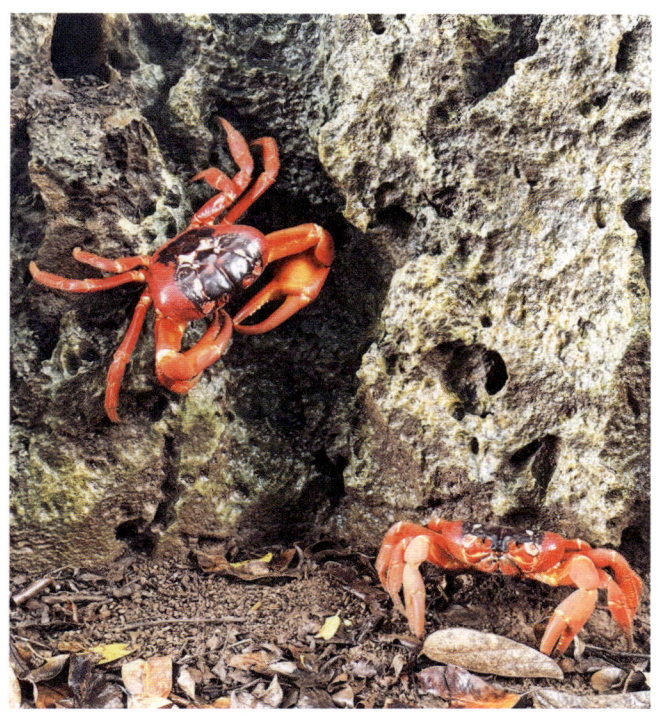

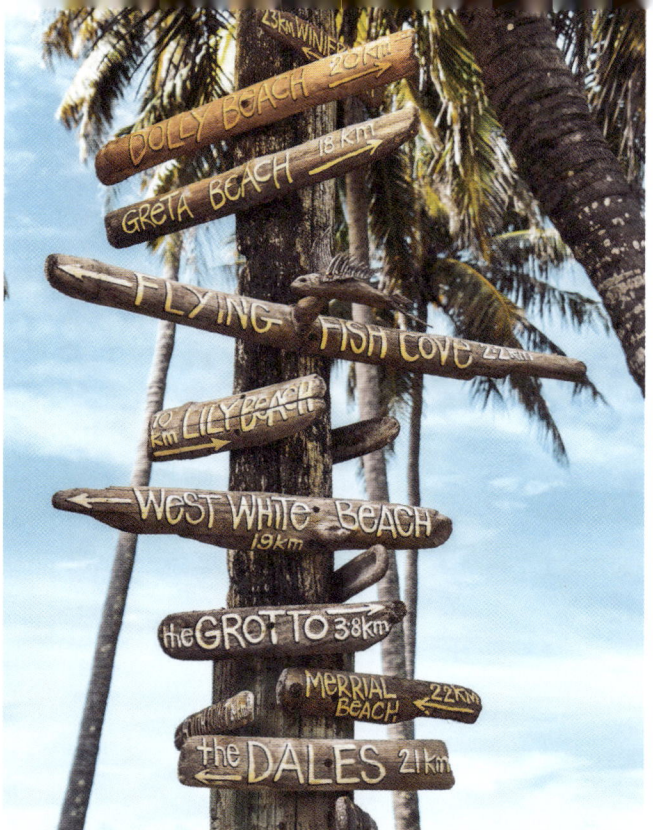

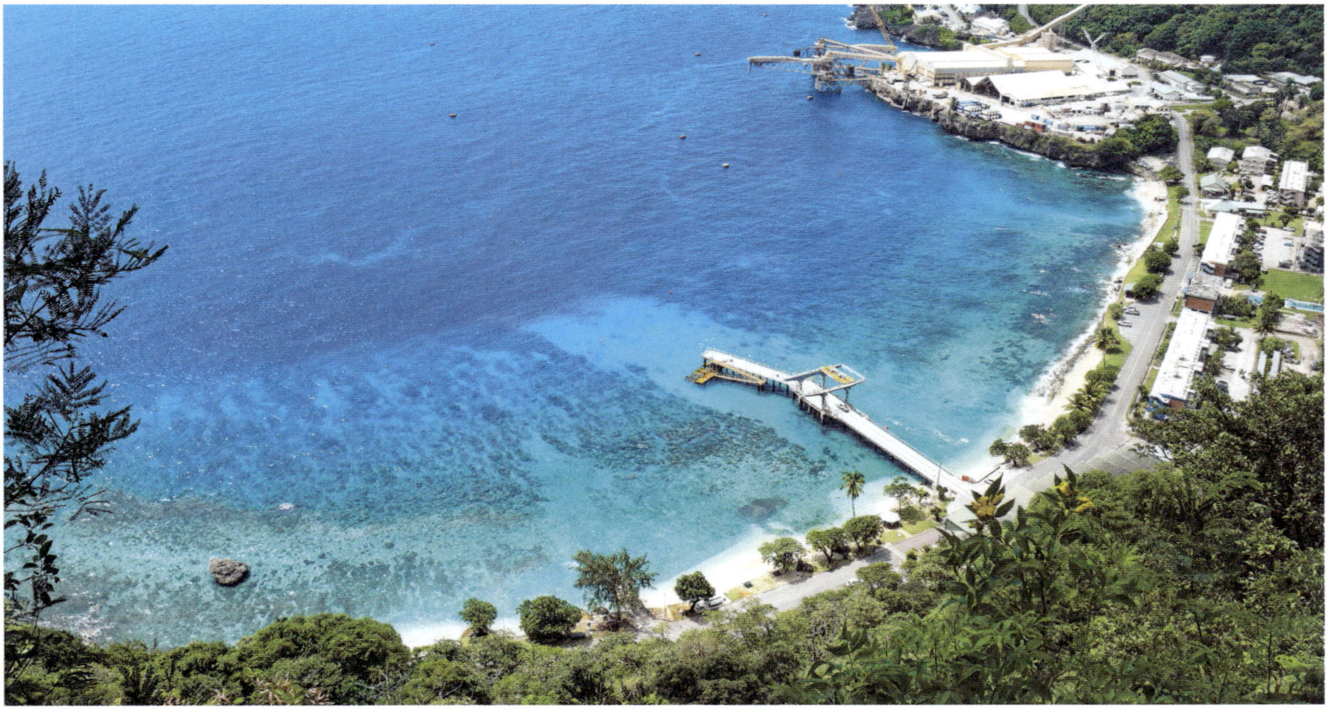

⊘ THINGS TO DO

There is so much to see and explore on Christmas Island. The first thing to do when you arrive is to jump on the **Christmas Island Orientation Tour** with **Indian Ocean Experiences**. The tours run the morning after each plane arrives, offering a guided tour of the township area, showing you places of interest around the island, sharing some of the island's history and culture, and pointing out different places to eat and shop. It's incredibly helpful and a great way to get an overview of the island.

After the tour, jump in your rental car and start exploring the different tracks of the island - taking you through the jungle, out to some beautiful viewpoints and beaches, with plenty of walking trails. Check out the views from **Territory Day Park**, with a great view of the Settlement, the mine and Flying Fish Cove. There's a great walking trail here to explore the rainforest and learn about the island's history. **Flying Fish Cove** is the best spot on the island for swimming and snorkelling, with a reef only metres from the shore that's full of corals and colourful fish. The waves can be a bit rough here sometimes, so it's better to go out between the tides (check ahead), but the water is beautifully warm.

Take a dip in the crystal-clear water of **The Grotto**. You might have to share this one with some red crabs, but the water here is a mix of freshwater and ocean water and is beautifully refreshing at about 5 degrees cooler than the ocean.

Follow the map to **Martin Point** to explore more of the jungle of **Christmas Island National Park**, where you're likely to find plenty of red crabs as well as the massive robber crabs. The views here are stunning and you can follow the walking track down to the beach. There's also **Hugh's Dale Waterfall** to stop at along the way.

Dolly Beach and Greta Beach are some of the best beaches to visit on Christmas Island, often getting turtles swimming in the water and nesting on the shore year-round. The road can sometimes be washed out throughout the wet season, so **Indian Ocean Experiences** also offers a half-day tour out there to check out the beaches and have a swim.

Lily Beach and **Ethel Beach** are also beautiful spots to visit, easily accessible by car.

Take a trip out to **The Blowholes** where a boardwalk takes you to see some of the most impressive blowhole spots, spraying water high into the air. It sounds like there's a fire-breathing dragon lying under the boardwalk, and there's a truly impressive view of the jagged coastline.

Opposite Aerial views over Christmas Island

Adventure awaits

On Saturday night head to Poon San to catch a movie at the **Outdoor Cinema**. Check the blackboard in the main roundabout for movie details during the week and bring your own cushion as the seats are a little hard.

To explore more of Christmas Island from the water, try one of the tours. **Wet 'N' Dry Adventures** offers scuba diving and snorkelling charters, as well as seabird watching charters. **Freedive Christmas Island** offers introductory free diving courses and guided seascooter tours. **Christmas Island Fishing & Adventure** offers fishing charters, as well as snorkelling and wildlife experiences.

ⓘ WHEN TO GO

Due to its position close to South-East Asia, Christmas Island experiences a tropical climate, with a definite wet and dry season and very high humidity from time to time. The dry season (between May and Sept), is generally the nicest time to visit, when days are often clear and sunny, with less rain and lower humidity. However, if you're hoping to watch the red crab migration, this generally begins after the first rainfall of the wet season (usually Oct or Nov but sometimes as late as Dec). A complicated phenomenon to plan for, the migration's exact timing and speed is determined by the phase of the moon.

ⓘ NEED TO KNOW

It can be difficult to plan a visit to Christmas Island, so we found it easiest to book through specialised travel agents **Indian Ocean Experiences** (indianoceanexperiences.com.au). They were able to create a custom itinerary and offer tailored advice, and also put together a package with lower prices than we could find if we had booked it ourselves. The owner of Indian Ocean Experiences, Lisa, lives on Christmas Island and has over 15 years' experience organising Christmas Island holidays. Highly recommend.

Alternatively, the **Christmas Island Visitor's Centre** can offer great advice and assistance in planning your visit. You can email them at office@christmasisland.net.au, give them a call on (08) 9164 8382 or pop into the visitor's centre on Gaze Rd when you arrive.

It is extremely important to have travel insurance when visiting Christmas Island. Due to the airport's location on the island, low cloud is a real issue for planes trying to land and take off, making flight cancellations and travel disruptions a regular occurrence. To avoid extra out-of-pocket costs, a domestic travel insurance policy is definitely a necessity.

Before you start exploring the island, stop by the police station and pick up a Personal Locator Beacon (PLB). Once you get out of the Settlement there is no phone reception around the island, so the PLB can notify the police if you get into any kind of trouble - whether you're lost or have car trouble, they encourage you to use it in any situation where you don't feel like you're okay. The PLBs are free to borrow and you can hold onto them for the whole time you're on Christmas Island.

Top left The mine on Christmas Island *Top right* Christmas Island Supermarket *Opposite* Exploring the wild tracks of Christmas Island

ISLAND HOPPING
Abrolhos Islands

CORAL COAST, WESTERN AUSTRALIA

Adventure awaits

Sitting 60km off the coast of WA is the archipelago known as the Houtman Abrolhos Islands, or more commonly, the Abrolhos Islands. About 10,000 years ago the Abrolhos Islands were part of the Australian mainland, during which time First Nations People were present as evidenced by Traditional tools located on Beacon Island, until the islands were separated from the mainland by rising sea levels. Made up of 122 islands, divided into three main groups, the Wallabi Group, Easter Group and Pelsaert Group, the Abrolhos Islands are surrounded by coral reefs and are a mecca for fishing, snorkelling, diving and birdwatching. The marine life is abundant and it's one of Australia's best areas for biodiversity. Abrolhos is a word derived from a Portuguese term which can be translated as 'open your eyes – keep good watch', and this is good advice for keeping your eyes open to spot wildlife.

The Abrolhos Islands are known for many tiny islands, covered in colourful fishing shacks and long jetties, jutting out over the water in all directions. There are 22 islands occupied at different times throughout the year, home to lobster fishermen and their families, who sustain the multimillion-dollar western rock lobster (crayfish) industry, which exports all over the world. It's a unique and dynamic environment.

The Abrolhos Islands are also home to the infamous *Batavia* shipwreck and the site of the mass murder that happened in 1629, when 125 men, women and children were murdered by mutineers following the shipwreck. The shipwreck is now one of WA's best dive sites, just off the coast of Beacon Island, with dive charters available from Geraldton.

➔ GETTING HERE

The best way to explore the Abrolhos Islands is on a scenic flight day tour, giving you the opportunity to see and experience the islands from the air as well as the ground. Book with either **Shine Aviation** (shineaviation.com.au) or **Nation West Aviation** (nationwestaviation.com.au). Tours depart from Geraldton Airport and are approximately 6hr long for the full-day experience. The day begins with a scenic flight, flying you low over the three groups of islands, and giving you a great view of them with plenty of photo opportunities. Your pilot and tour guide offer commentary throughout the flight, pointing out the different islands and points of interest along the way. You can also add on a quick detour flight over the iconic Pink Lake on your way home!

There are also plenty of fishing charters on offer from Geraldton if you're looking for fishing only; check out **Australia's Coral Coast** (australiascoralcoast.com) for all the options.

✓ THINGS TO DO

After your scenic flight your plane will land on the small dirt runway on East Wallabi Island, where you'll disembark and spend the day exploring the island. The beach is absolutely beautiful, with crystal-clear water and bright white sand stretching as far as the eye can see in both directions. A coral reef lines the beach, full of crayfish, colourful corals and plenty of bright fish, only a short swim from the shore. It's a great place for snorkelling, swimming or just relaxing on the sand. Your day tour includes morning tea and lunch on the island. Make sure you take a walk around the top of the island and see if you can spot the cute little tammar wallabies, which can often be spotted hiding in the shrubs during the day.

💤 STAY

Although there is no accommodation to book on the Abrolhos Islands, if you're looking to stay and explore a little longer, **Eco Abrolhos Cruises** (ecoabrolhos.com.au) offer five-day liveaboard cruises, giving you the unique chance to really absorb this interesting part of the world. You can take your time weaving your way through the many groups of the Abrolhos Islands, where you get to meet local fishermen, indulge in the freshest seafood, and spend your days soaking up island life, jumping in and out of the water all day long.

ⓘ MORE INFO

Alongside the crayfish industry, the Abrolhos Islands are known for pearling. Pearl shops **Chimere Pearls** and **Latitude Jewellers** in the heart of Geraldton sell pearls cultivated from the Abrolhos Islands.

To start planning your trip to the Abrolhos Islands, head to australiascoralcoast.com.

Opposite Aerial views over the fishing huts on the Abrolhos Islands

K'gari

The largest sand island in the world

FRASER COAST, QUEENSLAND

One of the most unique islands in Australia, and the largest sand island in the world, stretching for 123km along Queensland's Fraser Coast, K'gari is certainly a very special place. The island was officially renamed from Fraser Island to K'gari (pronounced *GUR-rie* or *gurri*) in June 2023, which is the local Butchulla People's Traditional name for the island. The name comes from their Dreaming creation story that explains how the island and surrounding lands were formed.

Each corner of K'gari offers a unique environment to explore. It's the only place on Earth where a luscious rainforest grows right out of the sand, with trees reaching more than 200m tall. It's home to more than half of the world's perched lakes, where depressions in the dunes are permanently filled with rainwater. It's where you can find the coloured sand cliffs of the Pinnacles, towering cliffs of oranges, reds, yellows and browns, and a stark contrast to the sparkling blue ocean they lie next to. It's a premier whale watching destination, with daily sightings during the season, and calves regularly spotted with their mothers learning to swim and play in the calm waters around the island.

There are many different ways to explore K'gari, from staying at the resorts, to bringing your own car and beach camping along the island. Bareboating is also becoming an increasingly popular way to explore K'gari from the water, allowing you the chance to explore more of the wild western coast of the island. No matter which way you visit, any time spent on K'gari is sure to be an adventure unlike any other.

TIME ZONE: AEST (GMT +10)
BEST TIME TO VISIT: Year-round
ACCESSIBLE FROM: Hervey Bay and Inskip Point
GETTING THERE: Ferry transfer
PHONE RECEPTION: Yes, in the main areas
WI-FI: Yes, at the resorts
DAYTRIPS: Yes
KID FRIENDLY: Yes
SOCIALS: @kingfisherbayresort, @fraserislandboatcharters
MORE INFO: visitfrasercoast.com, kingfisherbay.com, fraserislandboatcharters.com.au

THE BEST BITS

See the island from above on a 15min scenic flight with Air Fraser Island. Taking off and landing on the sand of Seventy Five Mile Beach, you'll be treated to breathtaking views of Lake McKenzie, Eli Creek, the *Maheno* shipwreck, the Pinnacles and more, with a wonderful aerial view of the epic K'gari.

Opposite Early mornings at Lake McKenzie

➔ GETTING HERE & AROUND

Two ferries connect K'gari to the mainland. The **Kingfisher Bay Ferry Service** (sealink.com.au/kgari-fraser-island) departs from River Heads near Hervey Bay four times a day, arriving at the small jetty at Kingfisher Bay Resort. It's a 50min trip, connecting with bitumen roads on the island. Not only is it the best option if you're staying at the resort, it's also the easiest. If you're heading to the eastern side of the island for beach camping, the **Manta Ray Fraser Island Barge** (mantarayfraserislandbarge.com.au) drops you straight onto Seventy Five Mile Beach after a short 10min trip across from Inskip Point. It's important to mention that Inskip Point is notorious for people getting bogged on both sides of the barge, so make sure you're prepared for the soft sand conditions if you head over this way.

Once you're here you will need your own 4WD, with most of the island's tracks and roads made up entirely of sand. There are also 4WD tour options available.

ⓩ STAY

The main resort on K'gari is **Kingfisher Bay Resort**, located on the western side of the island. Offering spacious rooms, three restaurants and four pools, it's a great spot to visit for anyone coming to the island, with the restaurants open to visitors who are not guests of the hotel as well. The small town of the resort is the largest on the island, where you can find a general store, petrol station, car wash, playground, laundry, and a day spa.

On the eastern side of the island, just steps from Seventy Five Mile Beach is **K'gari Beach Resort**. It has accommodation for every budget, including hotel rooms and two-bedroom apartments, as well as a lagoon pool, takeaway pizza, bakery, general store and petrol station.

Camping right on the beach is a favourite of many visitors to K'gari, with the chance to fall asleep to the sound of crashing waves and wake up to the sunrise. To camp on the beach you will need a vehicle access permit, as well as a booking at a designated camp area on the island. Bookings can be made up to six months in advance with Queensland Parks (parks.des.qld.gov.au/parks/kgari-fraser/camping).

For the ultimate K'gari experience, jump on a bareboat charter and explore the island from the water. **Fraser Island Boat Charters** (fraserislandboatcharters.com.au) and **Sweet Escape Yacht Charters** (sweetescapecharters.com.au) both offer the chance to be the captain of your own boat (no licence required) where you can explore the untouched western coastline of K'gari. Sleep aboard your yacht and head onto the island with your own tender whenever you like.

Above Whale watching season on K'gari *Opposite* Golden hour on a bareboat

Adventure awaits

⊙ DAYTRIPS

If you only have one day to explore K'gari, the best daytrip is with **K'gari Explorer Tours** (fraserexplorertours.com.au). The 4WD adventure departs from Hervey Bay and takes you to see the main highlights on K'gari, including Lake McKenzie, Seventy Five Mile Beach, Eli Creek, the historic *Maheno* shipwreck and the World Heritage-listed rainforest. You'll get around the island in their epic 4WD explorer bus, and the tour includes ferry transfers, lunch at K'gari Beach Resort, national park fees and courtesy pick up and drop off from locations around Hervey Bay.

⊙ FOOD & DRINK

There are only a handful of restaurants around the island. Kingfisher Bay Resort is home to **Sand & Wood** (Mon-Sun breakfast & lunch), with a menu of modern Australian cuisine and plenty of light snacks and fresh salads. The resort's new **Dune Restaurant** (Mon-Sun dinner) offers an Asian-fusion menu. **The Sand Bar & Bistro** (Mon-Sun lunch & dinner) offers a more casual dining experience, with pizzas and a traditional bistro menu, as well as takeaway. Grab a beanbag at the **Sunset Bar** near the jetty for cocktails on the beach; it's one of the best spots to watch the sunset.

The **Village Store** stocks a range of grocery items, snacks and alcohol, as well as gifts and souvenirs.

On the other side of the island, K'gari Beach Resort offers **McKenzie's On 75**, serving breakfast, lunch and dinner, as well as takeaway pizzas and light bites. There's also the **Eurong Bakery** for pies, sausage rolls and egg and bacon burgers, as well as a small general store.

If you're bareboating or camping on K'gari you will need to bring all of your food and drinks. The general store has a small range if you need it, but it's best not to rely on being able to do a large shop.

⊙ THINGS TO DO

With an impressive list of natural attractions to visit around K'gari, there's always something new to see and explore.

Start with **Lake McKenzie**, one of the most beautiful lakes in Australia. The freshwater lake has some of the clearest bright blue water close to the shore, before it drops off into deep blue only a few metres out. Surrounded by white sand and bushland, the water is lovely and warm and it's a great place for a swim. Another great place for a dip is **Lake Wabby**, the deepest lake on the island at the edge of Hammerstone Sandblow.

Opposite Wathumba Creek on the western side of K'gari

Eli Creek is definitely a favourite for anyone visiting the island; it's a cool freshwater creek that comes out of the rainforest and runs all the way down to the ocean. There's a boardwalk running alongside the creek and if you jump into the water at the end of the boardwalk the water will float you back to your car or the ocean at the other end. Definitely bring a floatie for this one, it's so relaxing.

Jump on a **whale watching tour** (July-Oct) to see the beautiful humpback whales on their migration through the waters surrounding the island. Or for an incredible once-in-a-lifetime experience, many tours also offer the option to get in the water and swim with the whales in their natural habitat.

Stretching for 75 miles, the iconic **Seventy Five Mile Beach** is an epic beach highway, which will actually take you hours to make it from tip to tip. Make sure you're driving at low tide (check ahead for tide times) and that your 4WD vehicle is prepared for sand driving. There are plenty of iconic places to stop along the beach, including the **Maheno** shipwreck which washed onto the shore around 1935. Sand blows across the wreck throughout the day and it becomes more and less visible with the tides, so visit at low tide to see more of the wreck exposed. A little further north, the towering **Pinnacle Cliffs** are quite a sight to see, with swirling patterns of red, orange, yellow, brown and white sands, and they seemingly come out of nowhere. At the northern end of the beach you can't miss the **Champagne Pools**. These rockpools are filled with crystal-clear water and are a great place for a dip after a long bumpy drive across the sand.

Kingfisher Bay Resort offers a range of immersive activities for their guests, with options for all ages. With activities including the Bush Tucker Talk & Taste, Junior Eco Rangers Program, Sea Explorer Cruises, segway tours and ranger guided walks and talks, there's always something to see and learn on K'gari. Grab a 'What's On' guide when you arrive for the full list during your stay.

On the western side of the island, **Wathumba Creek** is K'gari's answer to the Whitsundays' Whitehaven Beach. With sparkling blue water and white silica sand stretching as far as the eye can see, turtles and rays swimming in the shallow waters, and often not another person in sight, it's quite the untouched paradise. This one is only accessible on a bareboat charter or with your own boat, but it's such a wonderful spot to visit.

In the evening, jump on a **Sea Explorer Sunset Cruise** jet boat to experience the sunset from the water. Departing from the Kingfisher Bay jetty, there are complimentary drinks and snacks, good music and a thrilling jet boat ride to get you back to the resort once the sun has gone down. An epic way to end the day.

WHEN TO GO

K'gari is a great destination to visit year-round, with sunny weather throughout the year and not much of a rainy season. Spring is widely considered a great time to visit, as the weather gets warmer but there is little humidity. To experience whale watching from the island, visit between July and mid-October.

NEED TO KNOW

If you're planning to drive on K'gari, you will need to purchase a vehicle access permit from Queensland National Parks (qpws.usedirect.com/qpws). There are options for permits for one month or up to one year, which should be displayed on your dashboard at all times during your visit.

Also, always be aware of dingoes that might be running around the island. These are wild animals, so always keep your distance if you do come across one and make sure to pack away all food at campsites at night to avoid one coming to visit. The Queensland National Parks website has more information about dingo safety.

ON THE MAINLAND

Hervey Bay is the gateway to K'gari, and it's easy to add a couple of days to your itinerary to explore this sleepy coastal town. Jump on a **whale watching tour**, in season from July to mid-October, to get up close to these gentle giants as they stop for a rest in the waters of Hervey Bay. Take a walk down **Urangan Pier**, one of the longest in Australia stretching for almost a kilometre into the ocean. Visit the **Hervey Bay Regional Gallery** to see some of their unique touring and permanent exhibits. Enjoy the golden hour on a **Twilight Bay Sunset Cruise**, through the waters of the Sandy Straits.

Opposite top left Sea Explorer Sunset Cruise *Opposite top right* A special spot called One Tree *Opposite bottom* Pelican Banks is a favourite off the K'gari coast

Adventure awaits

Kangaroo Island

Where natural beauty meets great food and wine

SOUTH AUSTRALIA

There are not many islands to visit off the South Australian coast, but luckily Kangaroo Island or KI, as it's affectionately known to locals, has you covered in every way. From rugged natural beauty, spectacular beaches, a stunning national park and incredible wildlife encounters, to a delicious food and wine scene, KI has it all. It's an island that feels like a giant country town – quiet and peaceful even during its busiest periods, with plenty to fill your days with. In just a couple of days you'll feel like a local here.

People of the Ramindjeri, Ngarrindjeri, Kaurna and Barngalla Nations were all believed to inhabit the island around 16,000 years ago, before rising sea levels later caused it to separate from the mainland of South Australia. It's thought that the original First Nations inhabitants left Kangaroo Island around 2000 years ago, although it's not known why they left.

Deceptively large, Kangaroo Island is 155km long and 55km wide, which means it can actually take a while to get between different places around the island. In fact, it takes 2hr, 20min to drive across the whole island, from Cape Willoughby in the east to Flinders Chase National Park at the western end of the island.

With unique and wonderful places to explore on every corner of the island, KI is likely to have you coming back again and again to soak up its relaxed holiday vibe and explore more of its iconic natural beauty.

TIME ZONE: AEST (GMT +10)
BEST TIME TO VISIT: Summer months
ACCESSIBLE FROM: Cape Jervis or Adelaide
GETTING THERE: Flight or ferry
PHONE RECEPTION: Yes, but can be patchy outside of main towns
WI-FI: Yes, at the Kangaroo Island Visitor Centre and some accommodation
DAYTRIPS: Yes
KID FRIENDLY: Yes
SOCIALS: @authentickangarooisland
MORE INFO: tourkangarooisland.com.au, sealink.com.au/kangaroo-island

THE BEST BITS

If there's only one beach you visit on Kangaroo Island make it Vivonne Bay. With the most epic blue water, perfect swimming conditions, a wooden jetty that's ideal for fishing, and stunning views of the coastline as you drive down to the beach, it's one of our favourite spots on the island.

Opposite Our favourite beach on KI – Vivonne Bay

➲ GETTING HERE

SeaLink (sealink.com.au/kangaroo-island) operates a daily vehicle and passenger service between Cape Jervis on the mainland and Penneshaw on KI. The trip across takes about 40min with a departure generally every 45min to an hour. Dogs are allowed on the upper deck on board and you can also bring your car, caravan, boat or trailer across with you. Pre-booking is recommended to avoid missing out, especially during school holidays and peak periods.

You can fly to Kangaroo Island, with **QantasLink** offering regular flights between Kingscote Airport (KGC) on the island and Adelaide Airport, getting you to KI in 30min.

© GETTING AROUND

Without a doubt the best way to explore KI is by bringing your own car over on the ferry, giving you the freedom to explore every corner of the island. Rental cars are also available at both Kingscote Airport and in the town of Penneshaw when you get off the ferry. There are several unsealed roads around the island that take you to some of the best beaches and hidden hot spots, and while you can get by on many roads without a 4WD, make sure there are no issues with taking your rental car everywhere you want to go.

There are not many petrol stations around the island, with the main stations found in Kingscote and Penneshaw and smaller stations at Vivonne Bay, Parndana, American River and KI Wilderness Retreat (near Flinders Chase National Park). Always make sure you leave with a full tank for a day of exploring.

💤 STAY

There are eight different regions on Kangaroo Island (American River, Cygnet River, Kingscote, North Coast, Parndana, Penneshaw and the Dudley Peninsula, South Coast and West End), which all offer different accommodations. Kingscote is the main town, where most of the accommodation can be found, and is a good place to base yourself if you want to be near shops, restaurants and cafes. There are options across the island for every budget.

For somewhere luxurious to stay, look at **Hamilton & Dune** holiday houses, the newly renovated **Southern Ocean Lodge** which just reopened, more spectacular than ever, after burning down in the bushfires of 2019, or the eco retreat of **One KI**.

Top Relaxing on Stokes Bay *Bottom* Sea lion lounging at Seal Bay *Opposite* The Remarkable Rocks

There's a range of hotels and resorts, including **Kangaroo Island Seafront Hotel** and **Aurora Ozone Apartments** and even farmstays, such as **Cabn x Cape St Albans** and **Antechamber Bay Retreats**.

Some of the best campgrounds include **Kangaroo Island Seafront Holiday Park**, **Discovery Lagoon Campsite** and **Western KI Caravan Park**.

Around the island there are also a number of council-run campgrounds, which operate on a first-come, first-serve basis and cannot be booked. Fees apply for each location when you arrive and are paid via an onsite self-registration booth. Find out about the locations and facilities online (kangarooisland.sa.gov.au/recreation/camping-facilities).

⊛ DAYTRIPS

To experience the best of KI in only one day, **SeaLink** offers great daytrip tours, picking you up and dropping you off in the Adelaide/Tarndanya CBD. The **Experience Day Tour** is the ultimate choice, taking you to some of the iconic natural beauty sights around the island, including the Remarkable Rocks and Admirals Arch in Flinders Chase National Park, Seal Bay and the koalas and kangaroos at **Kangaroo Island Wildlife Park**. It includes return travel to KI by coach and ferry, a two-course lunch on the island, and gives you a glimpse into some of the best of this beautiful island.

⊚ FOOD & DRINK

There is no shortage of great places to eat and drink around KI, with a strong focus on local produce and a farm-to-plate style of dining. Opening hours can vary though, so check in advance before heading out.

Cactus Kangaroo Island in Kingscote and **Mille Mae's Pantry** in Penneshaw are both breakfast favourites. Try the lavender-infused biscuits, tea and scones at **Emu Bay Lavender Farm**. **Penneshaw Beach Bar** and **Prickly Pear Summer Cantina** in Kingscote both offer great food and vibes. **Vivonne Bay General Store** does a great burger after a visit to the Remarkable Rocks.

Head to **Kangaroo Island Spirits** to taste its award-winning botanical gin, as well as their unique vodka and whisky. For a locally brewed beer, **Kangaroo Island Brewery** offers a tasting paddle with four of their best local brews. To try some of the wine made on the island, **Dudley Wines**, **False Cape Wines** and **The Islander Estate** are great cellar doors.

Drakes supermarket is in Kingscote and there's an **IGA** supermarket in Penneshaw, as well as general cafes, pubs and takeaway shops in both towns.

Opposite Aerial view over Vivonne Bay

Adventure awaits

THINGS TO DO

Explore **Flinders Chase National Park**, home to some of KI's most beautiful natural attractions. **Remarkable Rocks** stand tall on a granite cliff, having been formed over 500 million years of wind, rain and pounding waves. They stand in unique shapes at the end of the park, overlooking the ocean and are a beautiful spot to come for the sunrise. Just down the road, **Admirals Arch** was also formed from thousands of years of erosion and is now home to hundreds of local seals that you can see below, soaking up the sun. Hold on to your hat as you walk down the boardwalk to Admirals Arch, as it can get extremely windy here. Above Admirals Arch stands **Cape Du Couedic Lighthouse**, built between 1906 and 1909. You can walk around it or book a stay in one of the lighthouse keeper's cottages.

Hop your way across some of the beautiful beaches that make up the KI coastline. **Vivonne Bay** on the southern coast, is a breathtaking spot to admire the coastline, with bright blue water contrasted by the red dirt road and bushland that surrounds it. **Stokes Bay**, on the north coast, is a beach hidden behind a walking path that will take you quite literally through the rocky cliffs that surround it, before you pop out to a beautiful beach dotted with warm rockpools, but be aware there is a rip here and the beach is unpatrolled. **Emu Bay**, also on the north coast, is the perfect beach for beach driving, a long, flat stretch of hard sand, where you can always find a spot to yourself. It's a great place for a beach barbecue or picnic, spending your day running in and out of the water.

Meet the locals at **Seal Bay Conservation Park** on the south coast, home to Australia's largest colony of more than 1000 wild sea lions. Jump on an early morning guided tour, as this is often when they're most active, to watch them emerging from their burrows and heading down to the water for their morning swim and sunbake. It's a great place to watch the young ones playing and chasing each other and surfing the waves back into the shore.

For more wildlife encounters head to **Hanson Bay Wildlife Sanctuary**, not far from the national park exit en route to Vivonne Bay, where the koalas roam freely between the gumtrees, snoozing and looking after their babies. The koalas here are free to come and go as they please, however we've always seen more than 30 of them when we've visited. You can also often see kangaroos jumping around the lawns of the sanctuary, particularly as the sun begins to set.

To get your adrenaline pumping, head to **Little Sahara**, where you can grab yourself a sandboard or toboggan and go sliding down the towering sand dunes. After a couple of times it can be a real mission to get back up to the top (they are super tall), but the speedy ride down is always worth it. You can also pre-book a buggy tour to explore the surrounding environments, including the coastline, and spot wildlife.

Pop into some of KI's unique spots, like the **Emu Ridge Eucalyptus Distillery** for tours and eucalyptus lollies and gifts; the **Island Beehive** to learn about Ligurian Bees which KI is a sanctuary for; or **Kangaroo Island Wool** where you can take an interesting mill tour and visit the new shop.

WHEN TO GO

The summer months from December to February are the most popular times to visit KI, when the weather is warmer and there are more sunny days. However, the whole island, including accommodation and ferry transfers can often be booked during these times, so make sure you lock in everything in advance. The shoulder seasons of spring and autumn are also great times to visit, with the slightly cooler weather allowing hiking and exploring to be a little more comfortable.

NEED TO KNOW

Outside of the main towns there is very limited phone reception, with much of the island being quite remote. Telstra has the most coverage across the island, but it's always a good idea to load maps and directions before you go.

ON THE MAINLAND

Whilst there is very little to see or do in Cape Jervis itself (other than hop on or off the ferry!), a visit to Kangaroo Island can be perfectly extended with some stops along the **Fleurieu Peninsula**. Hop along its iconic beaches through Second Valley, Port Willunga and the rolling cliffs of Sellick's Beach - a great place for beach driving. Visit nearby holiday towns like Victor Harbor (including **Granite Island**, *see* p.68), Port Elliot and Goolwa. Enjoy a tasting paddle of wines through the wineries of McLaren Vale; **Down The Rabbit Hole** is our favourite spot. Enjoy a 4WD adventure through **Deep Creek Conservation Park**, one of the most rugged and remote national parks in SA.

Opposite top left The exciting entrance to Stokes Bay *Opposite top right* Koalas at Hanson Bay *Opposite bottom left* Dolphins swimming off Penneshaw Beach *Opposite bottom right* The main road in Flinders Chase National Park

Hinchinbrook Island/ Munamudanamy

An untouched jungle paradise

CASSOWARY COAST, QUEENSLAND

Adventure awaits

For anyone looking to explore a raw tropical island paradise without crowds, untouched Hinchinbrook Island/Munamudanamy is the place to go. One of Australia's largest island national parks, Hinchinbrook is home to wild Jurassic jungle, challenging hiking trails, secret swimming holes and natural infinity pools boasting incredible views over the island. It's quiet, peaceful, and the ideal destination if you're looking to reconnect with nature.

Hinchinbrook Island is known as Munamudanamy and is the Traditional land of the Bandjin and Girramay Peoples. It's part of the UNESCO World Heritage-listed Wet Tropics of Queensland. It sees just 7000 visitors per year, with only around 40 people allowed to set foot on the island at any one time. The largest island on the Great Barrier Reef, Hinchinbrook is entirely a national park, and is famous for its range of diverse habitats, including luscious rainforests, beautiful sandy beaches, and unique mangrove forests.

Offering completely different and unique experiences, you can visit Hinchinbrook Island either on your own or as part of a tour, with options for cruising, beach camping, hiking and waterfall hopping. Many people head to the island each year to tackle the famous Thorsborne Trail, a multi-day hike across the entire island, while others want to take a dip in the stunning natural infinity pool at the top of Zoe Falls. No matter how you choose to spend your days, it's sure to be an adventure you won't forget.

TIME ZONE: AEST (GMT +10)

BEST TIME TO VISIT: April to Sept

ACCESSIBLE FROM: Cardwell and Lucinda

GETTING THERE: Boat transfer

PHONE RECEPTION: No

WI-FI: No

DAYTRIPS: Yes

KID FRIENDLY: Kids are welcome, however you will need to hike to get to any natural attraction, so be prepared and know their capabilities when planning your visit.

SOCIALS: @hinchinbrookway

MORE INFO: parks.des.qld.gov.au/parks/hinchinbrook, hinchinbrookway.com.au

THE BEST BITS

After all the hiking, when you finally get to the top of Zoe Falls, take a dip in the infinity pool and soak up the breathtaking views. It's one of the most magical spots on the island.

Opposite Views from the Zoe Falls infinity pool *Overleaf* Aerial views over the Hinchinbrook Channel

➔ GETTING HERE & AROUND

Hinchinbrook Island/Munamudanamy sits between Cairns in the north and Townsville in the south, and can be accessed from the towns of Cardwell and Lucinda. To get to Hinchinbrook Island you will need to either jump on a tour or organise a private charter boat to drop you off on the island. **Absolute North Charters** (absolutenorthcharters.com.au) offers camping transfers, as well as transfers for hikers tackling the Thorsborne Trail, with daily trips between Hinchinbrook Island and Lucinda, while **Hinchinbrook Island Cruises** (hinchinbrookislandcruises.com.au) offers transfers from Cardwell.

Once you're on the island, everything is accessible via hiking trails. It's a very remote and natural environment, with no cars, infrastructure or shops.

☾ STAY

Completely covered in jungle and rainforest, the only way to stay on Hinchinbrook Island/Munamudanamy is remote bush camping. There are several camping areas around the island, including beachside and bush camping options, that offer a completely off-the-grid, remote experience, with toilet facilities only available at a few of the camping areas. Some of the most popular campsites including **South Zoe Bay**, a stunning beachside camp at the entrance to Zoe Falls that offers toilets and picnic facilities; **South Macushla** is the perfect spot for boat camping (camp behind the crocodile barriers); and **The Haven (Scraggy Point)** offers a grassy camping area and is the only campsite on the western side of the island, with views overlooking the Hinchinbrook Channel (again, camp behind the crocodile barriers). Camping permits are required. Book through Queensland National Parks (parks.des.qld.gov.au/parks/hinchinbrook) or at the Hinchinbrook Visitor Information Centre in Ingham.

✹ DAYTRIPS

There are a few different ways to explore Hinchinbrook Island/Munamudanamy, with both half-day and full-day trips on offer, depending on where you want to go and what you want to see, with the most popular daytrips always including a visit to Zoe Falls. **Wild Hinchinbrook Adventures** (wildhinchinbrook.com.au) offers guided waterfall walks to Zoe Falls and Mulligans Falls, scenic cruises of the Hinchinbrook Channel, as well as fishing adventure charters of the channel and the Great Barrier Reef surrounding the island.

FOOD & DRINK

There are no shops on Hinchinbrook Island/Munamudanamy, which means you'll need to bring all your own food and drink supplies with you. If you're camping or on a multi-day hike, you'll need to bring food and drink supplies for the entirety of your trip (including drinking water), as well as cooking tools. It's important to note, open camp fires and cooking fires are not allowed within Hinchinbrook Island National Park as per the Queensland National Parks website. For those visiting on day tours, lunch, drinks and snacks are normally provided by the tour operators, but check when you book.

THINGS TO DO

With no shortage of beautiful natural attractions to soak up on Hinchinbrook Island/Munamudanamy, the only question is how are you going to spend your time there?

The most adventurous way to explore the island is by hiking the rugged **Thorsborne Trail**, internationally rated as one of the Top 10 walks on the planet. Taking you from Ramsay Bay to George Point, the challenging four-day hike will take you across 32km, through the island's misty mountains, tropical rainforests, stunning waterfalls and beautiful sandy beaches. You'll need to be prepared and bring all your own supplies, and you're also hiking through crocodile country, so it's definitely one for the more experienced hikers. Download the *Hinchinbrook Island Discovery Guide* from Queensland Parks and Wildlife (parks.des.qld.gov.au/parks/hinchinbrook/maps-resources) before you go, for all the information you need to know for your trek, including packing lists, information on camping areas, trail notes, maps, and facilities across the island. Note that the trail can be closed seasonally over summer due to extreme heat and heavy rainfall.

For those planning to visit the island on a daytrip, **Zoe Falls** is one of the most popular places to visit, with a refreshing swimming hole at the bottom of the falls and a stunning infinity pool at the top. It's a 25min, relatively flat bushwalk from the beach to Zoe Falls, and then a more adventurous (and steep) 15min hike to get up to the infinity pool at the top. It's a beautiful place to spend the day, swimming with jungle perch and turtles immersed in the rainforest.

Mulligan Falls is another favourite spot on the island, a short, easy walk that's accessible for the whole family. Approximately 2.5km return, you'll walk through the Jurrasic-like jungle rainforest, before you pop out at the sparkling pool at the bottom of the falls.

Adventure awaits

Top left Zoe Falls *Top right* Hiking Hinchinbrook Island *Opposite* The waterways of Hinchinbrook Island

There are also a number of shorter hikes to see a little more of the island's dramatic landscapes, including the **Haven Track** (1km return), the **Macushla to Cape Richards Track** (4.9km one-way) and **South Shepherd Bay** (7.6km return).

WHEN TO GO

Hinchinbrook Island/Munamudanamy has a unique climate, where daytime temperatures and humidity can be high year-round, and nights can be quite cool. April to September is considered the best time to visit the island, particularly for those planning multi-day hikes, when the humidity is lower and there is less rainfall.

NEED TO KNOW

With only 40 people allowed to camp on the island at any one time, it's highly recommended that you organise your camping permit in advance to avoid missing out - especially if you're planning on hiking the Thorsborne Trail. Group size is limited to a maximum of six people, with a maximum stay of two nights at each camping area. Permits can be purchased through Queensland Parks and Wildlife Service (parks.des.qld.gov.au/parks/hinchinbrook), and it's a good idea to also check the website for any park alerts or warnings - including for crocodiles - before setting off on your hike. For more information, stop into the **Hinchinbrook Visitor Information Centre** (44 Cooper St, Ingham) before you head over to the island.

ON THE MAINLAND

The Hinchinbrook Way stretches along the mainland from Cardwell in the north to Ingham in the south, with plenty to see and do. Take a dip in the bright blue waters of the **Cardwell Spa Pool**. Visit the incredible **Wallaman Falls**, the highest, permanent, single-drop waterfall in Australia, reaching 268m tall. Explore the epic **Paluma Range National Park**, home to Jourama Falls set amongst an incredible rainforest. Learn about the history and culture of the Nywaigi People at **Mungalla Station**, an award-winning cattle station rich in cultural experiences. Or, simply bakery hop your way through the tiny towns of the Hinchinbrook Way, with plenty of sweet and savoury treats to taste along the way.

ISLAND HOPPING
Dunk Island/ Coonanglebah

CASSOWARY COAST, QUEENSLAND

A short 20min boat ride, just 4km from Mission Beach, is Dunk Island/Coonanglebah. The largest of the Family Islands, most of the island is covered by Family Islands National Park, with pristine beaches that you're likely to have all to yourself and walking trails that meander through a dense tropical rainforest, leading you to lookouts that seem to pop out of nowhere, with views back across to Mission Beach.

Dunk Island has lived many lives. Known as Coonanglebah to the Bandjin, saltwater people, and Djiru, mainland people, meaning 'the island of peace and plenty', the island was used for tens of thousands of years as a source of food, accessed by bark canoes from the mainland once sea levels rose after the last ice age. In 1897 E.J. Banfield and his wife Bertha became the first European settlers on the island, living in a small beach hut for 26 years. The island was used by the Royal Australian Air Force during World War II.

The island's signature resort was built before the war in 1936 and was a popular spot for many decades, often welcoming big-name celebrities and Australian prime ministers for a stay. Unfortunately, it was hit by a couple of cyclones, causing severe damage and its closure after Cyclone Yasi in 2011. The remains of the resort can still be seen from the beachfront of the island, as they have struggled to find someone committed to rebuilding and reopening the resort over the last decade. The good news though is that there is a campground, so you can still stay on this island paradise.

These days Dunk Island/Coonanglebah is a quiet tropical paradise. It's a wonderful place for hiking, swimming and snorkelling and an island you'll often have mostly to yourself.

⊙ GETTING HERE

Being so close to the mainland, there are plenty of ways to explore and experience Dunk Island. The first is on a daytrip. **Myroo Adventures**, also known as **Dunk Island Adventures** (myrooadventures.com or quickcoast.com.au), offers a great daytrip across to the island from Mission Beach called **Dunk & Lunch**, with plenty of time to explore the island at your own pace, as well as a spectacular barbecue lunch onboard the ferry. Thom declared it the best day tour lunch we've ever had. He wasn't wrong. The tour allows plenty of time to explore the whole island, from hiking the rainforest-covered mountains to snorkelling the fringing reef around the island.

Alternatively, you can also hire a boat from Mission Beach and make your own way over to Dunk Island. **Mission Beach Boat Hire**, **Budget Boat Hire** and **Kurramine Boat Hire** all offer tinnies for you to make the most of Dunk Island from the water. Brammo Bay is the main anchorage on Dunk Island and there are three guest moorings there if you bring your own boat.

Top left Aerial views over Dunk Island/Coonanglebah and out to Mission Beach *Opposite top right* Beach baby on Dunk Island

✓ THINGS TO DO

There's plenty to explore on Dunk Island/Coonanglebah. For the adventurous, **Mount Kootaloo** offers a challenging 7km-return walk, taking you on a journey to the island's highest point, through the ancient fern forest, and past the remains of a World War II radar station, where you are presented with panoramic views of the Family Group of Islands. On the way back down you can continue along the circuit walking track of the island (which is approximately 11km and takes around 3hr or 4hr), through Palm Valley to arrive at Coconut Beach. For one of the island's favourite beaches and most lively snorkelling spots, follow the signs for **Muggy Muggy Beach**, at the end of the roughly 20min walk. Head to the spit for the calmest swimming conditions, with clear water and no rocks in the way. The main jetty at Brammo Bay is also a favourite local spot for fishing off the pier and also jumping and diving into the ocean, but if you decide to do it always exercise caution by checking tides and depth and understand the risks involved. On Saturdays and Sundays **What's Up Cairns** has equipment to hire on the beach, including stand-up paddleboards, kayaks, snorkelling masks and fins and stinger suits. You can also join a small group adventure stand-up paddleboard tour.

💤 STAY

Dunk Island/Coonanglebah has a great campground right on the beach, with hot showers, toilets, drinking water, barbecues and picnic tables. It even has mobile phone reception. Camping fees and bookings are managed by the Cassowary Coast Regional Council. Book online (dunkislandcamp.com.au) or at their office on Porter Promenade in Mission Beach.

MORE INFO

To find out more about Family Islands National Park, head online to Queensland Parks and Wildlife Service (parks.des.qld.gov.au/parks/family-islands).

Best of the Great Barrier Reef

Heron Island, Queensland 126
Lady Elliot Island, Queensland . . . 132
Island Hopping: Frankland Islands, Queensland 140
Lady Musgrave Island, Queensland 142
Fitzroy Island, Queensland 148
Island Hopping: Whitsunday Island, Queensland 157

Heron Island

The best place to see turtles nesting and hatching on the beach

SOUTHERN GREAT BARRIER REEF, QUEENSLAND

Imagine the clearest, brightest blue water you've ever seen in your life. It's perfectly warm all day and night, an unbelievable mixture of blues and greens swirling together as the waves move in and out from the shore. That is one of the things you will never forget about Heron Island. The colour of the water is simply unbelievable. Like someone has used a filter, or your eyes have increased the saturation. It honestly surprised me, every time I stepped out of our room, every day for our five-day visit. It's incredible.

Pair that water with the remarkable marine life and turtle experiences to be had on Heron Island, and it quickly becomes a can't-miss bucket-list destination. A snorkelling and diving hotspot year-round, Heron Island is known for its turtles, rays and reef sharks that you can swim with a few metres from the beach. Often spotted from the jetty, or even the sand, the underwater life here is phenomenal. It's easy to spend hours in the water exploring, only coming out when the tide gets too low to continue.

But one of the biggest drawcards of Heron Island is that it is a significant nesting location for Green Turtles and Loggerhead Turtles on the Great Barrier Reef. Nesting season occurs from November to March each year, when hundreds of turtles will make their way up the beach to build nests and lay their eggs. Then, from January until May, these eggs begin to hatch, with thousands of tiny baby hatchlings scurrying across the sand, making their mad dash to the ocean. It's an absolutely magical thing to see.

A complete island paradise, Heron Island will have you planning your return before you've even left.

TIME ZONE: AEST (GMT +10)
BEST TIME TO VISIT: During turtle season (Nov to March for nesting turtles, Jan to May for hatchlings).
ACCESSIBLE FROM: Gladstone
GETTING THERE: The Heron Islander ferry or helicopter
PHONE RECEPTION: No
WI-FI: Yes, purchase a voucher at reception
DAYTRIPS: No
KID FRIENDLY: Yes
SOCIALS: @heronisland
MORE INFO: heronisland.com

THE BEST BITS

Plan your visit during February or early March for the opportunity to experience both turtles nesting and baby turtles hatching on the same trip. The turtles nest and hatch all around the island, with guided turtle walks to help you find some action.

Previous Green turtle swimming around the Lady Musgrave Island pontoon *Opposite* Baby turtle hatchling emerging from their nest and heading for the ocean

The blues of Heron Island

⊙ GETTING HERE

Sitting 72km off the coast of Gladstone, Heron Island might take a little planning to get to, but it's absolutely worth the effort. There are regular flights between Gladstone and Brisbane/Meanjin available with both **Virgin Australia** and **Qantas**, with connections to all major cities.

From Gladstone Marina, Heron Island is easily accessible by the **Heron Islander Ferry**, which makes a round-trip five days per week (Mon, Wed, Fri, Sat and Sun), taking about 2hr each way. Check in half an hour before you're due to depart. There is a cafe at the marina serving breakfast and coffees if you need a little something before you board.

⊙ STAY

There are a number of different room types to choose from on Heron Island, ranging from the Turtle Rooms, set amongst the Pisonia Forest, to Beachside Rooms and even a Beach House. It's a good idea to choose your room based on where you would like to be located on the island, with some rooms opening right onto the beach, others offering sunset views with more of a cliff-drop to the water and others set more inland amongst the forest. Only a handful of rooms offer air-conditioning, which is important to consider if you're travelling during the summer months or with small children, however the ceiling fans in other rooms are very effective. The rooms are not serviced during your stay, but you can swap bath and beach towels at reception for fresh ones. Heron Island is a keyless property, but rooms can be locked from the inside and there is a safe available at reception should you need it.

As part of the resort, there is an outdoor pool near Baillie's Bar, as well as a complimentary laundry that you can use.

⊙ FOOD & DRINK

The one main restaurant on Heron Island is **Shearwater Restaurant**. Start your day in the morning with your complimentary buffet breakfast, to give you plenty of fuel for the day. Lunch and dinner are also offered, with a small a la carte menu for lunch, which also has a takeaway option, and a buffet selection or an la carte dinner menu. **Baillie's Bar** is quite the hub, with a large lounge area and outdoor seating overlooking the water and the resort pool. There are drinks, as well as snacks and sandwiches through the day, happy hour twice a day and an extensive cocktail list to taste

your way through. The **Heron Island Shop** also has a range of drinks, ice-creams and small snacks, as well as basic pharmaceuticals you might need like sunscreen, Panadol, seasickness tablets, swim nappies, souvenirs and beach essentials.

⊙ THINGS TO DO

The best way to tackle your day on Heron Island is to plan around the tides, which the staff will explain to you when you arrive. The tides can be quite dramatic, with high tide leaving you almost no beach to walk on, and low tide exposing the coral and the reef to the elements. Snorkelling off the beach is best during the two hours either side of high tide, when you can often find turtles, rays and reef sharks swimming close to the shore, as well as hundreds of colourful, tropical fish swimming amongst the reef. For the best snorkelling, jump in around the gantry or snorkel out to the shipwreck. Masks, snorkels and fins are complimentary to hire during your stay from the Marine Centre.

To explore more of the outer reef, jump on a **snorkelling or diving tour**. Taking you out to some of the most popular diving sites, including Heron Bommie, Blue Pools, Coral Canyons and Gorgonia Hole, you're sure to be met with an abundance of diverse marine life to explore. Heron Island also offers a range of certified **PADI Dive Courses**. It's important to note that there is a minimum age of eight years old for these tours.

Heron Island offers a huge schedule of **complimentary activities** so you can make the most of your time there.

> ### ISLAND HOPPER: WILSON ISLAND
> If you're looking for something a little more off-the-beaten track, take a couple of days to stay at Heron's little sister, **Wilson Island** (wilsonisland.com). An all-inclusive, adults-only retreat, Wilson Island has only nine glamping tents scattered around the island, which means no more than 18 guests at any one time. Talk about feeling like you have an island all to yourself. You can relax entirely here as all meals, drinks and snacks are included too. Just a 15min boat transfer from Heron, Wilson Island is the place to go for all the incredible wildlife and turtle experiences, mixed in with a little bit of luxury and seclusion.

Best of the Great Barrier Reef

There are island walks, reef discovery walks, bird walks, nature presentations and stargazing through the telescope at the helipad on the island itinerary year-round, as well as seasonal guided turtle hatchling and nesting walks, and a variety of evening talks throughout the year. When you board the Heron Islander catamaran you will be given a weekly schedule with all the activities, and you can pop your name down for any tour you would like at the Information Centre.

Stay dry and explore the reef on the **I-Spy Semi-Submersible tour**. Taking you out past the shipwreck and beyond, the semi-sub will get you right into the heart of the action underwater, without you getting wet. It's a great way to see unique corals and spot plenty of fish, rays and turtles swimming past.

Jump on a **guided kayak tour** to explore the reef from above. You can often spot plenty of rays, small sharks and sometimes even turtles on this tour, as your guide gives you some insight into the reef and the incredible coral life you're gliding across.

Take a tour of the **University of Queensland Research Station** that lies alongside Heron Island Resort, where researchers will give you a look into what they're investigating.

Kids aged between seven and 12 can discover the island's environment during the nature-focused **Junior Rangers Program**, where they'll participate in activities like island walks and birdwatching, and learn about the reef, coral and turtles. It runs during the Queensland school holidays.

Relax, restore and rejuvenate at **Aqua Soul Spa**. In the heart of the Pisonia Forest, the spa offers massages, face, body and skin packages to help you unwind in this island paradise. You can book treatments at reception but they often book out, so it's better to book in advance of your stay.

End the day with a peaceful **Sunset Cruise**, offering stunning views of the island from the water. Enjoy a cheese platter and a couple of drinks as you watch the sun sink below the horizon for the day. The cruise takes about 1.5hr and can be booked at the Marine Centre. There is an age limit of eight years old for this cruise.

WHEN TO GO

Heron Island and the Southern Great Barrier Reef is a great year-round destination, with warm temperatures throughout the seasons. The wet season is technically from January to March, it can be quite humid but there is little rainfall for a wet season. However, the best time to visit is of course during the turtle season - from October to March for nesting turtles and January to May for hatchlings. To give yourself the best chance of seeing both on one trip, plan your visit for February or early March.

NEED TO KNOW

There are many necessary rules and guidelines around observing turtles on Heron Island. For example, staying out of sight of any turtles coming to shore to nest, and having absolutely no lights on as they could disorientate the turtles. These guidelines are all extremely important as they allow the turtles to nest and hatch in the most natural environment possible, giving them the best chance of survival. You will be given a brief orientation when you arrive, but it's also a good idea to jump on a free turtle tour on your first night to get an idea of how things work before heading out to search for turtles on your own.

A quick note about the birds: turtle nesting and hatching season is also bird nesting season. Heron Island is covered in thousands of birds, often flying low and likely to poop on you at some point. Whilst it is a paradise for bird watchers, if you're not that keen on birds it is good to know before you arrive so you're aware.

ON THE MAINLAND

As the gateway to the Southern Great Barrier Reef, Gladstone is home to an impressive natural deep-water harbour that connects visitors to Heron Island from the mainland. Whilst visiting, check out the panoramic views from Auckland Point or Round Hill Lookout, wander through the **Tondoon Botanic Gardens** and try the fresh seafood at the **Gladstone Fish Market**.

Opposite top left The incredible water surrounding Heron Island
Opposite top right Family time on Heron Island *Opposite bottom* A turtle returning to the ocean after laying her eggs

Lady Elliot Island

Home of the Manta Ray

SOUTHERN GREAT BARRIER REEF, QUEENSLAND

At the southernmost point of the Great Barrier Reef, sitting approximately 80km north-east of Bundaberg, Lady Elliot Island is famous for its resident population of manta rays that can often be spotted swimming and feeding around the island all year-long. A proud eco-resort, Lady Elliot Island is also a leader in innovative sustainability programs and low-impact operations. One of the most unique little islands you will find in the Great Barrier Reef, there is something very special about Lady Elliot.

With a unique position on the reef, located between K'gari (*see* p.101) and Lady Musgrave Island (*see* p.142), Lady Elliot Island is too remote for boats, which means all visitors arrive via a short scenic flight. And what a way to arrive! From the air you can see the beauty of this island paradise, with an incredible view of the island and its surrounding reef lagoon. Then you land on the grassy airstrip, which runs the entire length of the island, and your adventure awaits.

Known as the Home of the Manta Ray, with more than 700 individual mantas identified by researchers in the waters surrounding the island, these gentle giants are completely magical to witness in their natural habitat. They are the world's largest ray, growing a wingspan of up to 7m and affectionately known as 'kites of the sea'. It is surreal and amazing diving or snorkelling amongst them.

Lady Elliot Island Eco Resort has a plethora of ecotourism awards and certifications under its belt, and strives to preserve the island's natural environment and ecosystem. It is 100 per cent solar powered and free of single-use plastic, and it partners with guests to offset all flight carbon emissions, as well as participates in a first-of-its-kind island restoration program. With friendly staff, delicious food and reef-front suites that are only steps away from incredible snorkelling, you will instantly feel at home.

TIME ZONE: AEST (GMT +10)

BEST TIME TO VISIT: Year-round

ACCESSIBLE FROM: Bundaberg, Hervey Bay, Brisbane and the Gold Coast

GETTING THERE: Scenic flight

PHONE RECEPTION: No

WI-FI: Yes, paid service available in the Departure Lounge

DAYTRIPS: Yes

KID FRIENDLY: Yes

SOCIALS: @ladyelliotislandecoresort

MORE INFO: ladyelliot.com.au

THE BEST BITS

Lady Elliot Island is the Home of the Manta Ray, with researchers identifying more than 700 individual manta rays swimming in the waters surrounding the island. While they can often be spotted year-round, the winter months (May-Aug) are the best time to see and swim with these gentle giants up close.

Opposite Heading to the beach on Lady Elliot Island

➔ GETTING HERE

Lady Elliot Island is the only coral cay island with an airstrip on the Great Barrier Reef; this means you get to start your island experience with a stunning scenic flight over the island and surrounding lagoon. It's an extraordinary way to arrive, with a beautiful bird's-eye view of the island as you land and take off. Whilst the closest and easiest access point is Bundaberg, flights are also available from Hervey Bay, Brisbane (Redcliffe) and the Gold Coast (Coolangatta). Flights to Lady Elliot Island are operated by a light aircraft, which are booked by the resort reservation staff when you make your booking. Strict luggage restrictions apply, so make sure you read all your booking confirmation information when you receive it.

ⓩ STAY

There are a range of different accommodation options at **Lady Elliot Island Eco Resort**, with two-bedroom beachfront units, glamping tents, reef units that are only a few steps from the lagoon reef and eco-cabins kitted out with bunk beds and shared bathroom facilities that are set a little further into the island. As guests staying on the island, the overnight rate also includes a full buffet breakfast and dinner, use of snorkelling equipment (including a mask, snorkel and fins) and a snorkelling lesson if you need one, as well as a snorkelling tour which includes a guided glass-bottom boat tour, and a full timetable of complimentary activities.

Around the island you can also find a saltwater pool, beach volleyball court, children's playground, air-conditioned Manta Lounge, a complimentary laundry and table tennis table.

⊛ DAYTRIPS

An incredible spot to spend the day, a Lady Elliot Island daytrip allows you to experience the best of the Southern Great Barrier Reef and this unique island all in one day. With daily departures from Bundaberg and Hervey Bay, the all-inclusive day tour includes return scenic flights, an island orientation tour, a glass-bottom boat/guided snorkel tour, snorkel equipment, and a delicious buffet lunch. With plenty of time for snorkelling, swimming with turtles and exploring the reef, the day tour is a great way to explore this beautiful part of the Great Barrier Reef.

Top Manta Ray on the reef *Bottom* Sunset at the lighthouse
Opposite The streets of Lady Elliot Island

Lady Elliot Island 135

FOOD & DRINK

There is only one place to eat on Lady Elliot Island - the **Beachfront Dining Room**. For guests staying overnight, a delicious breakfast and dinner buffet is included with your stay. At lunchtime you can choose between a buffet or an a la carte menu (we highly recommend the crab tacos). The food on Lady Elliot Island is absolutely outstanding - without a doubt, one of the best buffets we have ever experienced. There are so many options, with a menu that changes every day and tastes to please every palate. The **Lagoon Bar** offers drinks and snacks throughout the day, with an extensive cocktail menu, and the sprawling **Lagoon Deck** is the perfect setting for a meal, with views of the turquoise water of the lagoon.

As an eco-resort, there are no plastic bottles on Lady Elliot Island, so you will need to bring your own reusable drink bottle or purchase one from the gift shop to keep yourself hydrated during your stay. There are drinking water fountains to fill up your bottle around the island, as well as clean water from the taps in the guest rooms.

THINGS TO DO

The best thing to do on Lady Elliot Island is spend as much time as you can exploring underwater. **The Lagoon**, right in front of the resort, offers some of the best **snorkelling** opportunities you can find, with turtles often swimming close to the shore. The Lagoon is open for snorkelling at different times each day, depending on the tides, so check the activities board before you jump in.

Jump aboard a complimentary **glass-bottom boat and guided snorkel safari tour**, where your guides will take you out to explore some of the outer reef. The tour is included for all day and overnight guests and is a great introduction to the snorkelling around the island. There are also daily **snorkelling and diving tours**, exploring more than 20 dive sites around the island. In addition to The Lagoon, the western side of the island offers two snorkelling trails to explore: the Lighthouse and the Coral Gardens Trails.

With an extensive program of **complimentary activities**, there is always something to do, learn and experience during your stay at Lady Elliot Island Eco Resort. There are **snorkelling lessons**, **island discovery tours** and **fish feeding** each day, as well as a rotating program of **birdwatching tours**, behind-the-scenes **tours of the resort**, **guided reef walks** and even a **quiz night** once a week. There are also plenty of **guest speaker talks and special presentations** where you can learn about the ocean and

Opposite Lady Elliot Island from the plane

? WHEN TO GO

Lady Elliot Island is a great place to visit year-round, with sunny warm weather and not much of a wet season. The best time of year to visit is dependent on what kind of wildlife experience you're hoping for. Seasonal wildlife comes and goes throughout the year. The peak manta ray season is during late autumn and winter (May-Aug), turtle nesting season is summer (Nov-Feb), turtle hatching season is late summer and autumn (Feb-April), humpback whale migration season is in winter and spring (June-Oct) and sea bird season carries through spring and summer into autumn (Sept-April).

! NEED TO KNOW

As a coral island, it is particularly important to bring a pair of reef shoes (we found Crocs brand to be a good choice) with you to Lady Elliot Island. The coral shores can be sharp and painful to walk across, as can the seabed as you walk out to the reef, so reef shoes will be your best friend. There are some reef shoes to borrow during your stay, but sizes can be limited, especially for kids.

A quick note about the birds: turtle season is also bird nesting season. Lady Elliot Island is covered in thousands of birds during this time, often flying low and likely to poop on you at some point. Whilst it is a paradise for birdwatchers, if you're not that keen on birds it is good to know be aware before you arrive and even plan your visit accordingly.

> ### ON THE MAINLAND
>
> The closest mainland city to Lady Elliot Island is Bundaberg, sitting along the Burnett River and home to the iconic, award-winning **Bundaberg Rum Distillery**. If you have a few days to explore this vibrant town take a distillery tour and brew your own rum flavour, enjoy a leisurely river cruise aboard the Bundy Belle, check out the **Hinkler Hall of Aviation**, explore the macadamia orchard and take a self-guided tour of the **Bundaberg Barrel**, home of Bundaberg Brewed Drinks, makers of the famous ginger beer.

marine life. Check the activities board out the front of the Reef Education Centre for each day's activities, as well as a weekly schedule.

Go on the **walking trails** around the island. It takes about 45min to walk around the whole island on the coastal trail, or you can try some of the shorter walking trails, taking you through the shrubland, **Pisonia Forests** and heritage area of the island.

Spend some time in the **Reef Education Centre**, learning about the remarkable marine life that surrounds Lady Elliot Island. There are plenty of wall graphics, fact sheets and educational talks and videos so you can learn about the Great Barrier Reef, one of the most complex and biodiverse ecosystems in the world.

End the night with **sunset drinks at the lighthouse**. The best place on the island to watch the sunset, you can pre-order a charcuterie platter and purchase drinks at the lighthouse as you watch the sun set over the ocean.

Above Golden hour walks around the island *Opposite top* Sunset over Lady Elliot Island *Opposite bottom* The only island in Australia where you land on a grass runway

Lady Elliot Island

ISLAND HOPPING
Frankland Islands

TROPICAL NORTH QUEENSLAND, QUEENSLAND

The pristine Frankland Islands are a unique archipelago, sitting about 45km south-east of Cairns/Gimuy. There are five continental islands in the group – Normanby Island, High Island, Russell Island, Round Island and Mabel Island. All five of the islands are uninhabited, surrounded by healthy fringing reefs and home to plenty of marine wildlife, from turtles, giant clams and small sharks to a whole range of colourful reef fish. Manta rays, dugongs and whales can also sometimes be spotted swimming between the islands. Collectively they make up the Frankland Islands Group National Park.

The Frankland Islands hold special significance and are part of the Traditional sea country of the Mandingalby Yidinji and Gungandji Peoples. Since time immemorial to the present day, the Traditional Owners use these waters and islands to fish, hunt and gather food.

A trip to the Frankland Islands will leave you feeling like the ultimate explorer.

⊙ GETTING HERE

Offering one of the most unique reef and island daytrips, **Frankland Islands Reef Cruise** immerses you in the reef, the rainforest and the river. The tour begins in Deeral, seemingly in the middle of nowhere, where a small part in the mangroves of the river bed gives you access to a tiny jetty. It seems almost comical when you see it for the first time, this big reef ferry moored to this tiny jetty in the river. From the very first moment this daytrip feels completely unlike any other island experience.

The ferry, known as the *Turtle Islander*, is large and comfortable, with big semi-circle booths to make yourself at home. Morning tea is served as you depart for the day, and there's a bar serving drinks for the ride home. There are plenty of outdoor decks to soak in the scenery along the way. The day begins with a leisurely half-hour cruise down the Mulgrave River, winding your way towards the ocean, surrounded by the rainforest and the mangroves. Keep an eye out for crocodiles on the riverbank or even swimming alongside the boat.

✓ THINGS TO DO

From the mouth of the river it's only 10km across the open ocean before you arrive on **Normanby Island**. A unique triangle-shaped island, covered in sand and rainforest vegetation, this is your home base during the day tour. Arriving here is like being washed onto a deserted island for the day. During the cruise over you can sign up for activities to give you a rough itinerary for your day. Hit the water straight away with incredible snorkelling right off the shore. Home to some absolutely massive giant clams, as well as delicate little bommies and coral towers, filled with bright coloured tropical fish, Frankland Islands offers a unique snorkelling experience. You can also choose between a **guided snorkel tour** or an **adventure snorkel safari** if you want to go a little further off the beach. Or, you can jump into the **semi-submarine** to venture a little further offshore and explore the reef in some of the deepest parts. This guided tour goes for about half an hour, sharing information and insight about this part of the reef, with some of the best visibility from a semi-sub on the Great Barrier Reef.

After a morning of activities, head back to the island picnic area for a delicious cold buffet lunch, with salads, seafood, cold meats, sandwiches and fresh fruit to refuel on, before another afternoon of jam-packed activities. Join a guided **walking tour, led by a marine biologist and Master Reef Guide**, or head out for a paddle, with both stand-up paddleboards and kayaks available to use throughout the day. For the littlies there's even a **pirate treasure hunt**, to find buried treasure around the island. After a day of adventure and activities, the scenic cruise back through the river mangroves is definitely a great way to relax and unwind. Without a doubt, the Frankland Islands is sure to be one of the most unique days you've spent in the Great Barrier Reef.

☾ STAY

Bush camping is available on **Russell Island** and **High Island**. Both island camping areas have very few facilities, so you must be completely self-sufficient. Camping permits are required for both camping areas and fees apply for camping on High Island. The maximum stay is seven nights (or four

Top The reef at the Frankland Islands *Opposite* Aerial view over Normanby Island

nights during the Queensland school holidays, so check ahead). **Frankland Island Reef Cruises** can also provide island transfers for your camping adventure. To find out more and book your permit, head to Queensland Parks and Wildlife Service (parks.des.qld.gov.au/parks/frankland-group/camping).

ⓘ MORE INFO

To book your Frankland Islands daytrip, head online (franklandislands.com.au) or check out @franklandislands on Insta.

FRANKLAND ISLANDS FUN FACTS

Logically, the reef shouldn't even really be surviving around Normanby Island, due to its close proximity to the mainland and the amount of freshwater that floods into the ocean from the rivers during the wet season. However, the reef here is protected by a current that surrounds the island, stopping the freshwater from getting in and allowing the reef to flourish and thrive.

There is a lighthouse on Russell Island that was built in 1929 and it became a Commonwealth Island.

Lady Musgrave Island

The ultimate Southern Great Barrier Reef excursion

SOUTHERN GREAT BARRIER REEF, QUEENSLAND

Floating in the Southern Great Barrier Reef, Lady Musgrave Island is as picture perfect as you could imagine, completely untouched and undeveloped, with crystal-clear water lapping the shores. It's a tiny little heart-shaped island made up purely of coral and bird poop (yep, you read that right), protected by a beautiful turquoise blue lagoon that is absolutely teeming with marine life, including turtles, rays and sharks. Surrounded by 7000 acres of reef and lagoon, it's home to thousands of nesting seabirds, surrounded by coral reefs and is even a nesting site for green turtles in the summer months.

Right in the heart of the lagoon you will find the impressive Lady Musgrave HQ. It's a three-level pontoon built by the Lady Musgrave Experience team, and is completely wind- and solar-powered (and therefore boasts a zero-carbon footprint). It includes an underwater observatory and eight glamping beds on the top floor where you can spend the night on the reef. If you've ever dreamed of going to sleep listening to the waves and waking up to the sun rising from the ocean, right from your cosy bed, this is the place! Surrounded by beautiful warm lagoon water, you'll be hopping in and out of your snorkelling gear all day as the cheeky turtles keep you coming back for more.

Lady Musgrave is the only island in Queensland that is accompanied by a lagoon that you can navigate into by boat, which makes it the ultimate destination for a daytrip. Offering an action-packed day on the reef, from glass-bottom boat tours and guided island walks, to plenty of snorkelling and turtle encounters, you can really make the most of every minute when you take a trip with the Lady Musgrave Experience.

TIME ZONE: AEST (GMT +10)
BEST TIME TO VISIT: Year-round
ACCESSIBLE FROM: Bundaberg
GETTING THERE: Ferry with Lady Musgrave Experience
PHONE RECEPTION: No
WI-FI: No
DAYTRIPS: Yes
KID FRIENDLY: Yes
SOCIALS: @ladymusgrave_experience
MORE INFO: ladymusgraveexperience.com.au

THE BEST BITS

Lady Musgrave is a great spot for swimming with turtles and has exceptionally clear water. In fact, you're likely to see turtles popping their head above the water from the minute you arrive at the pontoon.

Opposite top left The underwater viewing platform on the pontoon *Opposite top right* There are plenty of turtles around Lady Musgrave Island *Opposite bottom* One of the most colourful parts of the Southern Great Barrier Reef

Lady Musgrave Island

Above Views from Lady Musgrave HQ to the island *Opposite* Aerial view over Lady Musgrave Island and the pontoon

➔ GETTING HERE

The best way to visit Lady Musgrave Island is on the **Lady Musgrave Experience**. With options for either a day tour or an overnight stay, the Lady Musgrave Experience's luxury catamaran, named the *Reef Empress*, departs each morning (at 7.15am) and returns each afternoon (at 5.30pm) from Bundaberg Port Marina and takes roughly 2hr, 15min each way. You can also use the *Reef Empress* as a ferry option, but only if you are planning to camp on the island. The Lady Musgrave Experience also offers a transfer service if you need a lift to and from Bundaberg or Bargara, or free parking at the marina.

💤 STAY

The **Lady Musgrave HQ Pontoon** offers the ultimate overnight experience for guests who want to spend a night on the reef. Here you can sleep in a reef- or island-view glamping bed - your own little spot on the pontoon with views out to the island and the reef. It's an incredible spot to watch the sun rise and set. An overnight experience includes all meals during your stay, VIP transfers from Bundaberg, and lots of optional activities during your extra time on the pontoon, including dive packages, snorkel safaris and turtle nesting and hatching tours (during season). There's also the option to sleep in HQ's underwater observatory bunk beds, where you can literally watch the fish and marine life swimming past you all night long.

Alternatively, you are also able to camp on Lady Musgrave Island. The campgrounds are only accessible by boat on the north-west side of the island. As you will be camping in the Capricornia Cays National Park you will need a permit from Queensland National Parks (qpws.usedirect.com/qpws). You will also need to be completely self-sufficient and bring all your own supplies, food and water.

⊛ DAYTRIPS

Most people visit Lady Musgrave Island on a day tour from Bundaberg. The team at Lady Musgrave Experience have created an epic daytrip itinerary so you absolutely get the most out of your visit, which includes a glass-bottom boat ride, guided island walk and plenty of time for snorkelling and turtle spotting. The day tour runs from 7.15am until 5.30pm.

🍴 FOOD & DRINK

The Lady Musgrave Experience includes all meals during your visit - buffet lunch, morning and afternoon tea for day guests, as well as breakfast and dinner for overnight guests. There is a bar on the pontoon where you can purchase drinks and extra snacks throughout the day, as well as onboard the *Reef Empress*.

✓ THINGS TO DO

You're in for an action-packed day whatever you do when you visit Lady Musgrave!

Take a **glass-bottom boat** ride with live commentary from the pontoon to the island where you can spot tropical fish, unique corals and even turtles swimming lazily under the boat. Once on the island you can take a **guided island walk**, where you will learn about the history of the island, the bird and marine life in the area, and the importance of this highly protected marine life area that serves as an important home for both birds and turtles. If you want to stay dry for a bit, check out the **underwater observatory**, where you can often see huge schools of fish swimming by.

But the highlight of your visit will no doubt be the **snorkelling**. With incredible clarity and warm water year-round, there's so much to see and explore under the surface. You're almost guaranteed to see turtles swimming around here, as well as plenty of colourful reef fish and sometimes even manta rays and small reef sharks.

If you're looking to get deeper into the ocean, you can choose to add on a **dive package**, with lagoon dive options for both certified and non-certified divers, and outer reef dives for certified divers.

If you're an overnight guest there's also the option to add a **night dive** for certified divers, as well as seasonal tours - either a **snorkel safari** to swim with the manta rays or **turtle nesting and hatching tours** on Lady Musgrave Island.

❓ WHEN TO GO

The Lady Musgrave Experience offers a wonderful experience year-round, with great weather and snorkelling conditions all the time. It's important to note that wildlife viewings vary seasonally, with turtle nesting season (Oct-Jan), turtle hatching season (generally Jan-April), and bird season (Oct-April) throughout the year.

Lady Musgrave Experience also offers a unique **Wellness & Yoga Retreat** a couple of times a year, which is a three-day retreat on Lady Musgrave HQ full of yoga, meditation and pilates, mixed in with lots of incredible snorkelling and ocean activities, as well as gourmet food. Check the website (ladymusgraveexperience.com.au/yoga-retreat) for the next available dates and complete itinerary.

❗ NEED TO KNOW

Both the overnight stays and day tours have limited numbers available, so it's a good idea to book your Lady Musgrave Experience in advance.

ON THE MAINLAND

To keep your coastal holiday experience going, book your stay around your visit to Lady Musgrave Island at Bargara. The sleepy beachside town is only 20min away from the marina with great sandy beaches and plenty of palm trees. It's a great place to jump on a tour to spot migrating whales (June-Oct), dolphins and even nesting turtles (Nov-March). You can find accommodation right on the beach, as well as caravan and camping options, with plenty of walking trails, playgrounds and fishing.

Lady Musgrave HQ

Fitzroy Island/Koba

Tropical North Queensland's easiest island getaway

TROPICAL NORTH QUEENSLAND, QUEENSLAND

Best of the Great Barrier Reef

TIME ZONE: AEST (GMT +10)

BEST TIME TO VISIT: April to Nov

ACCESSIBLE FROM: Cairns

GETTING THERE: Ferry transfer

PHONE RECEPTION: Yes

WI-FI: Yes

DAYTRIPS: Yes

KID FRIENDLY: Yes

SOCIALS: @fitzroyisland

MORE INFO: fitzroyisland.com

For one of the easiest and most-loved island getaways in Tropical North Queensland, you can't go past Fitzroy Island/Koba. Just a short 45min ferry ride from Cairns Marina, Fitzroy Island offers a laid-back island vibe, with sea turtles and giant schools of fish swimming around the jetty, resort rooms overlooking the ocean and open-air dining surrounded by palm trees. The scenery is simply spectacular, with the rolling hills of the tablelands on the horizon, it's the perfect spot for a quick island daytrip or a weekend getaway to soak up the sun.

A continental island that was connected to the mainland more than 10,000 years ago, Fitzroy Island is about 4sqkm in size, with 97 per cent of the island now classified as Fitzroy Island National Park. There's plenty to explore, with walking trails through the rainforest connecting you to secluded beaches, snorkelling tours to take you to the most colourful reef spots, and stand-up paddleboards and kayaks to hire, so you can spot turtles from the surface as you slowly paddle along.

Fitzroy Island is known as Koba to the local Gunggandji People (also sometimes spelled Gabar), meaning 'the first'. The Gunggandji did not have a permanent settlement on the island, instead visiting for brief periods and different ceremonies. Their main territory extends into the mountains surrounding Cairns/Gimuy, with their Dreaming stories recounting the time the water rose and the island became isolated from the land.

Stay at least one night to really experience the best of Fitzroy Island. When the last ferry leaves for the day and the sun begins to set over the mountains in the distance, the island suddenly becomes quiet and peaceful after the bustle of the day subsides. It's a magical moment, with some of the most beautiful sunsets in the tropical north as you overlook Welcome Bay.

THE BEST BITS

Fitzroy Island/Koba is one of the closest islands to the mainland where you can swim with turtles right off the beach. It's a favourite spot to see sea turtles feeding on seagrass close to the shore, as well as exceptional snorkelling conditions.

Opposite Nudey Beach

🡢 GETTING HERE

Arriving into Cairns Airport, it's only a 15min drive to get to the Reef Fleet Terminal at Cairns Marina. The **Fitzroy Flyer** (fitzroyisland.com) connects Fitzroy Island/Koba to the mainland with three daily transfers each way. It departs from the Marina at 8am, 11am and 1.30pm, and returns from Fitzroy Island at 9.30am, 12.15pm and 5pm. The midday services do not run in February and March. You will need to book in advance and check in at the Fitzroy Island Booking Centre on Spence St, 30min before your departure. The ferry ride takes about 45min to reach the island.

You can also take your own boat over to the island, with public moorings and anchorage available in the sheltered waters of the island. Get in touch with the resort to book if you're planning to stay overnight.

💤 STAY

Fitzroy Island Resort sits right at the end of the jetty, offering suites that look out to the ocean only a few steps from the water. You can literally see turtles popping their heads out of the water right from your balcony. There are plenty of different room types to choose from within the resort, although I would highly recommend choosing an option with a balcony and views of Welcome Bay to really add to your island experience. For self-contained accommodation, set a little further away from the main resort, the **Butterfly Bungalows** offer one- and two-bedroom options, with small kitchenettes, private outdoor decks and barbecue facilities. They're set amongst the luscious rainforest, directly across from the beach.

At the end of the main pathway, about a 5min walk from the jetty, is **Fitzroy Island Campground**. The grassy camping area has about 20 tent sites and a basic cold-water shower block, but you need to bring absolutely everything with you to camp here. The resort does offer camping gear for hire, including a tent, camp chairs, sleeping bags and mats, pillows and a beach wagon, if you'd rather not bring your own. Camping fees apply.

⊙ DAYTRIPS

It really becomes a choose-your-own-adventure situation when booking a daytrip to Fitzroy Island/Koba. Choose between a half or full day on the island, with optional extras for tours, equipment hire and glass-bottom boat rides, and spend the day exploring your own way.

Top Afternoon cocktail at Foxy's Bar & Cafe *Opposite* Sunset on Fitzroy Island/Koba

Fitzroy Flyer, **Fitzroy Island Adventures** and **Sunlover Reef Cruises** all offer daytrips to Fitzroy Island/Koba, with different inclusions and departure times, giving you plenty of flexibility to find a tour that works for you. To absolutely maximise your daytrip, book the Fitzroy Flyer going over at 8am and returning at 5pm. Those are the first and last ferries on the island each day, giving you the most possible time to explore the island.

🍸 FOOD & DRINK

Sitting right on the beachfront, **Foxy's Bar & Cafe** is the main food hub of the island, catering to everyone from resort guests to campers and daytrippers. Foxy's is the ultimate open-air, barefoot-island bar, with high benches overlooking the ocean, gorgeous sunset views and trivia games on the weekends. There are pool tables, a dance floor and a big sports TV. It offers morning coffees, lunch and dinner daily, and an all-day menu of light snacks and cocktails, with happy hour from 3 to 4pm, as well as takeaway meals, beer and wine.

Within the resort, **Zephyr Restaurant** is your go-to for breakfast on the island, as well as offering a night time a la carte menu for dinner, full of modern Australian dishes and locally sourced ingredients. Often booking out, with tables spilling across the outdoor terraces and into the resort foyer, it's a good idea to book your table at Zephyr's as soon as you arrive to avoid missing out.

For a quick bite to eat, the **Pool Bar** serves pizzas from 11am to 3pm, as well as drinks and a menu of cocktails, with happy hour from 3 to 4pm. Grab a drink in the pool at the swim-up bar, or stay dry at the high bar tables or deck chairs.

There is also a small **General Store** (Mon-Sun 9.30am-4.30pm) next to Foxy's that has a small range of drinks, ice-creams, sandwiches, pies and snacks, as well as souvenirs and island essentials, such as sunscreen.

⊙ THINGS TO DO

Fitzroy Island/Koba is a place of activities and adventures, with an endless list of things to do during your stay. Start with some equipment hire to explore the water. There are stand-up paddleboards (SUP) and kayaks to hire from **What's Up Cairns** on the beach (with guided SUP and kayak tours available), as well as snorkels and fins from the **Fitzroy Island Sports Hub** (FISH).

There is great **snorkelling** right off the beach in Welcome Bay, with bommies and the fringing reef to explore, and plenty of green turtles having a snack on the seagrass in the shallow water. To explore a little further, there are **snorkel safari guided tours**, which will take you around the island to Shark Fin Bay, for some truly exceptional snorkelling conditions, as well as **scuba-diving tours** and lessons. To stay dry, jump on a **glass-bottom boat tour**, and spend about an hour exploring the reef from above. It's one of the best glass-bottom boat tours we've ever been on, as you glide so close to the reef, with exceptional visibility.

Follow the walking trail across to **Nudie Beach**, Australia's number one beach in 2018, a spectacular little coral beach, surrounded by dense tropical rainforest and sparkling blue water. Keep your eyes peeled for cheeky monitor lizards who like to pop out for a little bit of sunshine every now and then. They can give you quite a fright if they sneak up on you. Hike up to the **Summit Lookout** or the **Lighthouse** for unparalleled views across the island. Both are graded as difficult hikes, so make sure you wear comfortable shoes and take plenty of water.

Take a tour of the **Turtle Rehabilitation Centre**, dedicated to taking care of injured and sick turtles before reintroducing them back into the ocean. You'll get to meet some of the turtle patients, as well as learn about turtle life on the

Opposite Aerial view over Fitzroy Island Resort

Great Barrier Reef and the reef restoration program. Or get hands on in protecting the reef yourself and jump onto the **Marine Conservation Program** (Mondays only), where you go behind the scenes to help out at the Turtle Rehab Centre, help remove drupella (coral eating snails) alongside the Reef Restoration Foundation, and contribute to the monitoring of the reef.

Fitzroy Island/Koba is a wonderful place for kids to be introduced to the activities of the Great Barrier Reef, with the **Junior Marine Biologist Program**, **Kids Bubblemaker Diving**, a school holiday program, and plenty of **arts and craft sessions** and junior activities. Fitzroy Island Resort also offers weekly activities for their resort guests, with plenty of options to keep the whole family entertained. There are guided walks, fish feeding, movie screenings, paint and sip or clay, jewellery making, bag painting and tie dye, to name a few. Some activities are included with your stay, while others will have an additional fee.

ⓘ WHEN TO GO

The dry season, between April and November, is the best time to visit Fitzroy Island/Koba, when the days are warm and there is less humidity around. Temperatures generally range from 19°C to 30°C. Throughout the summer months you can expect tropical showers throughout the day and higher temperatures and humidity.

ⓘ NEED TO KNOW

Stinger season is from October to May, where Irukandji and Box Jellyfish can be found around Fitzroy Island/Koba and the reef. During this time stinger suits are recommended, which can be hired from the Sports Hub in the resort.

Fitzroy Island is also mainly a coral beach island, so reef shoes are recommended for walking on the beaches, and in the water.

ON THE MAINLAND

With the marina located right in the heart of Cairns/Gimuy, a trip to Fitzroy Island/Koba is the perfect time to explore a little more of Tropical North Queensland's largest city. Take a dip in the **Cairns Esplanade Lagoon**. Indulge in a unique meal at **Dundee's Cafe & Restaurant** alongside the tropical fish, rays and reef sharks of the **Cairns Aquarium**. Shop at the iconic daily **night markets** on the Esplanade, or stop by **Rusty's Markets** for fresh fruit and veggies. Try a local brew at **Hemingway's Brewery** on the Cairns Wharf.

Left Monitor Lizard watching over Nudey Beach from the forest *Right* Where the rainforest meets the sea *Opposite* Cloudy sunset over Nudey Beach

ISLAND HOPPING
Whitsunday Island

THE WHITSUNDAYS, QUEENSLAND

Home to the iconic Whitehaven Beach, regularly voted one of the best beaches in the world, Whitsunday Island is the ultimate bucket-list daytrip island. The largest of the 74 islands that make up the Whitsundays, Whitsunday Island is covered in some of the whitest, softest sand in the world, made up of 98.9 per cent pure silica, with crystal-clear waters that are the perfect temperature to dive into, and a lookout over the sandbanks that cause the blue and white swirls of the coastline. This place is simply heaven on earth.

Whitsunday Island National Park sits within the Great Barrier Reef Marine Park, making it a protected area to keep the island in its beautiful natural state. Home to manta rays, turtles, humpback whales and plenty of colourful fish, there's always something to explore under the sea, or just kick back and enjoy the sand and the sunshine.

The Ngaro People of the Whitsundays have deep connections to the island and Whitehaven Beach. The sand here was named 'whispering sands' by the Traditional Owners due to the squeaky sounds it makes when you walk across it.

➔ GETTING HERE

Accessible from Airlie Beach on the mainland, as well as the Whitsunday resort islands - Hamilton Island (see p.40), Hayman Island (see p.9) and Daydream Island - there are plenty of different daytrip options to get out to Whitsunday Island to spend the day in paradise. From full daytrips, hopping past other iconic islands of the Whitsundays, including Hook Island and South Molle Island, to helicopters and seaplanes landing on the shore, beach grills, sailing yachts and exhilarating ocean rafting, there's a range of options to get out and visit Whitsunday Island.

✓ THINGS TO DO

All daytrip tours include plenty of time at **Whitehaven Beach**, the jewel of the Whitsundays and a can't-miss destination. Stretching for 7km, it's easy to find a spot all to yourself to enjoy your beach day. The pure silica sand on Whitehaven Beach actually doesn't retain heat, which means no matter how hot it is the sand is always cool and you can walk barefoot without burning your feet.

Most tours include shade, beach equipment and games, stinger suits (in season), and often lunch or morning/afternoon tea, depending on the length of your trip.

Make sure you choose a tour that also includes a stop at **Hill Inlet**. For some of the most spectacular and easily accessible views of the Whitsundays, you need to take the small walk to the Hill Inlet Lookout. From here you can see the swirling blue and white waters, best seen at low tide when the sand bars are fully visible amongst the water. The small beach at the base of the lookout, **Betty's Beach**, is often a great place to spot stingrays and turtles, swimming in the warm shallow water off the sand. If time permits, it's definitely one of our favourite spots for a swim or a paddle.

To experience the Whitsundays from above, jump onto a **scenic flight** from either Airlie Beach or Hamilton Island. Offering incredible views over the Whitsundays, including both Whitehaven Beach and Hill Inlet, this is one of the most beautiful regions in Australia to fly over. Absolutely stunning from the minute you leave until you land again. A 1hr-long scenic flight will also take you out to the Great Barrier Reef, where you can fly over the iconic **Heart Reef**, a small heart-shaped coral reef floating amongst the turquoise water. Book your flight around low tide, for the ultimate views over Hill Inlet.

⌂ STAY

If one day isn't enough and you want to spend a little longer in paradise, there are actually plenty of overnight and multi-day cruises around the Whitsundays, giving you the option to frolic in the waters here for longer. Or for the ultimate Whitsundays experience, rent your own **private yacht** and make your way around the islands at your own pace. With no boat licence required, you can load up the whole family or a group of friends onto your own catamaran and take to the seas, stopping wherever you like around the islands to jump in for a swim. It's the best way to find secret beaches and islands for yourself, visit popular hotspots like Whitehaven Beach and Hill Inlet without the crowds, watch the sun setting and rising from the water, and experience the Whitsundays in a completely unique way.

ⓘ MORE INFO

With plenty of tour operators offering trips it can be difficult to know where to start. For some award-winning tours of the Whitsundays, check out **Cruise Whitsundays** (cruisewhitsundays.com), **SeaLink** (sealink.com.au/whitsundays), **Sailing Whitsundays** (sailing-whitsundays.com), **Ocean Rafting** (oceanrafting.com.au) and **Red Cat Adventures** (redcatadventures.com.au).

Opposite Hill Inlet on Whitsunday Island

Off-the-beaten track

Cocos (Keeling) Islands, Indian
 Ocean Territories 160
Mackerel Islands, WA 168
Pumpkin Island, Queensland..... 174
*Island Hopping: Crab Claw
 Island, NT* 180
Torres Strait Islands,
 Queensland 182
Maria Island, Tasmania 189
*Island Hopping: Picnic
 Island, Tasmania* 195

Cocos (Keeling) Islands

Australia's most remote tropical paradise

INDIAN OCEAN TERRITORIES

Off-the-beaten track

TIME ZONE: Cocos Islands Time (GMT +6:30)

BEST TIME TO VISIT: April to Oct

ACCESSIBLE FROM: Perth

GETTING THERE: Virgin Australia flies to Cocos (Keeling) Islands (CCK) on Tuesdays and Fridays

PHONE RECEPTION: No

WI-FI: You can purchase wi-fi vouchers in advance from the Community Resource Centre (cocos.crc.net.au), which will give you wi-fi at hotspots all around the island, including at many accommodations: the Cocos Club, the Golf Donga, Salty's Airport Cafe, Trannies Beach, the Yacht Club, Pondok Abang on Home Island and the main shelter on Direction Island.

DAYTRIPS: No

KID FRIENDLY: Yes

SOCIALS: @cocoskeelingislands

MORE INFO: cocoskeelingislands.com.au

Floating in the Indian Ocean, miles away from anywhere else, you'll find the beautiful little atoll that is Cocos (Keeling) Islands. Known as 'Cocos' to the locals, the 27 islands that make up Cocos (Keeling) sit in an almost perfect circle, filled with the most incredible, crystal-clear, calm, warm water in the middle. The islands are covered in thousands of coconut trees, from one side to the other, and offer one of the most picturesque island settings you'll find in Australia.

The two main islands in the atoll are West Island – the tourist hub, where you will find most of the accommodation options, the visitor's centre, tours and activities and plenty of beautiful beaches – and Home Island, which is the cultural hub and where the local Cocos Malay People live. The community is small, with about 600 people calling Cocos (Keeling) home. A comfortable ferry connects West Island and Home Island, as well as Direction Island (on Thursdays and Saturdays), an island of palm trees, hermit crabs and breathtaking beach. The rest of the islands are uninhabited, though can be visited by boat or motorised canoe, and some can be camped on.

The water of the atoll is an underwater paradise, home to more than 500 species of fish, countless corals, molluscs, crustaceans and echinoderms, as well as green turtles, hawksbill turtles, manta rays, reef sharks and dolphins. It's a wonderful place for swimming and snorkelling, in some of the warmest, clearest water on the planet.

Cocos (Keeling) feels like the ultimate definition of island life. Coconut trees line the road on both sides, every beach you stop at is more beautiful than the last, tiny crabs scuttle quickly out of the way as you walk or drive along the road, the food is fresh and delicious. Time is slow and peaceful and there's no better place to unwind, relax and enjoy every moment.

THE BEST BITS

Make sure that you book an 'A' window seat for your departure flight from Cocos (Keeling) Islands. If you're lucky enough to be flying on a clear day, the views over the atoll and the lagoon as you leave the islands is nothing short of spectacular, and an 'A' seat absolutely offers the best views.

Previous The back roads of Cocos (Keeling) Islands
Opposite Daytrip to Direction Island

Above Direction Island *Opposite top* Hermit crab meeting in a coconut *Opposite bottom* Crabs cover the roads on Cocos (Keeling)

➔ GETTING HERE

Virgin Australia makes the round trip to the Indian Ocean Territories twice a week, travelling from Perth to Cocos (Keeling) Islands to Christmas Island (*see* p.91) on Fridays, and in the opposite direction on Tuesdays. The airport is in the centre of West Island, with the airstrip running right through the southern part of the island.

When travelling to the Cocos (Keeling) Islands you will be travelling through the Perth International Terminal and will need to clear customs and immigration at both ends. Travelling with your passport is highly recommended and the easiest way to travel (as well as being the only form accepted for children), however a Photo ID (such as a driver's licence) is also accepted.

© GETTING AROUND

Organise a rental car in advance to pick up when your flight arrives so you can explore the island at your own pace and get to all the best beaches on West Island. Book your car through the Cocos (Keeling) Islands website (cocoskeelingislands.com.au). Alternatively, a local bus service runs around the island, with stops around West Island Settlement and the Rumah Baru ferry jetty, and rides cost just 50c.

To explore the other islands, the ferry *Cahaya Baru* connects West Island and Home Island making regular trips between the two throughout the day, as well as Direction Island on Thursdays and Saturdays. At the time of our visit the ferry cost just $2.50 each way, but bring exact change to pay on board.

💤 STAY

There is a definite sense of pride in the accommodation options on Cocos (Keeling), with some truly beautiful properties offering waterfront locations, lagoon views and large open spaces only a few steps from the beach. Each holiday house has its own unique vibe, with plenty of options for families and larger groups, as well as smaller self-contained options. There are bed and breakfasts, historic homes, and award-winning cottages, as well as budget motel-style accommodation. Head online (cocoskeelingislands.com.au/accommodation) to book.

🍽 FOOD & DRINK

When you arrive at Cocos (Keeling) Airport, there will likely be someone handing out a 'What's On' guide, with everything to do on the island, including an up-to-date guide to the restaurants and cafes, and what will be open during your visit. You can also pick one up from the visitor's centre. There are only a couple of options for meals each day, with many restaurants and cafes open only at various days throughout the week.

Start at **West Island Supermarket** (Mon-Fri 8am-3pm, Sat 10am-3pm) if you want to cook at your accommodation or stock up on snacks. It's a very small supermarket with limited options, but it often has fresh bread.

The **Cocos Club** (Mon-Sun from 5pm) next to the airport is the only bar in town and the only place to buy takeaway alcohol.

Tropika Restaurant offers breakfast daily (7-9am), lunch (11.30am-1pm) and dinner (6-8pm), with small, simple menus that change daily, and delicious food.

Salty's Bakery & Grill is a little window eatery at the airport, offering toasties, coffee and baked treats from 7.30am on weekdays, as well as pizza and Malay food on Tuesday nights, fish and chips on Friday nights, and pizza night on Sunday nights. Salty's is also always open in line with planes landing and taking off, even if the regular schedule changes, so it's a great place to start when you land.

Overlooking the ocean **Surfer Girl Brewery** offers alfresco dinners with Italian night on Mondays and coconut night on Thursdays, as well as fresh coffee and brunch on Sunday mornings. Leave your name on the board out the front to book your spot.

There are also a couple of options on Home Island, with **Seafront Restaurant** and **Island Brunch Cafe** both open in the mornings and Seafront Restaurant also open for dinner some evenings.

Cocos (Keeling) Islands

✓ THINGS TO DO

Cocos (Keeling) Islands are the kind of place where you could find an endless list of things to do, or simply spend all your days lying in the sun under the palm shadows of a coconut tree.

Start your visit with a motorised canoe tour with **Cocos Islands Adventure Tours**. Island hopping your way across the atoll, the tour takes you swimming and snorkelling, spotting turtles in the water and offering spectacular views that you can't find from the land. It's a wonderful way to spend a few hours and explore more of Cocos (Keeling). The tours leave at different times each day depending on the tides, so it's a good idea to be booked into this one in advance, particularly if you're only visiting the islands for a few days. If you're not booked in advance pop over to the house at number 20 (just down from Saltmakers by the Sea) to check availability and tour times. These guys are also a great resource to chat to if you're looking to do any other tours and they can always recommend someone with a fishing charter or island-hopping boat.

Beach hop your way across West Island, with unbelievable beaches at the end of every road. Head north to **Trannies Beach** for a dip in the Indian Ocean, check out **The Spot** or **The Shack** for great surfing locations, or head south to **The Yacht Club** and **Kite Beach** for a dip in the calm serene lagoon. **Scout Park** is a great place for a barbecue or a snorkel, and at low tide you can even walk across to **Pulu Maraya** where turtles and tiny sharks can often be found amongst the reef. The **Rumah Baru Jetty** is an excellent place to spot marine life, with huge turtles and sharks, as well as giant trevally regularly spotted from the jetty.

Stop into the **'DONGA'** Golf Club, to play a round of golf across an international runway where you can often watch planes taking off and landing as you play. Mingle with the locals on a Thursday afternoon for a game of scroungers, or play your own game at this nine-hole golf course.

Take a daytrip out to **Direction Island** to spend a day on one of Australia's most beautiful beaches. It'll give you all the deserted island vibes you could wish for, and you'll feel like you have a whole island practically to yourself. Make sure you bring all your own food, water and beach supplies, including lots of sunscreen and insect repellent for the mozzies, as you'll be on the island for about five hours. Set up for the day under one of the shelters around the island and try and crack open your own coconut for a fresh, delicious beach snack.

Opposite Motorised canoe tour with Cocos Islands Adventure Tours

Off-the-beaten track

Indulge in a boho private picnic on the beach, set up by the team at **Cocos Picnics**. They create a beautiful environment right on the beach with grazing platters and drinks, perfect for a date night or to celebrate a special occasion.

Pop into the **Big Barge Arts Centre** (Tues-Wed 9am-12pm) to check out a stunning art gallery inside the hull of a rustic timber barge that has been done up and painted right on the beach, with their own **Sula Servery** offering morning tea by the ocean for gallery visitors. The Big Barge also hosts outdoor movies under the palms on Saturday nights. Check the blackboard at Club Cocos to see what's playing.

Jump on the **Home Island Tour** (Mon, Wed, other days on request; ask at the visitor's centre) for a guided trip over to Home Island, offering insight into the Cocos Malay lifestyle, cultural activities and a delicious traditional lunch. The tour gives you a more intimate understanding of Home Island and the culture and traditions of its people, rather than if you just visit yourself.

Explore more of the atoll with a **half-day boat charter**. There are a few different companies offering this, with fishing, scuba diving, island hopping, snorkelling, glass-bottom boat tours, and sea scooters all on offer and you can create your own itinerary depending on the boat you choose. The visitor's centre can help organise the best charter for however you would like to spend the day.

If you have a whole day to spare and you time it just right, Cocos (Keeling) is the only place in the world where you can **walk around an entire atoll**. It's about a 20km, 8hr walk, starting from Home Island's sailing club. You might need a local guide depending on the conditions, and you should definitely get advice from the visitor's centre on West Island and let them know when you're heading off so they can track your return, but what an incredibly cool way to spend a day.

❓ WHEN TO GO

With its position in the Indian Ocean, Cocos (Keeling) Islands has a unique weather pattern throughout the year. It is beautifully warm year-round, however January through to the end of April is peak cyclone and rain season, when flight cancellations are most likely. May to October is considered the trade wind season, when it can be quite windy (great for kitesurfing), but is generally sunnier and drier. You're probably likely to get a mixture of weather, no matter what time of the year you're here. Ramadan is also practised on the islands, with many restaurants, cafes and shops being closed during this time. The Hari Raya Puasa (end of Ramadan) celebration on Home Island is a great cultural experience to plan your trip around.

Above Exporing the lagoon in a motorised canoe *Opposite* Direction Island jetty

ⓘ NEED TO KNOW

It can be difficult to plan a visit to Cocos (Keeling), as there's limited information online and often very slow or non-existent responses to booking requests. We found it easiest to book our trip through specialised travel agents **Indian Ocean Experiences** (indianoceanexperiences.com.au). They are able to create a custom itinerary for you, depending on how long you want to visit the islands and what you would like to see and do, and they were able to offer prices we couldn't get ourselves. We highly recommend their services if you're planning a trip to either Cocos (Keeling) Islands or Christmas Island (*see* p.91).

It is extremely important to have travel insurance when visiting Cocos (Keeling) Islands. Due to its position in the Indian Ocean, flight cancellations due to unfavourable weather are a regular occurrence and travel disruptions happen often. We actually got stuck on the island for an extra couple of days due to Cyclone Herman getting in the way of the flight path from Perth.

Mackerel Islands

A barefoot paradise along the Pilbara coast

AUSTRALIA'S NORTH-WEST, WESTERN AUSTRALIA

Off-the-beaten track

For a completely one-of-a-kind, off-the-beaten track island adventure, you can't go past the Mackerel Islands. Sitting in the Pilbara region of Australia's north-west, the Mackerels are made up of ten pristine islands and atolls, about 22km off the coast of Western Australia. A barefoot paradise, the islands are a mecca for fishing, snorkelling and marine wildlife, with turtles using the island as a nesting ground in the summer months, whales migrating through the waterways in winter, and plenty of big game fish to be caught around the islands.

Of the ten islands, two welcome guests to stay – Thevenard Island and Direction Island. Thevenard Island is the main hub of the Mackerels, with beach houses set in the dunes overlooking the water, a small store for supplies, and plenty of moorings to stop on; while Direction Island offers the unique experience of renting your own island, with a sole beach shack on the whole island. The archipelago is quiet and peaceful, and the perfect escape when you're in need of a bit of a reset.

Accessible from both Exmouth and Onslow, the Mackerel Islands are open seasonally from April to October to stay, although if you have your own boat you can visit on a daytrip year-round. It's the kind of quiet island paradise that feels distinctly Western Australian and is a great addition to any Coral Coast or North Western adventure.

THE BEST BITS

Visit during July and August when you can see migrating whales right from your very own beach shack porch. If you fly in from Exmouth you can often spot whales from the plane at this time of year too.

TIME ZONE: AWST (GMT +8)

BEST TIME TO VISIT: April to Oct

ACCESSIBLE FROM: Onslow & Exmouth

GETTING THERE: Island ferry transfer or bring your own boat from Onslow, or fly in via charter flight from Exmouth

PHONE RECEPTION: Yes

WI-FI: No

DAYTRIPS: Yes, but only with your own boat

KID FRIENDLY: Yes

SOCIALS: @mackerelislands

MORE INFO: mackerelislands.com.au

Opposite Beachside cabins on Thevenard Island

Off-the-beaten track

GETTING HERE

There are a few different ways to get to the Mackerel Islands. Onslow is the closest access point on the mainland, with daily flights with **Virgin Australia** connecting Onslow (ONS) and Perth. The island transfer ferry runs twice a week, departing from its own private jetty in Beadon Creek, and it takes about 45min to get to Thevenard Island from Onslow. Alternatively, you can jump on a charter flight with **Ningaloo Aviation** from Exmouth to arrive on the island by air. The charter flight also takes around 40min, giving you a beautiful view of the North West coastline and even the chance of spotting migrating whales swimming around the islands on the way.

STAY

There are a handful of **beachfront cabins** to stay in on Thevenard Island. Sitting in the dunes, overlooking the ocean and with their own pathway straight down to the beach, there are two- and three-bedroom cabins available. The accommodation is large and spacious, complete with your own kitchen and living room and a large patio overlooking the boat moorings. There's air-conditioning, barbecue facilities and coffee machines, and everything you could possibly need during your stay.

You cannot sleep in your boat overnight here, so if you're hoping to stay at the island you will need to book a cabin.

FOOD & DRINK

The Mackerels are predominantly self-catering islands, which means you will need to bring all your food and drinks with you for the entirety of your stay (however, there is no BYO alcohol due to the island's liquor licence, so all alcohol must be purchased on the island). There is a small **grocery store** that has a small range of snacks, cooking supplies, drinks and toiletries if you forget anything or need a little extra, as well as the bottle shop with a range of alcoholic beverages to purchase.

Plan your visit around a **Dinner Under the Stars** (Tues and Fri) for a delicious dinner as the sun sets and the stars come out for the evening. The Mackerels team put on a delicious buffet spread, with a changing menu each night. It's a barefoot vibe, sitting under the fairy lights, making friends and sharing stories on family style tables. Pre-booking is essential to avoid missing out. This is a can't-miss evening on any Mackerels itinerary.

Above Welcome to the Mackerel Islands *Opposite top left* The main beach on Thevenard Island *Opposite top right* Exploring the waters around the Mackerels *Opposite bottom* Sunset on the Mackerel Islands

THINGS TO DO

The perfect islands to spend all your time outdoors and exploring the water, the Mackerels offer plenty of activities.

If you don't have your own boat you can rent an **Island Explorer Boat** (also known as plakas) for a half day or full day to explore the island from the water (requires a recreational skippers/boat licence). Since you're in the self-proclaimed fishiest waters of the Pilbara, try your luck at catching a **big game fish**, with fishing gear available for rent if you don't have your own. You might even get your photo on the island's wall of fame. **Snorkel** over the fringing reefs around the island, where you can spot plenty of tropical fish, colourful coral and little crabs a few steps from the shore. You can also rent all kinds of ocean equipment, with snorkels, bodyboards, kayaks and stand-up paddleboards, as well as a range of beach sport equipment for cricket and volleyball.

Take a trip out to **Back Beach** to explore the other side of the island to where you're staying, also known as the west end. It's a great place to watch the sunset from the picnic deck, with plenty of beautiful big shells and sea urchins to check out on the shoreline. To explore the island a little further, get dropped off at the west end and follow the roughly 6km track back to the main beach. You can also follow the **Island Eco Trail Walk** to complete a full lap of the island, about 12km all together and expected to take around 3hr or 4hr. There

are plenty of great places to stop and check out along the way, including the Coral Gardens, Turtle Dunes, Sandy Cay Lookout, Crayfish Corner and Stingray Beach.

For more guided experiences, there's a range of free tours to take advantage of during your stay, including the **Sunset 4WD Bus Tour**, **Back Beach Bus Trip** and **Island Sustainability Tour** to learn more about the island's solar farm and sustainable ecotourism.

During the school holidays there's a special **program of activities for the kids**, with **guided reef walks** at low tide, kids **fishing clinics**, **guided home reef snorkel tours** and **sunset boat cruises**.

ⓘ WHEN TO GO

Thevenard Island is open seasonally (April-Oct), if you're looking to stay on the island. However, if you have your own boat you can visit the islands on a daytrip year-round. Fishing around the Mackerels is always great, but the best months are considered to be April and May. During July and August you can see migrating whales making their way past the island, and you can often even spot them from the shore or your beach cabin patio. During the summer months turtles make their way onto the beach for nesting, with baby hatchlings often emerging from February to April. You can often swim with turtles off the shore year-round too.

ⓘ NEED TO KNOW

With only a handful of beach cabins available to book, make sure you lock in your dates as early as possible to avoid missing out - especially during the school holiday period.

ON THE MAINLAND

While you're in Onslow be sure to pop into the Mackerel Islands' sister resort, **Onslow Beach Resort**. The Beach Club offers meals and drinks overlooking the Indian Ocean, and is a great spot to watch the sun set. If you're pairing your Mackerel Islands' getaway with a visit to Exmouth, make sure you give yourself plenty of time to explore **Ningaloo Reef** where you can experience swimming with whale sharks (March-Aug). Take a boat cruise through **Yardie Creek**. Stop for a dip in the famous **Turquoise Bay**. Watch the sunset at **Charles Knife Canyon**. And after a day of adventure, grab a bite and a brew at **Whalebone Brewing**.

Opposite Aerial views over the Mackerel Islands

Pumpkin Island

One of Australia's best-kept secrets

CAPRICORN COAST, QUEENSLAND

Off-the-beaten track

TIME ZONE: AEST (GMT +10)
BEST TIME TO VISIT: Year-round
ACCESSIBLE FROM: Yeppoon
GETTING THERE: Pumpkin Island ferry (Mon, Wed, Fri, Sun)
PHONE RECEPTION: Yes
WI-FI: Limited wi-fi available in the Sunset Lounge
DAYTRIPS: No
KID FRIENDLY: Yes
SOCIALS: @pumpkinisland
MORE INFO: pumpkinisland.com.au

Pumpkin Island is the ultimate destination to feel like you've washed up on a deserted island. Catering to up to only 34 guests at a time, it's easy to not see anyone else for hours, and to feel like you have the whole island completely to yourself. A leader in eco-tourism, with no reception desk, shops or restaurants, and only a handful of cute cottages dotted along the shoreline amongst the coconut trees, Pumpkin Island is quiet, peaceful, and the ideal place to do absolutely nothing. It's absolutely one of Australia's best-kept secrets and definitely an island you'll want to add to your bucket-list.

Sitting only 14km off the coast of Yeppoon, just above the Tropic of Capricorn, Pumpkin Island is pure beauty. The tiny island amounts to about 6 hectares in total (450m long and 150m wide) and is completely powered by the sun and the wind. Pumpkin Island strives to be as sustainable as possible – saving water and power, minimising carbon emissions and conserving and protecting the natural environment. Part of the Southern Great Barrier Reef Marine Reserve, the surrounding water is teeming with coral reefs and marine life, and there are plenty of great lookout points from which to see different views around the island.

Pumpkin is where you can immerse yourself in the romance of island life, by spending slow days wandering around the island boardwalks, lazing in hammocks by the ocean or swimming in the shallows. Keep an eye out for turtles and dolphins swimming past, and even whales during the season (June–Nov). Take advantage of the island's equipment and go kayaking or stand-up paddleboarding, snorkel amongst the coral reefs or even try collecting your own oysters off the rocks. Grab a cocktail in the evening and a spot in the Sunset Lounge to watch the sun drop below the ocean.

One of the most incredible things about Pumpkin Island is that you can actually rent the entire island out. It's the dream destination to gather together a group of family or friends for a special occasion or just a relaxing group getaway, and enjoy your very own private island. Can you think of anything better?

THE BEST BITS

The best part of Pumpkin Island is the chance to just relax. Kick back in a hammock, watch the sun rising and setting each day, swim in the ocean, wander slowly around the island and see if you can spot turtles and dolphins swimming by. You're on island time here, with nothing to do but chill.

Opposite Sunset on Pumpkin Island

Off-the-beaten track

Above The Sunset Lounge *Opposite top left* A unique warning sign in the tropics *Opposite top right* Island info at the Sunset Lounge *Opposite bottom left* DIY meals from the Waterline *Opposite bottom right* You'll feel welcome as soon as you arrive on the island

➲ GETTING HERE & AROUND

Rockhampton Airport (ROK) is the closest airport to Pumpkin Island, with most interstate flights connecting through Brisbane. From the airport you will need to organise a transfer to make the 45min drive to Yeppoon's Keppel Bay Marina. The **Pumpkin Xpress** ferry service travels between the island and Keppel Bay Marina, making a return trip on Mondays, Wednesdays, Fridays and Sundays. The trip takes between 30 and 40min depending on the tides; check the schedule on the website (pumpkinisland.com.au) for accurate departure times. The cost of the ferry is additional to the accommodation fee. If you're bringing your own boat, Pumpkin Island also has a mooring available for guests.

Once you're here, everything is just a short stroll away, with boardwalks around the whole island, taking you anywhere you need to go.

💤 STAY

There are five cottages and two bungalows scattered around the island. Each has two bedrooms, and their own kitchen, living room and bathroom, private deck with a barbecue, and all face the sunset. They are perfectly sized for families, with each cottage accommodating four to six guests. Book directly on the Pumpkin Island website (pumpkinisland.com.au) for the most accurate availability, as well as to see photos of each cottage to choose where to stay. Children under 16 stay for free and discounts are offered if you book a longer stay.

The cottages only have 12V power in them, so you will need to bring a USB charger to charge your phone, or any cameras or smaller electronics that you might be bringing with you. There is 240V power in the Sunset Lounge if you need it.

Alternatively, if you're lucky enough to have a large group of family or friends to travel with, you can actually book out the whole island, for the ultimate private island experience. How incredible would that be?! Once you divide the total cost by everyone in your party, it works out about the same as an average hotel room on any other island.

FOOD & DRINK

Pumpkin Island is a self-catering island, with no restaurants or shops, so you need to bring absolutely everything with you for your stay. There are two ways you can do this. The first is to completely self-cater yourself - you do your grocery shopping before you get to the marina and bring everything you need across with you on the ferry. You can also choose to buy your groceries online and have them delivered to the marina before you depart. The second, highly recommended, option is to pre-order all your meals from the award-winning **Waterline Restaurant** in Yeppoon. You can select your meal ingredients (to make your own meals) from a menu up to 10 days before your departure and then Waterline will take care of everything else. The meals are fresh and delicious, with plenty of variety and generous portion sizes. Pick up your meals from Waterline (within Keppel Bay Marina) 30min before your ferry departure, and when you arrive on Pumpkin Island your food will be taken to your accommodation, along with your luggage, which includes all the ingredients, condiments, recipes and cooking instructions. Your cottage will be equipped with all cooking utensils, pots and pans, etc.

There is a bar in the **Sunset Lounge**, which offers cocktails and drinks each evening as the sun sets between 5pm and 7pm. You can also purchase drinks to take back to your room if you wish. If you would like the bar to open in the evening, make sure you visit before 1pm and tick the box on the little blackboard so the management knows you want them to open.

THINGS TO DO

The main thing to do on Pumpkin Island is just *relax*. Surrender yourself to island time, leave your shoes in your room, find yourself a beach chair and enjoy your incredible surroundings as you unwind in this beautiful setting. But if you start to get itchy feet, there are still plenty of things to do.

Explore the water from a **glass-bottomed kayak** or **stand-up paddleboard**, both available for use free of charge from the activities hut on the main beach, and try to spot turtles swimming around you. If you want to get wet there is also **snorkelling** gear to use, with plenty of reef around the island to check out.

Walk around the whole island and check out the views. Our favourite lookout is the giant frame that gives you a beautiful view around the main beach. The beach looks completely different from this spot depending on if the tide is in or out.

Spend the afternoon **fishing** right off the beach but note that you will need to bring your own fishing gear. There are plenty of delicious fish to catch, including mackerel, trevally, rock cod, coral trout and squid. If you're interested in **deep-sea fishing charters** this can also be arranged too, with many charters operating out of Keppel Bay Marina. You can also hire a tinnie from Pumpkin Island management, for either a half- or full-day.

When the tide is low you can walk across to **Little Pumpkin Island**, where there's another whole island to explore. There are plenty of lookout points to see the view of Pumpkin Island and birds to watch. Just make sure you're back well before the tide comes in, otherwise you might be swimming back to Pumpkin!

WHEN TO GO

Pumpkin Island is a perfect year-round destination, with warm water and a sub-tropical climate, and an average temperature of 25°C every day of the year.

NEED TO KNOW

Book your stay on Pumpkin Island as early as possible, with the island often booking out over a year in advance. Check out the website for the most accurate availability.

Also, stingers may be present in the water from November to May. Stinger suits are recommended.

ON THE MAINLAND

Yeppoon is the gateway to Pumpkin Island, a charming little seaside town, most famous for its incredible **beachfront lagoon pool**, complete with an infinity pool overlooking the ocean. There's plenty to see and do around Yeppoon too, with snorkelling and diving opportunities right off the shore, **Byfield National Park and State Forest** to explore only 30min away and full of natural swimming holes and stunning forest, and the favourite **Emu Park**, home to the ANZAC Memorial walk and the Singing Ship sculpture.

Opposite Lookout views over Pumpkin Island

ISLAND HOPPING
Crab Claw Island

TOP END, NORTHERN TERRITORY

Crab Claw Island is a truly unique little corner of the Northern Territory (NT). Sitting on the south-western side of Bynoe Harbour, it's still a little off-the-beaten track but actually accessible by dirt road throughout most of the year. However, during extreme high tides, particularly in the wet season, the road can be completely flooded by the rising water, giving Crab Claw its island status. Crab Claw Island is a favourite for fishing, mud crabbing, birdwatching and bushwalking. It's a great spot to relax for a couple of nights and soak up that balmy Top End vibe.

The NT's answer to a barefoot beach club, Crab Claw Island is home to a small resort of sorts, with cabins surrounded by palms, campsites in the red dirt, and an open-air restaurant overlooking the water. It is distinctly 'The Top End'. Quirky and wonderful, with summertime temperatures year-round, inviting calm water that is completely off-limits due to its resident crocodiles, peacocks wandering along the beach, wallabies hopping through the campgrounds, and a changing menu of local favourites.

➔ GETTING HERE

There are a few different ways to explore Crab Claw Island. If you have your own 4WD, it is a 130km drive from Darwin/Garramilla, which takes about 1.5hr, but check ahead for the tides when the road in gets flooded. There are plenty of signs along the way to point you in the right direction. You can also opt for a charter helicopter or aeroplane flight, which will get you there in 15-20min, offering spectacular views over the Top End coastline and waterways.

If you're not planning to stay, you can also visit Crab Claw Island on a daytrip. Cruise over from Darwin/Garramilla with **SeaLink** on a full daytrip from Cullen Bay, which includes an indulgent all-Australian seafood buffet. Generally operating on Saturdays through the dry season, check the schedule in advance to confirm available dates.

✓ THINGS TO DO

Crab Claw Island is heaven for those who love the outdoors. Rent a tinnie, available for full- or half-day hire, and hit the water for some of the best fishing in the NT. More than 30 species of fish, including the iconic barramundi, can be found in the waters of the harbour. Before you cast your line though, make sure you sign up for the NT's **Million Dollar Fish competition** (milliondollarfish.com.au), as you never know what you might catch out there! **Mud crabbing** is also popular in the creeks and rivers that surround the resort, with plenty to be caught during the dry season. Or if you just want to explore a little further, there are five islands sitting within the harbour to check out, including **Crocodile Island** and **Knife Island** just off the shore of Crab Claw. On land, there are plenty of **bushwalking trails** around the island to explore as well - just make sure you take plenty of water when hiking in the Top End heat.

For the ultimate experience, you can visit Crab Claw on a **Top End Heli Pub Crawl**. Taking you to four of the Top End's iconic remote pubs - Crab Claw Island, Darwin River Tavern, Goat Island Lodge and Noonamah Tavern, you'll have 1hr on each island, as well as around 1hr of scenic helicopter flying between the pubs.

For my favourite time on Crab Claw Island, make sure you wake up early to watch at least one sunrise. Top End sunrises can't be beaten.

💤 STAY

If you're planning to stay on Crab Claw Island for a couple of nights there's a range of different cabins to choose from, with **beachfront cabins** overlooking the water, **retreat cabins** nestled in the palm garden, and **family cabins** that sleep six guests.

There's also a **campground** with 19 powered campsites, a pool and shared facilities, with plenty of room for caravans and motorhomes.

ⓘ MORE INFO

Head to the island website (crabclawisland.com.au) for more information and to book your stay. For heli pub crawls, book online (helifish.com.au). To book a cruising daytrip to Crab Claw Island, check the schedule and reserve through SeaLink (sealink.com.au/darwin).

Opposite top Aerial view over Crab Claw Island *Opposite bottom left* Island beach walks *Opposite bottom right* Beware of crocodiles around the island

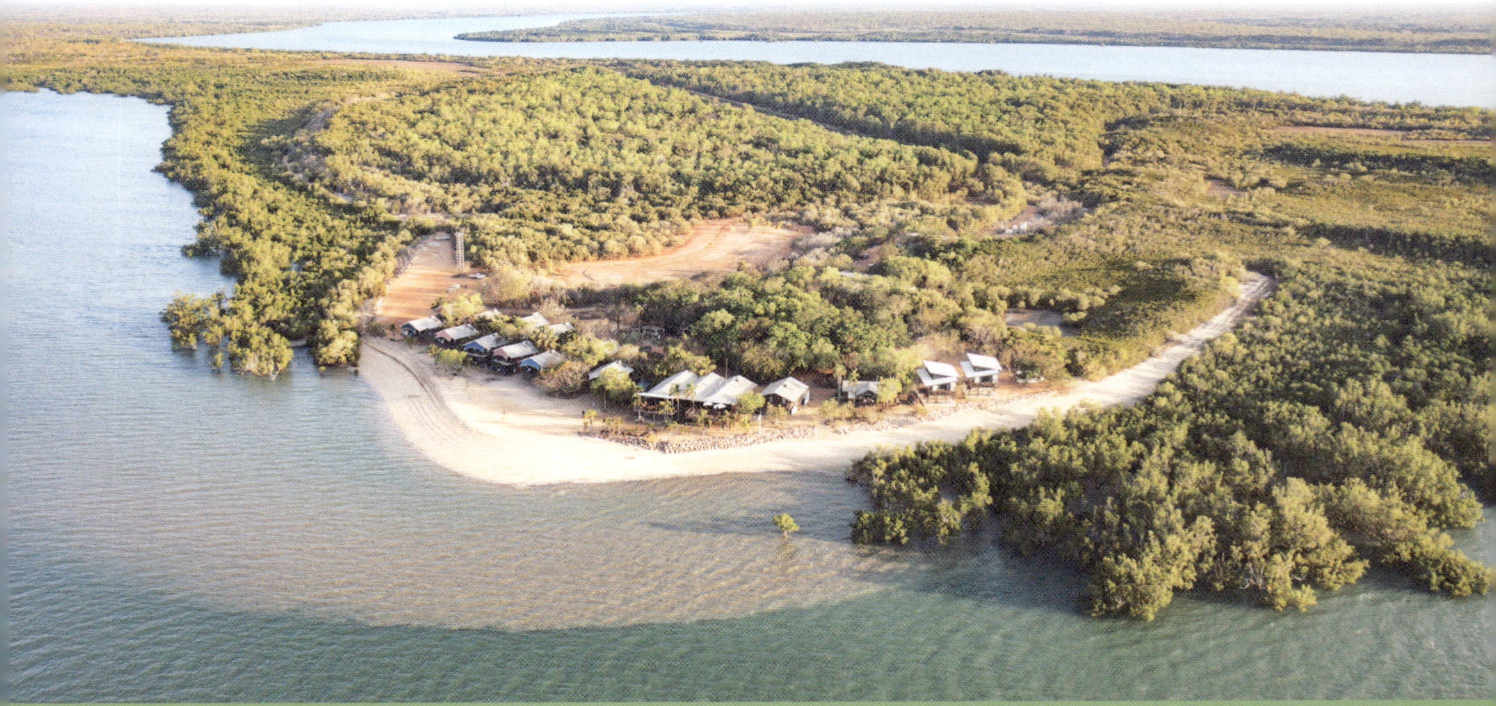

DONT RISK
YOUR LIFE
BEWARE OF
CROCODILES

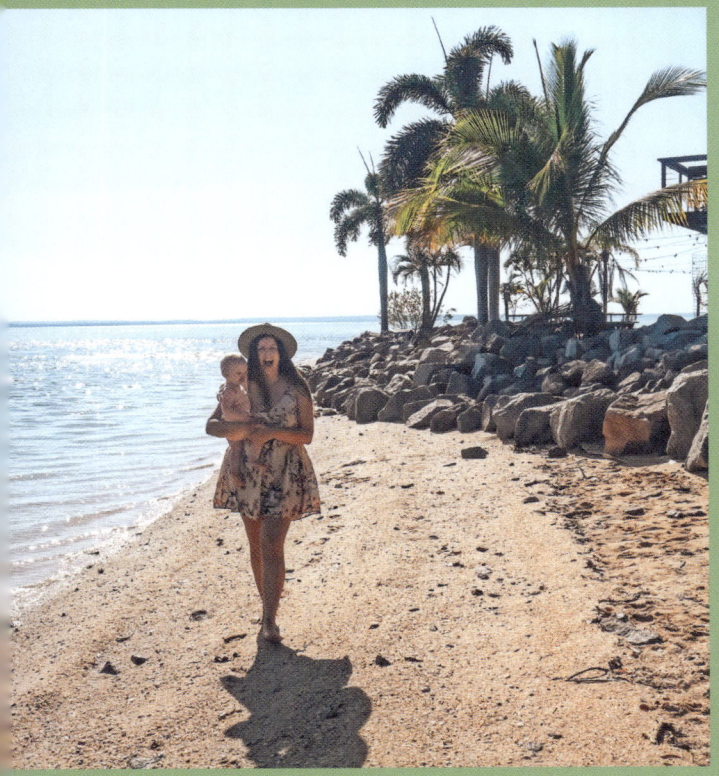

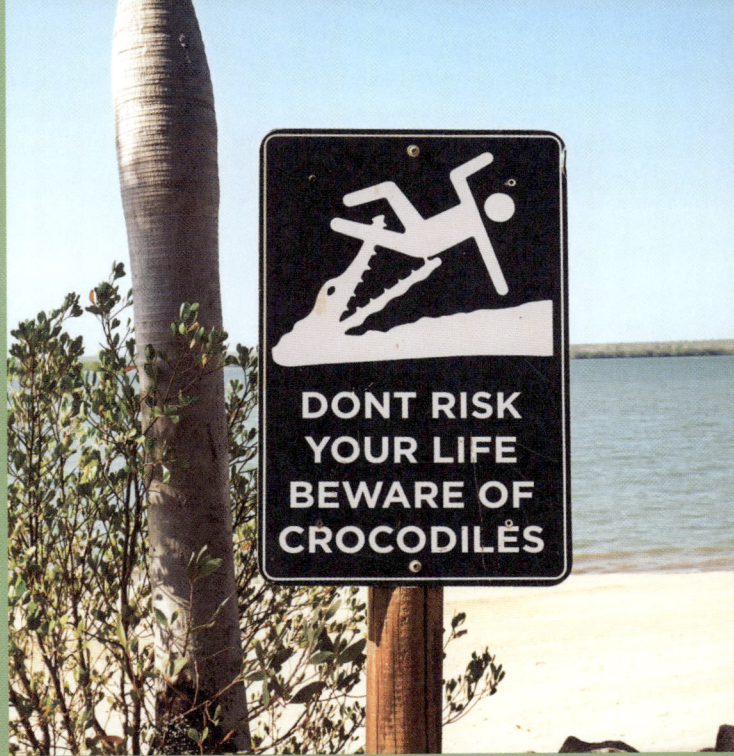

Torres Strait Islands

Immerse yourself in culture and tradition by the sea

TROPICAL NORTH QUEENSLAND, QUEENSLAND

Off-the-beaten track

Sitting quietly between the tip of Queensland and Papua New Guinea are the beautiful Torres Strait Islands. An archipelago of around 275 islands, surrounded by some of the most beautiful clear azure water you've ever seen, the Torres Strait Islands are part of Australia, but feel like a world all of their own. With friendly welcoming locals, sharing their culture and way of life with anyone who visits, it's easy to feel instantly at home in the Torres Strait.

The most northern part of Australia, the Torres Strait Islands are home to around 4500 people who live across 14 of the islands. The largest population can be found on Thursday Island/Waiben (around 3000 people), the main island within the peninsula. The Traditional Owners are the Kaurareg People, with a history dating back tens of thousands of years.

Explore the Torres Strait Islands from the tip of Australia at Cape York, or fly into Horn Island/Ngurupai from Cairns/Gimuy to start your cultural adventure. To soak up everything the Torres Strait has to offer, take the time to island hop across the islands to explore some of the local culture, World War II history, beautiful landscapes and great food on offer.

There are three main islands to hop your way across during your visit to the Torres Strait. Thursday Island/Waiben is where you will find most of the accommodation, places to eat and best beaches; Horn Island/Ngurupai is where you can take a tour of World War II sites, as well as visit the museum and art gallery in the small town of Wasaga; and Friday Island is home to Kazu Pearl Farm which offers a delicious seafood and Japanese lunch.

TIME ZONE: AEST (GMT +10)
BEST TIME TO VISIT: May to Sept
ACCESSIBLE FROM: Cairns and Seisia
GETTING THERE: Flight from Cairns or ferry from Seisia
PHONE RECEPTION: Yes
WI-FI: No
DAYTRIPS: Yes
KID FRIENDLY: Yes
SOCIALS: @peddellsthursdayislandtour
MORE INFO: straitexperience.com.au, peddellsferry.com.au

THE BEST BITS

Learn more about the local culture and traditions with a visit to Gab Titui Cultural Centre to see dancing and performances. It's sure to be a highlight of your visit to the Torres Strait.

Opposite The blues of the Torres Strait Islands

Off-the-beaten track

➔ GETTING HERE

Horn Island Airport (HID) is the only airport in the Torres Strait Islands, with Qantas offering regular flights there from Cairns. Once you're on Horn Island/Ngurupai there are several small ferry services which connect the islands together. Keep an eye out for **McDonald Charter Boats** to take you over to Thursday Island. If you're heading to the Torres Strait from Cape York, **Peddells** offers a passenger ferry connection between Seisia and Thursday Island/Waiben, which takes about 1hr, 10min.

💤 STAY

Base yourself on Thursday Island/Waiben, described by the locals as the heart of the Torres Strait Islands. There's a small number of motels, holiday homes and guest houses available to book, and most are within walking distance of the main streets and local restaurants.

Strait Experience offers one of the best websites (book.straitexperience.com.au/accommodation) to search for accommodation options, with options on Thursday Island/Waiben, Horn Island/Ngurupai and the Cape York Peninsula.

✱ DAYTRIPS

To explore the best of the Torres Strait Islands in only one day, **Strait Experience** (straitexperience.com.au) has a tailored day tour departing from Cairns/Gimuy full of landscape, culture and community. You'll get to immerse yourself in Traditional dance performances, learn from local artists and enjoy a delicious feasting-style lunch buffet. Most of your day is spent with the mainland Torres Strait communities in Bamaga and Seisia, as well as a trip to Pajinka - at the very tip of Australia, where you can experience local culture and traditions first hand.

If you're already at Cape York, the best way to explore the islands is on a day tour through **Peddells Ferry**. Making trips across to Thursday Island/Waiben daily, on your arrival you can jump on the **Peddells Bus Tour** with a local guide, who'll take you to some of the best sights around Thursday Island and tell you about the local history, culture and traditions. After the tour you'll have plenty of free time to explore the island on your own, before heading back to the ferry in the afternoon and making your way back to Cape York.

Opposite top Cultural performance in the Torres Strait *Opposite bottom left* Welcome to Thursday Island *Opposite bottom right* Thursday Island waterfront

🍴 FOOD & DRINK

The **Torres Hotel** is technically Australia's Top Pub - the most northern pub in all of Australia. You have to stop here for a beer and it's a great place for lunch and dinner as well, but order small because the portion sizes are absolutely huge.

Douglas St on Thursday Island/Waiben is the main street in town, where you can find many cafes and small restaurants, as well as the grocery store for snacks.

Uncle Frankies Cafe is a favourite for locals and visitors, and is a great place for breakfast or lunch **Bobby's Snack Bar** is a great stop for on-the-go snacks. Or head to **Makai Cafe** for a coffee and chat with the locals.

✓ THINGS TO DO

Start your visit to Thursday Island/Waiben with the **Peddells Bus Tour**. Hosted by a local guide, the bus tour takes you to some of the main highlights around Thursday Island, including the **Green Fort Lookout**, **Thursday Island Cemetery** and **Gab Titui Cultural Centre**. It's a great way to get your bearings and learn a little more about the history and people of the island.

To immerse yourself in the local culture, stop in for a visit at **Gab Titui Cultural Centre**. Wander through the art gallery here, where you can see all kinds of artworks, historical artefacts, masks and headdresses, as well as learning more about the land of the Kaurareg Nation, the Traditional Custodians of the Kaiwalagal Region, which includes the inner islands of the Torres Strait. There are incredible dances and performances to experience too, which share the stories about the land and the sea.

Head to **Green Fort Lookout** at sunrise or sunset for the best views across the islands. From the top you can see all the way out to Horn Island/Ngurupai, Prince of Wales Island, Hammond Island and Friday Island, and even to the mainland of Australia on a clear day. Green Fort is one of the most well-preserved 19th-century forts still standing in Australia, and it was manned during both world wars.

Visit **Kazu Pearls** on Friday Island, a working pearl farm owned by Kazuyoshi Takami. You'll be treated to a presentation about pearl farming and how they extract the pearls, and you can buy pearls harvested straight from the farm, before sitting down for a delicious Japanese lunch. The tour goes for about three hours and generally runs at 11.30am and 2.30pm. Book ahead by calling Kazuyoshi on (07) 4069 1268 at least one day in advance.

For World War II history head to Horn Island/Ngurupai, where you can take a guided bus tour with **Torres Strait Heritage** (torresstraitheritage.com) of significant wartime sites around

Above Australia's northernmost pub *Opposite* Kazu Pearl Farm on Friday Island

the island, including the air base, as well as a visit to the famous **Torres Strait Heritage Museum and Art Gallery**.

Get off-the-beaten track with a visit to **Prince of Wales Island**. Remote, quiet and completely off the grid, Prince of Wales Island is where the locals have their holiday houses. There are plenty of waterfalls to explore, and **Bluefish Point** is said to be one of the best fishing spots in the region. The island used to be a cattle station, so you might still see the odd wild cow wandering around it.

To see the islands from above, jump on a 2hr scenic flight with **Strait Experience**. Departing from Horn Island or Bamaga on the mainland, it's an epic way to see the islands, and really give you some perspective of the unique landscapes that make up the Torres Strait Islands and the northernmost tip of Australia.

WHEN TO GO

During the winter months, between May and September, is considered the best time to visit the Torres Strait Islands, when the weather is hot and dry and you can expect clear sunny days. The **Winds of Zenadth Cultural Festival** is held on Thursday Island/Waiben every second September (odd years) and is when communities of the Torres Strait showcase their individual customs and cultures in an exciting and vibrant celebration, giving visitors a great insight into the local culture.

NEED TO KNOW

The main language spoken on the islands is Torres Strait Creole - also known as Brokan and Yumplatok. It's spoken across all of the islands, as well as in the West Papuan border area, Cape York and many island communities around mainland Australia. There are two other languages spoken on the island as well, Western-Central Torres Strait and Eastern Torres, although most people know and will speak to you in English.

ON THE MAINLAND

The closest part of the mainland to Torres Strait Island is **Cape York**, the northernmost tip of Australia, and around a 1030km drive north of Cairns along mostly dirt roads. It's quite the challenge to get there, however if you're visiting from Cape York make sure you snap a photo at the 'tip of Australia' sign at Pajinka, stopping to take a dip in the refreshing **Fruit Bat Falls** and **Twin Falls** on your way there. Once you make it all the way to Cape York, grab a celebratory drink at the **Loyalty Beach Campground** and always keep an eye out for crocs near the water.

Maria Island

Extraordinary landscapes with an abundance of wildlife

EAST COAST, TASMANIA

With beaches of bright blue water, colourful painted cliffs and an abundance of wildlife, including plenty of wombats and one of the healthiest populations of Tasmanian devils you can find, Maria Island is certainly a special place. Sitting on the East Coast of Tasmania, and pronounced *Mariah*, Maria Island quickly becomes a highlight of any Tasmanian itinerary. Home to a World Heritage–listed convict site, and being an island where walking and cycling are the only ways to get around, it's easy to feel like you've stepped back in time on Maria Island.

There's plenty of history to explore on Maria Island. The Traditional Owners of the island are the Palawa People and their culture can be traced back to more than 40,000 years. Convicts were settled on the island and sentenced to hard labour from 1825, and there was once a population of 500 people on the island. Today you can still explore the Darlington Probation Station, one of the most intact examples of a convict station in Australia with a collection of convict-era buildings to wander through.

There is also plenty of natural beauty to experience on Maria Island. From the beautiful secluded bays and beaches, to McRaes isthmus and the abundance of wombats, wallabies, kangaroos and Cape Barren geese wandering across the island, it's a natural paradise waiting to be explored. A Tasmanian favourite of anyone who makes the journey, Maria Island is sure to leave a lasting impression.

THE BEST BITS
Pitch a tent on the lawns of Maria Island and wake up in the morning to wombats on the grass right outside.

TIME ZONE: AEST (GMT +10), with daylight savings time (GMT +11) in effect from Oct to April

BEST TIME TO VISIT: Dec to March

ACCESSIBLE FROM: Triabunna

GETTING THERE: Ferry transfer

PHONE RECEPTION: Very little

WI-FI: No

DAYTRIPS: Yes

KID FRIENDLY: Yes

SOCIALS: @mariaislandwalk, @encountermaria

MORE INFO: encountermaria.com.au

Opposite Wombats on Maria Island

GETTING HERE & AROUND

Triabunna on the East Coast is the gateway to Maria Island. It's around a 1.5hr drive from Hobart or 2.5hr from Launceston. From Triabunna, **Encounter Maria Island** (encountermaria.com.au) operates a ferry to and from the island several times a day, which takes about 30min to get across to the island. You can buy tickets in advance or at the Maria Island Gateway building when you arrive. You will need to check in at least 45min before your ferry's scheduled departure time, and show your National Parks Pass when you check in. Once you're on the island the only way to get around is on foot or by bicycle. You can either bring your own bike with you, or hire one from Encounter Maria Island. You will need to book a bike at least 24 hours before your ferry departure, and they can book out in advance during peak periods.

STAY

There are two ways to stay on Maria Island, the most popular of which is to camp. There is a large **campground** behind the sand dunes at Darlington where you can pick your own campsite and pitch a tent. There's easy access to the beach and it's a great spot to watch the wombats in the early mornings and evenings. You will need to bring all your own camping gear, food and drinking water with you on the ferry, but the campground does have fireplaces with firewood to keep you warm in cold weather, free gas barbecues and toilet facilities. You don't have to book, but there are camping fees to be paid at the Maria Island Gateway (Charles St, Triabunna, across the road from the wharf) before you board the ferry. There are also campsites available at French's Farm and Encampment Cove, around a 3hr or 4hr walk (1hr or 2hr bike ride).

Alternatively, if you're not keen on camping, there is some basic accommodation available at **Maria Island Penitentiary**. Within the old penitentiary building in Darlington there are nine rooms with bunk beds, accommodating up to six people each, with one larger room for 14 people. It's super basic, with picnic-style tables and chairs and a wood heater, but saves you bringing camping gear and gives you the opportunity to stay at a World Heritage-listed Convict Site. Bookings can be made up to six months in advance, and are recommended, especially during busy periods, as all rooms are often booked out. Contact Sheffield Visitor Information Centre (03 6491 1179) to make a booking. There is a communal mess hall, which has power for charging phones (there's no electricity in the rooms), and a kitchen including gas cookers and sinks (no

Opposite **McRaes Isthmus**

fridges, bring your own esky), as well as a communal toilet block available nearby. You'll need to bring all your own food and drinking water, as the island has no fresh drinking water.

There are also no showers or laundry facilities on Maria Island, and you can find the closest in Triabunna (corner of Vicary and Charles St).

For both campers and guests staying at the penitentiary, there are trollies available at the Darlington Jetty to help you transport all your gear and food up to the penitentiary or campground (about a 500m walk).

DAYTRIPS

When booking your ferry across to Maria Island there is an option for a same-day return ferry, giving you the choice to visit the island for the day or even just a few hours. To make the most of your visit, jump onto the first ferry of the day at 8.30am and then return back to Triabunna on the last ferry of the day at 4.15pm. Once you're on the island you can explore at your own leisure. **Maria Island Tours** (mariaisland.tours) also offers day tour options from Hobart/Nipaluna which include return transfers from Hobart to Triabunna, a sightseeing cruise, tour of Darlington Probation Station and a buffet lunch.

FOOD & DRINK

Whether you're camping on Maria Island, staying at the penitentiary accommodation or even just visiting for a day, you will need to bring all your own food and drinks (as well as things to cook with). There are no shops or restaurants on the island, so you will need to be completely self-sufficient. This also includes enough drinking water for the duration of your stay, as there is no fresh drinking water available either.

THINGS TO DO

From the convict settlement to the white sand beaches, there's plenty to see and explore on Maria Island. Start your trip in **Darlington**, the tiny hub of Maria Island, and the UNESCO World Heritage-listed convict site that has been preserved since the 19th century.

Take a walk out to the spectacular **Painted Cliffs**. These beautiful sandstone cliffs are 'painted' in swirling stripes of oranges, reds and yellows, and are a can't-miss sight. Best visited at low tide, it's a 4.3km-return walk to the cliffs. For a prehistoric look at the island, the **Fossil Cliffs** are the place to go to see 300-million-year-old fossils (4.5km-return walk). The **Bishop and Clerk** walk takes you 620m above sea level, with the summit offering views over the island and out to Freycinet Peninsula (11km return). For the most challenging walk, head to the top of **Mount Maria**, which rises 711m above sea level (16km walk which takes around 8hr), but offers unparalleled views around the island.

If you've got plenty of time to kill, head out to **McRaes isthmus**, the narrow neck of sand that holds the two sides of Maria Island together. On one side the waves of Riedle Bay crash to the shore, while on the other side of the isthmus the waters of Shoal Bay can be completely still and calm.

For the most experienced hikers, the **Maria Island Walk** (mariaislandwalk.com) is a four-day award-winning hike that completely immerses you in the landscapes of the island. Hiking through the wilderness and out to sandy white beaches, sleeping under the stars amongst the diverse wildlife, it's easy to see why this hike is listed as one of the Great Walks of Australia. More of a luxurious hike experience, Maria Island Walk covers accommodation (including private wilderness camps and a night at Bernacchi House in Darlington), fully inclusive meals, private guides, and a hiking pack with everything you need for your journey.

ⓘ WHEN TO GO

Due to its wild and unpredictable Tasmanian climate, consider visiting Maria Island during the warmer months, from December to March. Whilst this definitely doesn't guarantee that it's going to be warm (summer in Tasmania can still be quite cool), these months often have the best weather, with higher temperatures and less wind and rain than in other seasons. If you're planning a visit during school holidays consider booking your ferry and penitentiary accommodation in advance, as they can both book out.

ⓘ NEED TO KNOW

As Maria Island is a national park, you will need to purchase a Parks Pass before you visit from Parks & Wildlife Tasmania (passes.parks.tas.gov.au). If you're just visiting for the day or one night (up to 24 hours) you can purchase a daily pass, however if you're planning to stay for a little bit longer you will need a holiday pass which is valid for up to two months. Parks Passes can be used at all national parks across Tasmania, so take advantage during your visit and stop into a couple of the state's stunning national parks.

ON THE MAINLAND

Visit Maria Island on an East Coast Tasmanian road trip, to explore more of this beautiful region. Hike to **Wineglass Bay Lookout** for beautiful views over the Hazards, or stop in to try a local drop at **Devil's Corner Cellar Door**. Beach hop along the stunning **Bay of Fires/larapuna**, home to some of Tasmania's most picturesque water surrounded by huge granite boulders covered in red and orange lichen. Try a fresh oyster plucked straight from **Great Oyster Bay**. Pull in to check out the **Little Blue Lake**, a natural phenomenon resulting from the pioneering mining days of South Mouth Cameron.

Opposite above Darlington *Opposite below left* Waking up to wombats at the campgrounds

194

ISLAND HOPPING
Picnic Island

EAST COAST, TASMANIA

If you've ever dreamt about your own private island in the rugged wilderness of Tasmania, Picnic Island, a tiny privately owned island, surrounded by the stunning mountains and scenery of Freycinet National Park, can be your own little oasis to take some time to slow down and unwind. Accommodating up to 10 people at a time, it is the perfect place to curl up in front of the fire with a wine in winter. You'll be completely immersed in the beautiful landscapes that surround you here. It is really a unique spot for island hoppers – quiet and peaceful, and the kind of place that makes you feel like time stands still in one moment.

There's an abundance of wildlife, including the island's very own penguin colony, who can be spotted coming back to their burrows on the shore for the evening after sundown. You're likely to spot whales, dolphins and seals jumping around in the waters surrounding the island.

The tiny island has a complex history. Until about 200 years ago, the Palawa People travelled to the island for many thousands of years on bark canoes, using the island for collecting food. Their shell middens can still be seen on the western end of the island. In the 1820s the island was mined for sandstone using convict labour. The island has been owned by the same family now for the last 20 years, who built the stunning lodge that stands there today, designed by Tasmanian architect John Latham.

Depending on the time of year you visit, and the weather conditions at the time, everyone that visits Picnic Island can have a completely unique experience. With sunny hot days in summer, where the water is perfectly calm and crystal-clear, to wild winter days, with howling winds and crashing waves, it might be the most unique island retreat in the country.

➔ GETTING HERE

The closest main town of Coles Bay is roughly an equal distance from both Hobart/Nipaluna and Launceston airports, so it doesn't matter which you choose to fly into. From each airport it is about a 2hr drive to reach Coles Bay. From there, **Freycinet Aqua Taxi** (email info@freycinetadventures.com.au or call (03) 6257 0500) can get you across to the island, along with your luggage. You organise your transfers directly with the water taxi to align with your flight times. If you want to head back to mainland Tasmania at any time during your trip, for daytrips or to restock supplies, you will also need to organise a water taxi. If you want to arrive in a little more style, **Above & Beyond** (aboveandbeyond.flights) can organise for you to arrive on a seaplane from Hobart.

✓ THINGS TO DO

You can spend your days exploring, fishing, swimming and relaxing. It's a beautiful place for photography, especially **astro-photography** on a clear night, as well as simply taking in the landscapes.

If you choose to take a daytrip back to Coles Bay, it's in the perfect location to either have an adventure or do absolutely nothing and soak up the scenery. You can hike your way to the **Wineglass Bay Lookout**, which offers stunning views across Freycinet National Park. Take an **Oyster Bay Tour** and taste some of the freshest oysters in the region. If you're visiting in summer, hop your way across some of the beautiful beaches, including **Honeymoon Bay**, **Hazards Beach** and **Richardsons Beach**, all with stunning clear water to swim in. Before you go to Picnic Island, stop for a tasting paddle at **Devil's Corner Cellar Door** - the best place to stock up on wines for your getaway.

💤 STAY

There are five bedrooms, accommodating up to 10 people on Picnic Island, as well as communal living and dining areas. The island will only take one booking at a time, which means you will always have the whole island to yourself. You will need to bring all your own food and drink supplies to the island for the duration of your stay. If you're planning on visiting during school holidays or peak periods, definitely book your stay well in advance to avoid missing out.

MORE INFO

For more information head to picnicisland.com.au or check out its Instagram at @picnic_island.

Opposite top Aerial views over Picnic Island *Opposite bottom* The accommodation on Picnic Island

island towns

Lord Howe Island, Pacific Ocean, NSW 198
Norfolk Island, Independent Territory 205
Flinders Island, Tasmania 210
Island Hopping: Cockatoo Island/Wareamah, NSW 217
King Island, Tasmania 218
Phillip Island/Millowl, Victoria 227
Bruny Island/Lunawanna-alonnah, Tasmania 232

Lord Howe Island

Home to the world's southernmost coral reef

PACIFIC OCEAN, NEW SOUTH WALES

On a clear day, the flight into Lord Howe Island is simply breathtaking. A somewhat crescent-shaped island comes into view, surrounding a lagoon of sparkling azure water, with two impressive mountains watching over the island at one end. Home to the world's southernmost true coral reef, spectacular beaches, palm tree-lined roads, dynamic hiking trails and a welcoming local community, it's easy to see why Lord Howe Island deserves its UNESCO World Heritage status.

Lord Howe Island is around 600km off the coast of NSW, roughly in line with Port Macquarie. Thought to be the last island that was discovered in the world, in 1788, Lord Howe Island considers itself to be 'the last paradise'. And there's no doubt that Lord Howe Island is not only a paradise, but an extremely rare and unique little island. The remains of a now-extinct volcano, dating back more than 7 million years and eroded to just 5 per cent of its original size, Lord Howe Island is 11km long and 2km wide. The island was uninhabited for millions of years, with no record of First Nations People having lived there.

With only around 445 permanent residents (as of 2021 census), and visitors restricted to just 400 at a time, it's always quiet on Lord Howe Island; it's the Pacific Ocean's version of a small country town. The only destination in Australia that's free from snakes, crocodiles, stingers, dangerous sharks or poisonous spiders, it's an outdoor lover's dream, and a great place to immerse yourself in nature – or to simply kick back and relax.

Island towns

TIME ZONE: Lord Howe Island Standard Time (GMT +10:30), half an hour ahead of Sydney, with daylight savings (GMT +11) in effect from Oct to April

BEST TIME TO VISIT: Sept to May

ACCESSIBLE FROM: Sydney

GETTING THERE: QantasLink has daily flights from Sydney Airport

PHONE RECEPTION: No

WI-FI: Yes

DAYTRIPS: No

KID FRIENDLY: Yes

SOCIALS: @visitlordhoweisland

MORE INFO: lordhoweisland.info

THE BEST BITS

Head to Signal Point, only a short walk from the main beach, for the most iconic Lord Howe Island views over Lagoon Beach and the famous twin peaks of Mount Gower and Mount Lidgbird.

Previous The Flinders on Flinders Island *Opposite* Early mornings at Ned's Beach

Island towns

GETTING HERE

Just a 2hr flight from Sydney, **QantasLink** offers daily flights to Lord Howe Island Airport (LDH). There are extremely strict luggage requirements, as you're flying on a light aircraft. Checked luggage can't weigh more than 14kg per bag, or you risk it being offloaded, and only a small handbag or backpack is allowed with you in the main cabin, as there is no overhead storage for carry-on suitcases. All accommodation offers complimentary airport transfers in your stay, so be sure to advise them of your flight times before you take off.

GETTING AROUND

Once you're on Lord Howe Island, bicycles are the main form of transport to get around. Available for rent for just $10 per day from **Wilson's Hire Service**, there are cycling paths around the whole island. The island is quite hilly though, so it's best to stay close to the main street. There are a handful of automatic rental cars on the island too, although they often book out well in advance. In the evening, your accommodation courtesy bus will drop you off for dinner, with the restaurant's courtesy bus dropping you back home when you're done.

STAY

With a strictly limited number of beds on Lord Howe Island, it's important to organise accommodation as soon as you start planning your trip, generally before even booking flights. Have a look at options close to the main street (the corner of Ned's Beach Rd and Lagoon Rd), to avoid having to ride up a steep hill every time you need to go back to your room (speaking from experience, it gets tiring quickly). **Beachcomber Lodge**, **Blue Lagoon Lodge**, **Somerset Apartments** and **Pine Trees** are all in great locations, making it super easy to go from your room to the beach and to get food whenever you like.

For luxury accommodation, **Capella Lodge** is the best of the best on the island. With an infinity plunge pool overlooking the iconic twin peaks, a restaurant serving a menu of delicious local produce, and just nine intimate suites, it's the ultimate destination for a celebratory island getaway.

There's also a handful of beautifully designed holiday homes scattered across the island, including **Island House**, **Bowker Beach House**, and **Blue Peter Beach House**, as well as **Arajilla Retreat**, the island's premier retreat nestled under a canopy of Kentia Palms and Banyan Trees.

Opposite top left Swinging at The Crooked Post *Opposite top right* Walking amongst the banyan trees *Opposite bottom* The best view over Lord Howe Island from Signal Point

FOOD & DRINK

Like many islands around Australia, the restaurants on Lord Howe Island operate on different days and opening hours can vary, so it's a good idea to book in advance to avoid missing out.

Anchorage Restaurant is the main food spot on the island, open for all meals (Mon-Sun). Right in the heart of the main street, directly across from the lagoon, the on-site bakery also offers fresh bread, as well as house-made pies, pastries and sandwiches for takeaway options.

Thompson's Store is a great lunch and takeaway spot, with delicious burgers, fish and chips, gourmet rolls and salads, as well as the go-to coffee spot.

Lord Howe Island Brewery can be found within a Kentia Palm nursery, with a menu of local brews to try (Thurs-Sat from 1pm). There are brewery and nursery tours (Thurs 4pm), woodfired pizza, smoked meat rolls and drinks surrounded by the brewery's own veggie garden.

The Crooked Post is an island favourite for a sunset cocktail. With views over the lagoon and all the way to the mountains, this spot doubles as the local physio in the morning, transforming into the hot spot for a drink in the afternoon. With a menu of signature cocktails, often created with Lord Howe Island Gin, and Taco Tuesdays from 12pm, cooking tacos on the barbie out the front, this little shack is always abuzz.

Sunset Bar & Grill (Mon, Tues, Fri and Sun dinner) at the Lord Howe Island Golf Club offers one of the best meals on the island.

Coral Cafe (Mon-Sun breakfast and lunch, Mon, Wed & Thurs dinner) is located at the Museum, with burgers, sandwiches and wraps on the menu.

Driftwood Bar & Restaurant is the newest go-to spot, with amazing Asian-inspired cuisine, taking advantage of the fresh fish that's caught daily on the island.

The **Bowling Club** is open five nights a week (Tues, Wed-Thurs, Sat-Sun) for a good Aussie pub meal. You'll really feel like a local here.

Love Lord Howe can set you up with a private boho picnic in some of the island's most stunning locations, complete with grazing platter and bubbles.

If you feel like having a **sunset dinner by the beach**, there are communal barbecues at many of the 11 beaches around the island. Grab some supplies from the store or have fresh fish delivered to your door, and head down to the beach for a picnic dinner by the water.

⊘ THINGS TO DO

Get to know Lord Howe Island intimately on **Chase 'n' Thyme's All Corners of the Island Tour**. Taking you on a journey from past to present, locals Peter and Janine show you some of the best spots and share the island's history, giving you an insight into local life. Book this one before you arrive via the booking form on its website (chasenthyme.com), to avoid missing out.

Hop your way across the best beaches, from **Lagoon Beach** and **Old Settlement Beach**, both of which are great calm snorkelling spots, to the epic surf breaks at **Blinky Beach**. At **Ned's Beach** you can buy a cup of fish food from the info hut on the shore and feed the colourful fish that swim in the shallow water. It's also a great snorkelling spot, with turtles regularly spotted here.

Jump on a glass-bottom boat tour with **Lord Howe Environmental Tours** to explore some of the colourful reefs that sit within the lagoon. Stopping at a few different spots to snorkel along the way, including **Erscotts Hole**, there's a beautiful underwater world to explore, with little reef sharks and turtles often spotted in the lagoon waters. **Upper Settlement Beach** is also a great place to spot turtles, usually around an hour before high tide, having a snack on the seagrass.

Catch yourself the fish of a lifetime on a fishing tour with **Sea Lord Howe**. With fishing trips to suit everyone, including half-day, full-day and sunset options, they catch some monster fish in the waters that surround the island. Brad the tour guide is a sixth-generation Islander, so he knows all the secret spots to catch the biggest fish.

Embark on one of Australia's best day hikes and head to the top of **Mount Gower**, one of the two main peaks overlooking the lagoon. Covered in rainforest, with a cloud forest near the top and incredible views from the summit, it's a real accomplishment for anyone who tackles it. You'll need a guide for the journey, and fifth-generation Islander Jack Shick is the man to find.

There are also plenty of smaller hikes to take around the island, including Malabar Hill, Kim's Lookout, Valley of the Shadows and Goat House Cave.

Play a round of golf at one of the prettiest golf courses in the world at **Lord Howe Island Golf Club**. Dotted with palm trees, with views out to the twin peaks, it's the picture-perfect place for nine holes of golf.

Right in the middle of the lagoon there's a teeny tiny island called **Rabbit Island** (or sometimes, Blackburn Island). You can rent a kayak to get there and hike your way to the top (it's not very tall), for a completely different view of the lagoon and the island. You'll be standing right in the middle of it!

⊘ WHEN TO GO

A great island to visit year-round, Lord Howe Island has pretty consistent weather throughout the year, with temperatures averaging 25°C during summer and 19°C during the winter months. September to April is considered the best time to visit the island, with warmer weather and less rainfall providing excellent conditions for swimming, snorkelling and ocean activities.

⊘ NEED TO KNOW

There is not a scrap of phone reception on Lord Howe Island, in fact, most locals don't even own or use mobile phones. Wi-fi is available at many of the accommodation options, as well as in the main street for a fee per GB, however its strength is dependent on the good clear weather, so it's not always 100 per cent reliable.

The Lord Howe Island Visitors Centre (Mon-Fri 9am-1pm, Sun 10am-1pm) located inside the museum is worth popping into to find out more about the island. You can also give them a call on (02) 6563 2114.

Left The Crooked Post *Opposite* Sunrise over Ned's Beach

Norfolk Island

Australia's own South Pacific island

INDEPENDENT TERRITORY

Watawieh, welcome to Norfolk Island!

There's something so special about this little island floating in the South Pacific. It's the kind of place where every single driver waves as they pass each other driving down the road (it's called the Norfolk wave); where cows have right of way as they wander unfenced around the island – often stopping traffic to cross the street; and where you're welcomed with a giant smile wherever you go. Everyone on Norfolk is so friendly, making you feel instantly at home even on your very first visit.

Sitting approximately 1600km off the coast of Sydney and measuring just 8km by 5km, Norfolk Island might be little, but it's bringing big energy. Boasting some of the best beaches in the South Pacific, UNESCO World Heritage Sites, national park walking trails with unbelievable views, and the tallest fern trees on the planet, there is so much diversity. Descendants of *Bounty* mutineers and Polynesian families live here, meaning Norfolk has a culture, history and identity all of its own and also its own unique language – *Norf'k Laengwij*.

Norfolk Island will keep you busy for days, from hikes that twist and turn around the island, to afternoon swims in the crystal-clear water, plenty of places to stop and eat along the way, and of course the incredible night sky. Norfolk is a Gold Level Dark Sky Town and there are hardly any lights at all, which makes the night sky exceptionally beautiful. Whether you're visiting for a weekend, a week or longer, there is plenty to see, do and explore around Norfolk.

Himii staat, let's go!

TIME ZONE: Norfolk Island Time (GMT +11) with daylight savings time (GMT +12) from Oct to March

BEST TIME TO VISIT: Summertime between Oct and April

ACCESSIBLE FROM: Sydney and Brisbane

GETTING THERE: Qantas flies from Sydney & Brisbane international terminals

PHONE RECEPTION: Only with a Norfolk Island sim card

WI-FI: Yes, for a fee

DAYTRIPS: No

KID FRIENDLY: Yes

SOCIALS: @norfolk.island

MORE INFO: norfolkisland.com.au

THE BEST BITS

Make time for a swim in the warm, clear water at Emily Bay; take a picnic and check out the cliff-top views of Anson Bay; grab an afternoon drink at the Norfolk Island Brewery and make friends with some of the locals, before dinner at the Homestead Restaurant, and watch the sunset at Puppies Point.

Opposite Looking over Emily Bay

🡒 GETTING HERE

Norfolk Island is a 2hr flight from Brisbane/Meanjin or a 2.5hr flight from Sydney, with **Qantas** flying between both several times a week. While it is considered a domestic island, flights to Norfolk Island leave from the international terminals at both Brisbane and Sydney, so leave enough time if you're making a connection. Passports are the preferred form of ID when travelling to Norfolk Island (and only form accepted for children), but an Australian driver's licence or ID card is also accepted.

Ⓒ GETTING AROUND

Despite Norfolk's small size, there are more than 120km of roads to explore, taking you to every part of the island, so make sure you rent a car to get around. Rental cars often book out early during school holidays and long weekends, so it's always a good idea to book early.

💤 STAY

There is a wide variety of accommodation on Norfolk Island, with hotels, cabins, holiday houses, apartments and homesteads to choose from.

If you're coming to explore the island, check out options such as **Aloha Apartments** and **Castaway**, right around the main street - Taylors Rd - to be within easy walking distance of plenty of cafes, restaurants, boutique shops and everything you might need.

If you're hoping to unplug and unwind during your stay, with views of the rolling green hills or the ocean perhaps, check out **Shearwater Scenic Villas** or **Tintoela Homestead & Cottages**.

🍴 FOOD & DRINK

The restaurants and cafes across Norfolk Island all have different trading days and hours, which can be tricky to keep track of and they often change without notice. When you arrive, pick up an 'Eating Out' guide from the visitor's centre for the most current information.

Start your day at the **Golden Orb Cafe** (Wed-Sun) or the **Olive Cafe** (Thurs-Tues), both offering great breakfast menus and takeaway options. Stop by **Prinke Eco Store** (Mon-Sun) for a coffee and to stock up on organic foods and local products and gifts.

Norfolk Island Brewing at Castaway is a great spot if you're looking for something that's open in the afternoon. Try their local brew with a cheese plate or lunch if you're peckish.

Dinner at **The Homestead Restaurant** is a must - a beautiful 1930s island home that has been converted into a restaurant offering a delicious menu. Book online for dinner reservations (Thurs-Sat).

Bounty Bar & Grill (Wed-Sun lunch, Tues-Sun dinner) is the island's grill and steakhouse, offering a great menu full of local meats and produce.

Immerse yourself in local life at **Norfolk Island Fish Fry** (Tues and Thurs), for a delicious dinner of local dishes, salads and homemade coconut bread, alongside some of the freshest fish you've ever tried. With live music and a breathtaking cliff-top sunset, it's sure to be an evening that will keep you dreaming of Norfolk Island after you're back home.

Left The 200-year-old Moreton Bay fig trees *Opposite top* Aerial view over Norfolk Island *Opposite bottom* Convict ruins at the Kingston UNESCO World Heritage Site

✓ THINGS TO DO

There are literally 101 things to do on Norfolk Island, with activities for every type of traveller. Start your visit with an **Orientation Tour** run by **Pinetree Tours**, where you will learn about Norfolk's convict and Tahitian history, as well as get a good overview of the island. It's a great way to get your bearings before you take off on your own.

Spend the day at **Emily Bay**, the most picturesque, calm beach surrounded by pine trees, with coral reefs to snorkel around and a platform to jump off. Or hop on a glass-bottom boat tour if you prefer to stay dry and see the underwater life from above.

Make sure you drive up to **Lone Pine** for an epic view of the bay and the whole coastline. Also stop by **Slaughter Bay** as well, another great spot for snorkelling.

Explore **Norfolk Island National Park**, where you can drive to the top of **Mount Pitt** for a 360-degree-view of the island, walk under the tallest pines on earth and keep an eye out for the famous green parrot. There are plenty of hiking trails to adventure a little further if you want to explore more of the park. Take a picnic up to the **Captain Cook Lookout** for stunning views over the islands.

Visit the convict ruins at **Kingston UNESCO World Heritage Site** - once a harsh settlement for banished British prisoners. You can learn about the history of the area at the four Kingston museums nearby. If you're feeling brave, jump on a night-time **lantern ghost tour** through the ruins. Or play a round of golf at **Norfolk Golf Club**, one of the only golf courses in the world located within a World Heritage Site.

Book a guided trek to neighbouring **Phillip Island**, for landscapes that will make you feel like you're on another planet. In fact, its nickname is the 'Uluru of the South Pacific'. Part of Norfolk Island National Park, Phillip Island is made up of incredible colourful cliffs of red, yellow and pink soil that need to be seen to be believed. Hike down to some of the most secluded beaches at **Anson Bay** and **Bumboras Beach**. Not for swimming, but for beautiful walks. Take a photo amongst the roots of the incredible 200-year-old **Moreton Bay Fig Trees**. While you're here follow the walking track through **Hundred Acres Reserve** to Rocky Point, a local favourite fishing spot.

For a magical night under the stars and thousands of fairy lights, head to **Wonderland by Night** (Pinetree Tours run this tour on Wed and Sun nights) to celebrate Norfolk's identity with a collection of Old Time Island Stories, traditional Norf'k language, poetry and conversation over a hot cuppa.

Opposite The countryside of Norfolk Island *Top* Slaughter Bay

? WHEN TO GO

With a lovely subtropical climate, Norfolk Island is a great destination to visit year-round. The warmest months are between October and April, sharing similar weather to Sydney/Warrang.

To completely immerse yourself in Norfolk Culture, plan your visit around **Foundation Day** (March) or **Bounty Day** (June) where there are historical re-enactments, parades, wreath-laying, and an abundance of local food to enjoy.

! NEED TO KNOW

There is no phone reception for regular Australian sim cards on Norfolk Island. When you arrive you can purchase a Norfolk Island sim card if you need to use your phone. Plans start from $30 for a tourist mobile plan. You can also purchase internet hotspot vouchers which can be used in different spots around the island. Most accommodation has wi-fi options, although you will likely need to pay per GB. The RSL is the only place in town with free wi-fi.

You can find an ATM at the Commonwealth Bank on the main street, but credit cards are accepted across the island.

To book tours when you arrive, pop into the **Norfolk Island Visitors Information Centre** on Taylors Rd (Mon-Sun from 8.30am). You can also give them a call from mainland Australia or Tasmania on 1800 214 603 or from Norfolk Island on +6723 22147. They can also give your passport a special Norfolk Island stamp!

Flinders Island

Tasmania's best-kept island secret

BASS STRAIT, TASMANIA

The eastern side of Bass Strait is home to the Furneaux Group of islands, the largest of which is Flinders Island. Anchored alongside the other 50 or so mostly uninhabited islands that make up this archipelago, Flinders Island is a wild place, with rugged granite mountains sitting alongside perfectly calm clear bays, the Darling Ranges running through the middle of the island, wombats burrowing on the side of the road, and an incredible food scene.

Tasmania's largest island (and Australia's sixth-largest island), Flinders Island is about 75km long and 40m wide. More than 65 shipwrecks are dotted along the 120 stunning beaches that make up the coastline of Flinders Island, which you will likely find you have all to yourself to explore. It's home to about 1000 people, mainly farmers and fishers, all of whom will give you a wave as you drive past. There is a small First Nations community of around 70 people who live on Cape Barren Island, also known by its Traditional name truwana, just south of Lady Barron.

Be prepared to switch onto 'island time' during your visit to Flinders Island. Time moves slowly, there's no traffic to share the road with, and it might seem like the restaurants and businesses open at different times every single day – but that's the beauty of it. You'll have all the time in the world to stop at every beach or lookout you spot along your drive. It's calm and quiet, and the perfect country island to disconnect and recharge in nature.

THE BEST BITS

Head to Trouser Point Beach for an incredible relaxing beach day, with crystal-clear calm waters and looming mountains in the background. The scenery is absolutely phenomenal, and Flinders Island is one of the most unique island destinations we've experienced.

TIME ZONE: AEST (GMT +10), with daylight savings time (GMT +11) in effect from Oct to April

BEST TIME TO VISIT: Summer and autumn

ACCESSIBLE FROM: Launceston & Melbourne (Essendon)

GETTING THERE: Sharp Airlines is the only airline that flies to Flinders Island (FLS)

PHONE RECEPTION: Yes - Telstra only

WI-FI: Check with your accommodation

DAYTRIPS: No

KID FRIENDLY: Yes

SOCIALS: @visitflindersisland & @flindersisland

MORE INFO: visitflindersisland.com.au

Opposite Aerial view over Lady Barron

➔ GETTING HERE

Sharp Airlines (sharpairlines.com) flies to Flinders Island (FLS) from Launceston daily and Melbourne (Essendon) several times a week. During peak times flights can be booked out quite far in advance, as there are only 19 people on each flight.

For those looking to camp, you can also bring your car and camping gear to Flinders Island on **Bass Strait Freight** (bassstraitfreight.com.au). The service accepts passenger and vehicle bookings and departs from Bridport in Tasmania and takes about 7hr to get to Flinders Island, docking at Lady Barron. Check the website for the schedule as the service times vary, depending on the season.

© GETTING AROUND

There's no public transport on the island, so book a car to pick up from the airport when you arrive with **Flinders Island Car Rentals**, so you can explore the whole island.

💤 STAY

There are two main areas to stay on Flinders Island, the central hub and main town of Whitemark, and the smaller seaside town of Lady Barron. Both offer basic accommodation styles, with easy access to restaurant options and small local stores. But the best way to experience Flinders Island is by booking one of its exquisite holiday homes. Popping up all over the island are incredible unique little stays, from beach houses to farm stays and mountain lodges immersed in nature and beautifully designed.

The **Mountain Seas Lodge**, at the foot of Mount Strzelecki, offers both mountain and ocean views, with private walking trails and waterfalls and a seasonal cafe right on the property. It's a great corner of the island to be completely in nature.

There are quite a few authentic farm stays, including **Wombat Lodge** and **Dwarf Cottage** in Killiecrankie or **Echo Hills Cottage** at the base of the Darling Ranges.

There's also no shortage of beachfront stays, such as **Allports Beach House**, **Palana Beach House** and **The Nest** in Palana, and **Nautilus** and **The Crayshack** in Killiecrankie.

If you're coming to Flinders Island to camp, you can find campgrounds at **All Ports**, **Yellow Beach**, **Trouser Point** and **North East River**. You will need to be self-sufficient as there are no powered campsites and no shower facilities available, so if you need to recharge batteries or are looking for a hot shower you'll need to book a night of accommodation. Fires are not permitted on any Furneaux Island.

🍽 FOOD & DRINK

No matter where you choose to eat on Flinders Island you'll be sure to have a good meal, with menus full of fresh local produce.

The Flinders Wharf is the perfect place to start with a seasonal menu full of local island produce, and located right on the jetty with views of the water. It's a striking modern building, with all different seating options and plenty of local products and gifts to purchase. It's also a great place to watch the sunset during Happy Hour on Fridays.

Grab some fresh fish and chips or check out the specials from the colourful **Flinders Island Food Van 7255** (Thurs-Sun 12pm-4pm).

Cate Cooks (Wed-Sat) is a small tuckshop and cafe that always seems to have people sitting out the front. Pop in here for your coffee fix in the morning, as well as seasonal food, sweet and savoury treats and take-away meals.

Head to **Flinders Island Bakery** (Mon-Fri 7am-4pm) for fresh bread and pastries in the morning.

The **Interstate Hotel Bistro** (Mon-Sun breakfast, Mon-Fri lunch, Mon-Sat dinner) in the centre of Whitemark offers an extensive menu with delicious meals. It's an easy go-to after a day of exploring.

Top Trouser Point Beach *Bottom* Lunch at The Flinders *Opposite* Flinders Island Airport

Flinders Island

Down south in Lady Barron, the **Furneaux Tavern** offers lunch and dinner daily, with a cosy little dining room and great outdoor space overlooking the water.

There's also a decent **IGA supermarket** in the main street of Whitemark, as well as a smaller **general store** in Lady Barron.

✓ THINGS TO DO

Spend your time exploring the island at your own pace, driving the dirt roads between beaches and lookouts, stopping whenever something catches your eye. **Visit Flinders Island** (visitflindersisland.com.au) has put together some epic drive itineraries, focusing on either the north, south or centre of the island for you to follow, and pointing out plenty of local secrets along the way.

In the north, **Killiecrankie Bay** is a favourite for both visitors and locals alike, a pretty, calm beach at the bottom of the impressive Mount Killiecrankie. Try your luck fossicking for the elusive Killiecrankie 'diamond', or try your luck at Diamond Creek, about 2km along the beach. Further north, **Palana Beach** offers a beautiful dramatic coastline, surrounded by hundreds of boulders sitting along the shoreline. Head all the way to the end of the road for the best views that stretch across to Inner Sister Island. On the way up to Palana Beach make sure you keep an eye out for wombats along the side of the road. You'll be able to see heaps of wombat burrows on the left-hand side as you drive north, often with a cheeky wombat peering out at you. Keep going up to **North East River** to stand at the most northern tip of the island, a great spot for wildlife and fishing.

In the centre of the island, head up to **Walkers Lookout** for a 360-degree view of the island, including the Darling Ranges rising up through the middle. Explore the main town of **Whitemark**, and stop in at **The Purple Swamphen** to check out their range of handmade gifts and souvenirs; there are sometimes orphaned wombats to visit at the store. The **Furneaux Distillery** has created Australia's Maritime Whisky and Untamed Gin, truly flavours of the island. Sitting within the Flinders Wharf, you can visit the distillery for a tour or a tasting by appointment (call 0438 025 705). **Whitemark wharf** is also a great spot to go for a fish, where you're likely to catch squid and trevally.

Tackle the coastal walk from **All Ports Beach** to the spectacular **Castle Rock**, a massive, orange lichen-covered granite boulder standing tall along the beach of **Marshall Bay Conservation** area. Some of the other favourites in this area are **Sawyers Beach**, **Lillies Beach** and the views from Settlement Point. Take a drive out to **Patriarch Wildlife Sanctuary**, a volunteer-run conservation reserve, where you can get up close with wallabies, wombats and cape barren geese.

In the south, explore the small town of Lady Barron. Pop into the **Unavale Vineyard** (Mon-Sun 11am-4pm) to try some of Flinders Island's local wines. There are grazing platters available at the cellar door and vineyard tours to explore amongst the vines.

Check out **Trouser Point Beach** for arguably one of the most beautiful beaches on Flinders Island, as well as the neighbouring **Fotheringate Beach**, and explore the surrounding **Strzelecki National Park**. Hike to the top of Mount Strzelecki, the highest point on the island at 756m tall. It's a challenging walk, but offers panoramic views across the whole island on a clear day. It's also one of Tasmania's Great Short Walks. Head to **Yellow Beach** for a great swimming and snorkelling spot to spend an afternoon or to check out the views across Franklin Sound.

? WHEN TO GO

The summer and autumn months, generally between December and April, are often the best time to visit Flinders Island, when the weather is warm with little rain, perfect for getting outdoors and exploring the island.

The third weekend in January is the **Furneaux Islands Festival**, which celebrates island community, culture, food and music with plenty of events across three days. A highlight of the festival is Sunday's Community BBQ Day with live music, entertainment for the kids, culture circles and a delicious barbecue lunch by local chefs. It's definitely a great time to organise your visit to Flinders Island.

! NEED TO KNOW

Flinders Island has its own app (flindersisland.app) which will be a great help during your time on the island. Save it to your phone's home screen for instant access to restaurant and business opening hours, visitor information, events and activities, hiking guides and essential services. In particular it's super helpful for knowing what food and drink options are open during your visit, as many have changing opening hours and are either only open for a few hours, or closed several days of the week.

Opposite Beach house on Killicrankie Bay

ISLAND HOPPING
Cockatoo Island/ Wareamah

SYDNEY, NEW SOUTH WALES

If you're looking for a city island escape, why not one smack bang in the middle of bustling Sydney/Warrang? Sitting in the middle of Sydney Harbour is the little-known Cockatoo Island/Wareamah. Home to historic landmarks, award-winning accommodation and a UNESCO World Heritage–listed Convict Site, it offers a completely different insight into Sydney, and is one few people take the opportunity to explore.

Known as Wareamah in the Dharug language, the island sits within the waterways and homelands of the Wallumedegal, Wangal, Cammeraygal and Gadigal Peoples. The island was used as a meeting place for these groups, who share the Dharug language. From the late 1830s until 1869, the island held convicts, and the prisoners included First Nations People. There was a daring escape by convict Frederick Ward, known as Captain Thunderbolt, and his wife, Mary Ann Bugg, a Worimi woman, aided him by swimming from Balmain to help him escape. The island held a branch of the Aboriginal Tent Embassy in 2000. These days the island is considered a nationally significant place and is looked after by the Sydney Harbour Federation Trust.

With a unique harbourside, waterfront campground, self-guided tours around the island, a historic dockyard, great dining options and exciting seasonal events, Cockatoo Island is an easy daytrip or weekend away.

GETTING HERE

The easiest way to visit Cockatoo Island is by hopping on the public ferry. The F3 and F8 services depart daily from Circular Quay and Barangaroo, making the short journey to Cockatoo Island. You can find ferry times on the Transport NSW website (transportnsw.info/travel-info/ways-to-get-around/ferry). You can also get across to Cockatoo Island with a water taxi, private boat or kayak.

Opposite top Aerial view of Cockatoo Island in Sydney Harbour
Opposite bottom Convict ruins

THINGS TO DO

Take a journey through Cockatoo Island/Wareamah's history, including its convict- and shipyard-era days, on a guided tour around the island. There are plenty of different options to choose from, including the **Convict Prison Tour**, **Dark Past Tour** or **Sandstone to Steel Tour**, just to name a few, or if you're up for a fright, jump on their adults-only after dark **Ghost Tour** (for ages 18+). The guided tours run on a weekend schedule, with group bookings available on weekdays. There is also a selection of audio self-guided tours that you can choose from. Pop into the island's visitors centre to find out more.

There's a range of fun and free experiences to check out around the island, from the **beanbag cinema** in the Convict Precinct, to a giant outdoor chess set, **lawn games**, a **harbourside basketball court**, and plenty of grassy places to enjoy an afternoon picnic overlooking the harbour and Sydney's skyline.

You can grab a bite to eat at either the **Marina Cafe & Bar**, a harbourside hangout with a diverse pub-style menu and a stunning outdoor beer garden (cafe menu daily, kitchen menu offered Thurs-Sun), or head to **Cockatoo Overboard** with more quick takeaway-style options, as well as hot, cold and alcoholic beverages all served with an incredible harbour view. Opening hours for both change depending on the season, so check their websites for the most up-to-date information.

Cockatoo Island is also a favourite spot to spend New Year's Eve. Staying right in the heart of Sydney Harbour you'll have the best views of Sydney/Warrang's iconic fireworks over the Harbour Bridge. Accommodation and packages for New Year's Eve book out well in advance, so plan ahead.

STAY

There are a few different accommodation options on Cockatoo Island/Wareamah. A top favourite is the **harbourside campground**, with views across the water right from your own little deck. With basic and deluxe camping options to choose from, you can check into a pre-set-up tent, all ready for you to start enjoying your getaway. There are tent options that cater for between two and six people, with toilets and hot showers available at the campground.

There's also a range of **holiday houses** and **harbourview apartments** in different locations all across the island, as well as a cute little studio apartment in the island's former fire station.

MORE INFO

To find out more and start planning your visit to Cockatoo Island/Wareamah, head to cockatooisland.gov.au or check out their socials at @cockatooisland.

King Island

An island version of a quiet country town

BASS STRAIT, TASMANIA

TIME ZONE: AEST (GMT +10), with daylight savings time (GMT +11) in effect from Oct to April

BEST TIME TO VISIT: Summer and autumn months

ACCESSIBLE FROM: Launceston, Melbourne (Essendon), Hobart & Burnie

GETTING THERE: Sharp Airlines, REX Airlines and King Island Airlines fly to King Island from various places in Tasmania and Victoria.

PHONE RECEPTION: Yes, but Telstra only

WI-FI: Free wi-fi at the Currie library and outside the Currie post office (with Telstra air), or at the King Island Hotel if you're having a meal. Check with your accommodation if you need wi-fi during your stay.

DAYTRIPS: No

KID FRIENDLY: Yes

SOCIALS: @visitkingisland

MORE INFO: kingisland.org.au

King Island is so much more than you might imagine. Sitting about halfway between Tasmania and Victoria, at the western end of Bass Strait, it's a unique place known for its fresh local produce, with particularly delectable cheese, steak and crayfish, and is home to deserted white sand beaches, stretching as far as the eye can see, rolling green hills covered in cattle, sheep, wild turkeys and peacocks, jagged coastlines and shipwrecks dotted all around the island. It also boasts some of Australia's best golf, with three courses for you to choose from.

Larger than you might expect, King Island is approximately 64km long and 27km wide. It takes just under an hour to get from Cape Wickham in the north down to Grassy in the south, with the main town of Currie sitting almost in the middle. It's essentially an island country town, where everyone knows everyone, the main street has only six shops and the farmer fills in for the butcher when he's on holiday. You'll feel like a local as soon as you arrive, with a wave from every car you pass on the road.

King Island is a great spot for viewing the Aurora Australis, if you're visiting at the right time (most commonly during winter between May and Aug), or for a spectacular sunset on a clear evening, when the most incredible afterglow falls over the island as the misty fog rolls in. With a plethora of hidden gems to explore, from the iconic colourful Boathouse – the restaurant with no food, to the resident little penguin colony at the tip of Grassy Harbour, King Island is sure to exceed your expectations.

THE BEST BITS

Before you leave, make sure you pop into the King Island Butcher and grab some steaks to take home with you. The steaks from King Island are mouth-wateringly delicious, with all recommendations from locals saying the very best are found at the butchers.

Opposite top left Orange granite boulders on the beach at Disappointment Bay *Opposite top right* A dusk glow over King Island *Opposite bottom* Disappointment Bay

King Island

Island towns

➔ GETTING HERE & AROUND

Sharp Airlines (sharpairlines.com) is the main airline servicing King Island (KNS), with flights from Launceston, Melbourne (Essendon), Hobart and Burnie. They are small planes, with only 19 seats, so it's definitely a good idea to book in advance. **REX Airlines** (rex.com.au) also offers flights to the island from Melbourne (Tullamarine) and Burnie, and **King Island Airlines** (kingislandair.com.au) offers a daily service from Moorabbin Airport.

Book a car with **King Island Car Rental** to pick up at the airport on your arrival. With no public transport, you will definitely need a car to explore the island.

💤 STAY

There are plenty of different options when deciding where to stay on King Island, from **luxury beachfront holiday homes** to budget motel rooms and everything in between. To stay right in the heart of the action, check out a self-contained A-frame cabin at **Island Breeze Motel**. Only a short walk or drive from Currie and with beautiful views over the hills, these little cabins are not only super cute, but have everything you will need, including their own kitchen, laundry and outdoor deck.

For the ultimate luxury stay you can't go past **Bass Lodge** and **Shore House**. With their beachfront locations, set on the dunes and overlooking the ocean, these houses are exquisitely designed, both with their own fireplaces, private outdoor saunas and sunken timber hot tubs, offering a complete sanctuary during your stay. There are also plenty of accommodation options for families and larger groups travelling together.

🍴 FOOD & DRINK

When you arrive on King Island make sure you pick up a 'What's Happening On King Island This Week?' flier from the airport, for all the most up-to-date opening hours of restaurants and eateries. From there, you can start to make a plan of where to go each day.

Wild Harvest (Mon-Sun, bookings essential) offers a can't-miss dining experience, with a seasonal menu of local produce that changes throughout the year. It's a great place to taste local steak and crayfish or experience its six-course degustation menu on a Saturday.

View Dining (Tues-Sun) located in the King Island Golf and Bowling Club offers a great modern menu, with sweeping views over the ocean and the golf course.

The **King Island Bakehouse** is open daily (times vary), and you can stock up on homemade pies and sweet treats for the day before you head out on your adventures.

The **King Island Hotel** is open for lunch and dinner (Mon-Sun), with a great pub menu, or head to the **Grassy Club** for a buffet meal with the local miners.

Make sure you grab a steak from the **King Island Butchery** to cook up yourself - it's the best steak on the island.

For a completely unique and very King Island dining experience, grab your own food and take it down to **The Boathouse** (at the end of Lighthouse St). Known as the 'restaurant with no food', this little boathouse sits on the rocky shore of Currie Harbour and is spectacularly designed and decorated by local artists. Everything you need is here, including cooking facilities, cutlery, plates, cups, etc. Just make sure you clean up your dishes and leave it as you found it.

Above Cape Wickham Lighthouse *Opposite top* Beer garden at the King Island Brewhouse *Opposite bottom* A-frame cabins at the Island Breeze Motel

To taste some of the best of King Island, head to **King Island Brewhouse** (Thurs-Sun) for a tasting paddle of their latest brews and views over the hills. You can't miss an afternoon cheese plate at **King Island Dairy** (Mon, Wed, Fri, Sun). There are tastings at the Cheese Store and we highly recommend the delicious baked brie and a glass of wine. **King Island Distillery** (Wed-Sun) offers tastings of their bespoke gin, vodka and whiskey, as well as distillery tours.

⊘ THINGS TO DO

Spend the day at one of King Island's stunning beaches. **Disappointment Bay** is a definite favourite, with large red coloured boulders scattered across the sand. **Little Porky Beach** and **Martha Lavinia Beach** are also great surf spots, with strong powerful waves, so always be careful in the water. For a calm, peaceful swimming spot, check out **Penny's Lagoon**, a rare 'suspended lake' (one of only three in the world), where the freshwater is held by compacted sand and organic matter. There's no stream or underground aquifer that feeds into or flows out of the lake.

For some of the most dramatic views of the rocky King Island coastline, head south to **Seal Rocks**. A short boardwalk takes you to a lookout with waves crashing onto the rocks below. Check out the unique **calcified forest**, the remains of an ancient forest that's more than 7000 years old. An easy 1.3km (return) walk will take you there, with views across the forest at the halfway point.

If you're looking for a guided tour, check out **King Island Tours** (kingislandtours.com), who offer small group tours through the eyes of a local. They have plenty of options, from 4WD adventure tours to get you out to every corner of the island, to DIY fishing tours and indulgent food tours.

Check out **Cape Wickham Lighthouse**, standing tall on the northern point of the island. At 48m tall it is actually the tallest lighthouse in Australia, guarding King Island since 1861.

King Island Historical Museum (Tues, Thurs, Sat-Sun 2-4pm) is the place to go to learn more about King Island's history, including the many shipwrecks, mining, sealing and agriculture. The **Cultural Centre** (Mon, Wed-Sun 1-4pm daily) offers exhibitions and workshops, showcasing local artists and community projections, so you can learn a little more about life on King Island today.

Play a round of golf at one of the most exciting golfing destinations in the world. With two 18-hole courses on the island - **Ocean Dunes** and **Cape Wickham Golf Links**, and a 9-hole course in the heart of Currie, you could easily spend your whole trip on the green.

Opposite Aerial view over Disappointment Bay to Rocky Point

Head to **Grassy Harbour** at dusk to watch the resident little penguin population coming out of the water to their nests for the night. Thousands of penguins come in from the water each night, waddling their way across the road to the shrubbery as the sun sets. When you get to the harbour, follow the signs around to the penguin colony. For the best chance of viewing the penguins, park your car across the road, close to one of the small lampposts that line the road and wait for them to come out. Before you know it, the whole road seems to be lined with penguins!

ⓘ WHEN TO GO

The summer and autumn months, from December to around the end of April, are the best time to visit King Island, when the weather is warm and dry and the conditions are great for exploring. The **Festival of King Island** (also known as FOKI) is held on the first weekend of February each year in the natural amphitheatre of Currie Harbour. Plan your visit over this weekend for two days of live music, a 100m water slide, raft races, pie-eating competitions and all kinds of other activities to celebrate King Island. Some of the other annual island events include the **King Island Show** (first Tues in March), **King Island Golf Open** (Nov long weekend) and **Pheasant Weekend** (June, King's Birthday long weekend).

ⓘ NEED TO KNOW

You can plan your whole trip to King Island on its website (kingisland.org.au), with all the options and availability right in one place, including accommodation, car hire and tours. Accommodation, car hire and experiences can book out pretty early on King Island - especially during the summer months and any event long weekends. Book in advance to ensure you don't miss out.

Above The Boathouse *Opposite* Seal Rocks Lookout

Phillip Island/Millowl

Home to some of Australia's most unique wildlife

GIPPSLAND, VICTORIA

Phillip Island/Millowl, one of Victoria's only accessible islands, is an island full of adventure, wildlife, and natural beauty. Less than a 2hr drive from the city of Melbourne/Naarm, Phillip Island is a local favourite, with families flocking to its beaches in the summertime, adventure parks, heritage farms, epic mazes and activities to keep the whole family entertained for days on end. Although it only takes 25min to drive from one end of the island to the other there is so much to see and do here, it can be hard to know where to start!

Known as Millowl to its Traditional Owners, the Boon Wurrung/Bunurong People, the island has been part of the homelands of the Yallock-Balluk People for tens of thousands of years. The Traditional Owners used the island in the summer months to feast on shellfish, fish, small marsupials and mutton birds. Ochre has been found across the island and on Churchill Island, used as body decorations during ceremonies.

Phillip Island is home to an abundance of wildlife, with more penguins than people (40,000 adult penguins to be specific) in the world's largest little penguin colony, as well as Australia's largest fur seal colony, plenty of koalas snoozing lazily in the gum trees above and kangaroos hopping along the roads. Whether you're coming to relax on the beach, or hit the hiking trails and explore the rugged coastline, Phillip Island is a great weekend away right on the city's doorstep.

THE BEST BITS

Phillip Island is home to extraordinary wildlife experiences. From the tiny little penguins that waddle onto the shore each night and koalas nestled high into the trees, to boat cruises to spot seals, dolphins and even orcas (killer whales) during the winter months, there's an incredible amount of wildlife to see on this little island.

TIME ZONE: AEST (GMT +10), with daylight savings time (GMT +11) in effect from Oct to April

BEST TIME TO VISIT: Dec to March

ACCESSIBLE FROM: Melbourne

GETTING THERE: Car or public transport options

PHONE RECEPTION: Yes

WI-FI: Yes

DAYTRIPS: Yes

KID FRIENDLY: Yes

SOCIALS: @phillipisland

MORE INFO: visitphillipisland.com.au

Opposite Australia's largest colony of fur seals swimming alongside Wildlife Coast Cruises

→ GETTING HERE

Around 90min from Melbourne or just over a 2hr drive from Tullamarine airport, Phillip Island/Millowl is an easy road trip out of the city following the major highways. Rental cars can be picked up at the airport or take your own car to explore. There is a **V/Line Coach Service** connecting Melbourne to Cowes each day which departs from Southern Cross Station in Melbourne's CBD, or you can catch the **Western Port Ferries** (westernportferries.com.au) passenger ferry from the Mornington Peninsula.

💤 STAY

There are plenty of accommodation options, with holiday houses, caravan parks, hotels and resorts, farmstays, backpackers, and even glamping options. To be right in the heart of the action, base yourself close to Cowes, the main town. You can find everything you need here, including grocery stores and petrol stations, bars and restaurants, and the visitor's centre.

Check out **Waikiki Beach Front at Smiths**, **Marlin Beachfront Smiths Beach** and **Sault Phillip Island** for beautiful coastal holiday homes.

NRMA Phillip Island Beachfront Holiday Park and **Anchor Belle Holiday Park** are caravan parks with access to the beach and only a short walk from the main street in town.

The **Waves Apartments** and **Phillip Island Apartments** offer modern, spacious accommodation right in the heart of Cowes.

For something different, stay on an authentic working farm, at **Five Acres** or **Ripples 'N' Tonic**, to wake up to farm animals in the morning.

⊛ DAYTRIPS

It's easy to create your own daytrip to Phillip Island/Millowl from Melbourne/Naarm, by either taking your own car or renting one from the airport or the city. There are also a handful of full day small group tours that depart from Melbourne, including all your activities for the day. With a range of options to choose from, check the activities before you book to ensure your tour includes what you want to see.

🍴 FOOD & DRINK

Boasting an incredibly diverse selection of restaurants, cafes, breweries and bars, Phillip Island/Millowl offers cuisine from all around the world.

Start your day with breakfast at **The Store**, **The Waterboy Cafe** or **Wild Food Farm and Cafe** for a homestead-style farm-to-table menu.

Head to **Saltwater Phillip Island**, **Beach HQ** and **Hotel Phillip Island** for excellent food with ocean views. The **Wooli Tavern** has a great vibe, with an outdoor beer garden, live music and classic pub meals.

For international flavours, you can find delicious Italian food at **Isola Di Capri** or **Pino's Trattoria**, Asian fusion at **Bang Bang Bar and Restaurant** or a great tapas menu and colourful cocktails at **The Lost Cowe**.

Taste a local wine at Phillip Island's two award-winning wineries, **Phillip Island Winery** and **Purple Hen Winery**, or heard out to **Ocean Reach Brewing** and **Phillip Island Brewing Co.** for a local boutique beer. Grab a punnet of strawberries during summer from **Phillip Island Strawberries** and make sure to stop at the **Phillip Island Chocolate Factory** for delicious handmade chocolates.

The **Churchill Island Farmers Market** (first Sat of each month, 8am-1pm) is a great place to pick up fresh produce from the Gippsland region.

✓ THINGS TO DO

With 101sqkm to explore, there's always a new adventure wherever you go on Phillip Island/Millowl.

Head out early in the morning to hike to **The Pinnacles at Cape Woolamai** for the sunrise. The walking trail begins in the Surf Life Saving carpark, and is about 2km long. It's pretty spectacular, especially at sunrise or sunset, with the rocky coastline glowing golden. Cape Woolamai is also a fantastic surf beach, with some of the best breaks on the island.

Step back in time with a visit to **Churchill Island Heritage Farm**, which is recognised as the site of the first agricultural pursuits in Victoria. Since the 1850s Churchill Island has been continuously farmed with all kinds of local produce. These days the farm lets you experience the way life used to be, with cow milking, sheep shearing, whip cracking and wagon rides. You can also take a walk around the farm and meet some of the local highland cattle, Clydesdale horses and baby animals.

Take a walk around the tree-top boardwalks at the **Koala Conservation Centre** to get up close and personal to Australia's cutest furry creatures snoozing lazily in the gumtrees.

Opposite top left Koala snoozing in the trees at the Koala Conservation Centre *Opposite top right* Sunset over Cowes Beach *Opposite bottom* Cowes jetty

Island towns

Hop on board with **Wildlife Coast Cruises** and head out to visit Australia's largest colony of fur seals swimming and playing together around Seal Rock. There are literally thousands of seals out here, and they love to put on a show for visitors, jumping around and swimming close by the boat.

Embark on an 'Antarctic Journey' at **Nobbies Ocean Discovery**, which plunges you into the world of the Southern Ocean and Antarctica through a number of interactive and immersive experiences throughout the exhibit. Feel the freeze in the Antarctic Chill Zone, check out thermal imaging, explore the Sound Lab and Research Station to learn more about the sights and sounds of Antarctic wildlife.

Hike your way around the island, with plenty of **walking trails** to follow with great views. For coastal walks, check out **Pyramid Rock**, **Kitty Miller Bay** and **Forrest Caves**. **Rhyll Inlet** offers a great inland bushwalk.

Hit the water with **Ocean Adventures Phillip Island** for wild water activities, including jetboat tours and thundercat racing boats. With unique views of the incredible coastline and entertaining commentary during the tour, you're sure to have a great time exploring the island from the water! Bring a jacket for this one, as you're likely to get a little bit wet.

Get your adrenaline pumping at the **Phillip Island Grand Prix Circuit**, which is home to some huge motor racing events each year, including the Australian Motorcycle Grand Prix (Oct), the Superbike World Championship (Feb) and the V8 Supercar Series. You can get into the action yourself by taking a speedy drive around the track with a real race car driver, or for something a little calmer, you can drive a go-kart around a smaller replica of the circuit.

Indulge your inner child or take your kids to **Amazen Things**, home to astounding illusions, insane puzzles, maxi mini golf and its signature giant 3D maze. Confuse yourself in the Magic Manor, get shrunk down to be super tiny on Puzzle Island, or see if you can make your way out of the giant maze.

> ### ON THE MAINLAND
> The small town of **San Remo** is the gateway to Phillip Island/Millowl, however with the island's close proximity to the mainland it doesn't really feel like there's much difference between the two. An authentic fishing village with a laid-back vibe, San Remo is best known for its pelican feeding by the pier at noon each day, and its abundance of seafood restaurants offering fresh locally caught fish. For a great lunch stop on the way over to the island check out **San Remo Fisherman's Co-op**.

In the evening, head out to the **Penguin Parade**, which takes place every night at dusk, for the chance to see the cute little penguins waddling out from the ocean and back to their nests on the shore. The **Penguin Discovery Centre** has built a fantastic boardwalk so that you can watch the penguins finding their nests, feeding their babies and interacting with each other on the shore. The penguins start to emerge from the ocean at sunset, and access to the viewing areas opens about an hour before the estimated penguin arrival time.

ⓘ WHEN TO GO

Head to Phillip Island/Millowl during the summer months (Dec-March) to take advantage of the warmer weather and longer days. However, the weather can be quite temperamental at any time, as well as a bit colder than in Melbourne/Naarm. No matter what time of year you visit, bring a jacket and some warmer options, especially for the Penguin Parade and going out in the evenings.

ⓘ NEED TO KNOW

For more information and recommendations when you arrive, pop into the Phillip Island Visitor Information at 895 Phillip Island Rd, Newhaven.

Above The Wooli Tavern in Cape Woolamai *Opposite* Bring your own van for the best Phillip Island stay

Bruny Island/ Lunawanna-alonnah

From delicious local produce to dramatic landscapes

TASMANIA

Island towns

Bruny Island/Lunawanna-alonnah is close enough to Hobart/Nipaluna for a daytrip, but far enough away to spend a whole weekend or more. It's covered with long dry grass, tall gumtrees and an abundance of wildlife hopping across the road, and surrounded by both calm blue waters and wild seas. Made up of a north and south island, held together by the iconic and narrow isthmus called The Neck, it's a place for foodies, hikers, nature lovers and those wanting to immerse themselves in a piece of Tassie's great outdoors.

Traditionally known as Lunawanna-alonnah to the Traditional Owners, Bruny Island has a rich First Nations history, dating back to a time before Tasmania, as we know it, even existed. It was also a stop for some of the earliest European explorers, with the first visit to the island around 1642.

Stretching for approximately 100km, Bruny Island is deceptively large and covered in beautiful rugged landscapes. From white sand beaches and dramatic cliff-faces, to the striking South Bruny National Park, the natural beauty of the island is rivalled only by the fresh produce. Allow yourself plenty of time to taste your way across the island, with wineries, cheese makers, oyster farmers, berry growers and chocolatiers offering samples of their delicacies.

THE BEST BITS

Taste your way across Bruny Island/Lunawanna-alonnah, with offerings from cheese and oysters to chocolate and berries, and of course you can't go past a glass of the island's premium wines or signature whisky.

TIME ZONE: AEST (GMT +10), with daylight savings time (GMT +11) in effect from Oct to April

BEST TIME TO VISIT: Dec to March

ACCESSIBLE FROM: Kettering

GETTING THERE: Ferry transfer

PHONE RECEPTION: Yes

WI-FI: No

DAYTRIPS: Yes

KID FRIENDLY: Yes

SOCIALS: @brunyislandau, @tourismbrunyisland

MORE INFO: brunyisland.org.au, brunyisland.com

Opposite Views over The Neck

Island towns

GETTING HERE & AROUND

From Hobart, it's about a 40min drive to Kettering where you catch the **SeaLink Bruny Island** ferry service (sealink.com.au/bruny-island) across to the island. The ferry runs every half hour during the summer months and peak holiday periods, with more than 20 services a day, and operates on a first-come, first-served basis. You can't book a specific departure time, simply head down to the wharf and join the line. It takes only 20min to get across to Bruny Island/Lunawanna-alonnah from Kettering. Passengers travel for free, while you only have to pay for vehicles, including cars, caravans, bikes and trailers. Once you're on the island it's best to have a car to get yourself around, as stops can be quite far away from each other.

STAY

Bruny Island/Lunawanna-alonnah has an abundance of cute properties on Airbnb and self-catering cottages that have popped up across the island. Make sure to check the location when booking properties as some are quite remote surrounded by bushland. **Bruny Boathouse**, in the town of Alonnah is only a few steps from the water and offers stunning views across the D'Entrecasteaux Channel and out to Satellite Island. **Sheepwash Bay** on South Bruny offers rustic luxury with outdoor bathtubs overlooking the ocean, and is also home to the famous Bruny Baker. **Hundred Acre Hideaway Retreat** gives you your own wood-fire hot tub to relax in, on a private deck overlooking South Bruny National Park and immersed in the wilderness.

Stay on your own private Tassie island at the **Satellite Island Summer House**, in the heart of the D'Entrecasteaux Channel. Only a short 5min boat ride off Bruny Island, this luxe accommodation is the ultimate private island getaway.

DAYTRIPS

It's easy to create your own daytrip to Bruny Island/Lunawanna-alonnah from either Hobart/Nipaluna or the Huon Valley. Simply head across to the island in the morning, spend your day driving across it, and stop in at all the tiny stores, quiet beaches and hiking trails you desire, and then head back to the ferry to return to the Tasmanian mainland at the end of the day. **Bruny Island Safaris** also offer guided tours across Bruny Island from Hobart, if you'd prefer to travel with a group.

Opposite top left Oyster stop at Get Shucked Oysters *Opposite top left* Cape Bruny Lighthouse *Opposite top left* Pick up fresh bread and treats from the Bruny Baker

FOOD & DRINK

With incredible food, drinks and local produce to try across Bruny Island/Lunawanna-alonnah, your only question will be where should you start? Check ahead for opening times though as hours can vary.

Pick your own strawberries, raspberries, blackberries and blueberries at **Bruny Island Berry Farm**, or try berries on pancakes, in ice-cream and their famous jam. Immerse yourself in the eucalyptus forest with a delicious cheese plate at **Bruny Island Cheese Co**. Try some of the freshest oysters at **Get Shucked Oyster Farm**, farmed in the waters right off Bruny Island. Stock up on tasty treats at **Bruny Island Chocolate**, or head to the iconic bread fridge by the side of the road for fresh sourdough, Anzac cookies and loaves of bread from the **Bruny Baker**.

The island is not only a feast for foodies, but a wine and whisky destination too. **Bruny Island Premium Wines** offers an extensive menu of tapas, gourmet burgers, platters and tacos, all made with local island produce, as well as its signature wines list to taste from, with alfresco dining surrounded by the vines and rolling yellow hills. At **Bruny's House of Whisky** you can taste test your way through its award-winning menu of single-malts, or head up to the restaurant to experience their whisky and fine food pairings.

If you're looking for a good dinner menu, **Hotel Bruny** is the place to go for pub classics and fresh Tassie seafood. It also claims the title of the southernmost pub in Australia.

THINGS TO DO

Hike your way across the island, to find some of the most dramatic landscapes that you just can't get to by car. The **Cape Queen Elizabeth Walk** is one of the best, a 2hr return (12km) moderate hike that follows the trail between Big Lagoon and Little Lagoon and climbs up Mars Bluff. Best attempted at low tide, the highlight of this walk is the Bruny Island Arch, an incredible archway made of jagged rocks standing in the middle of a white sand beach.

On South Bruny, the **Labillardiere Peninsula Walk** takes from 5hr to 7hr (18km return), where you will hike around the whole peninsula, including across beaches, dry forests, Mount Bleak and coastal headlands. There are a lot of steep walks and rocky trails on this walk, so come prepared.

Explore **South Bruny National Park** at the bottom of South Bruny, where towering cliffs overlook long sandy beaches and the surrounding ocean. The park is home to **Cape Bruny Lighthouse**, Australia's second-oldest lighthouse - built in 1835. It can be found at the very tip of the island, standing 13m tall. You can also climb to the top on a tour with **Bruny**

Island towns

Island Safaris. **Cloudy Bay** within the national park is a favouite spot for surfers, with windy conditions offering great swell.

See the island from the water on a cruise with **Pennicott Wilderness Journeys**, an award-winning 3hr cruise exploring some of the rugged coastline of the island. Taking you alongside some of Australia's highest sea cliffs and to the powerful spot where the Tasman Sea meets the Southern Ocean, you're likely to spot seals, dolphins, migrating whales and a plethora of birds during the tour.

For the most spectacular views across the island, tackle the 279 stairs to the top of **The Neck**, a viewing platform halfway across the isthmus where North Bruny and South Bruny connect. A great spot during the golden hour and at sunset, when the sky really puts on a show. At The Neck you'll also find the **Truganini Memorial**, a celebration of the life and resilience of Truganini, a First Nations woman who endured unthinkable crimes throughout her life and worked tirelessly to protect her people. You can sometimes spot little penguins here after dusk, as they make their way out of the ocean and back to their burrows.

WHEN TO GO

Plan your visit to Bruny Island/Lunawanna-alonnah during the summer months, from December until March, to take advantage of the warmer weather. It's the best season to immerse yourself in nature, the great outdoors and all the related activities the island has on offer. There are more ferries during the summer months and everything on the island is open, while a much smaller selection of stays open for winter.

NEED TO KNOW

You will need a Parks Pass from Parks & Wildlife Tasmania (passes.parks.tas.gov.au) to visit South Bruny National Park. Purchase in advance online, as there's nowhere to purchase it once you arrive at the park.

ON THE MAINLAND

Pair your visit to Bruny Island/Lunawanna-alonnah with a few days in Hobart/Nipaluna to really soak up the Tassie vibes. Head to **Salamanca Market** on a Saturday morning for all kinds of locally grown produce and locally made products. Check out the views from the **kunanyi/Mount Wellington**, where it can even snow during the summer months. Grab a beer at the historic **Cascade Brewery**, where you can sip on the country's longest continuously brewed beer. End your day with a sunset cruise along the **Derwent River**, a great way to see some of Hobart's famous landmarks.

Above Lunch on Bruny Island *Opposite* Satellite Island

INDEX

A
A Day at Dirk tour, Dirk Hartog Island WA 87
Above & Beyond Tas. 195
Abrolhos Islands WA 98-9
Absolute North Charters Qld 118
Adelaide Hills wineries SA 68
Adelaide SA 109
Admirals Arch, Kangaroo Island SA 115
Air Frontier NT 34
Airlie Beach Qld 9, 10, 25, 40, 43, 45
Allports Beach, Flinders Island Tas. 213, 214
Allports Beach House, Flinders Island Tas. 213
Aloha Apartments, Norfolk Island 206
Amaroo on Mandalay, Magnetic Island Qld 58
Amazen Things, Phillip Island Vic. 231
American River, Kangaroo Island SA 110
Amici Restaurant, Hayman Island Qld 13
Amity Point (Pulan), North Stradbroke Island Qld 76, 79, 80
Anchor Bay, Lizard Island Qld 5
Anchorage Restaurant, Lord Howe Island NSW 201
Anson Bay, Norfolk Island 205, 209
Antechamber Bay Retreats, Kangaroo Island SA 112
Aqua Darts snorkelling, Lizard Island Qld 6
Aqua Restaurant, Hayman Island Qld 13
Aqua Soul Spa, Heron Island Qld 131
Arajilla Retreat, Lord Howe Island NSW 201
Arcadia, Magnetic Island Qld 59
Arcadia Village Pub, Magnetic Island Qld 59
Arthur Bay Lookout, Magnetic Island Qld 60
Atherton Tablelands Qld 6
Aurora Ozone Apartments, Kangaroo Island SA 112
Australia's Coral Coast, Geraldton WA 98
Australia's Last Sunset, Dirk Hartog Island WA 88

B
Back Beach, Thevenard Island WA 171
Back Beach Bus Trip, Thevenard Island WA 173
Baillie's Bar, Heron Island Qld 128
Bali Hali Reef, Whitsundays Qld 13
Bam Bam Restaurant, Hayman Island Qld 13
Bamaga Qld 185
Bandjin People 26, 116, 122
Bang Bang Bar and Restaurant, Cape Woolamai, Phillip Island Vic. 228
Barangaroo, Sydney NSW 217
Bargara Qld 145, 147
Basin, The, Rottnest Island WA 55
Bass Lodge, Loorana, Flinders Island 221
Bass Strait Tas. 210-15, 218-25
Bass Strait Freight 210
Batavia (shipwreck). Abrolhos Islands WA 98
Bathurst Island NT 33, 34-5, 36
Bay of Fires Tas. 193
Beach BBQ, Moreton Island Qld 64
Beach Cafe, Moreton Island Qld 64
Beach Club, Hamilton Island Qld 43
Beach Hotel, Point Lookout, North Stradbroke Island Qld 79
Beach HQ, Cowes, Phillip Island Vic. 228

Beachcomber Lodge, Lord Howe Island NSW 201
Beachfront Dining Room, Lady Elliot Island Qld 136
Beacon Island, Abrolhos Islands WA 98
Bedarra Island/Biagurra Qld 26-31
Bedarra Island Resort Qld 29, 30
Belle Holiday Park, Phillip Island Vic. 228
Betty's Beach, Whitsunday Island Qld 157
Big 5 Marine Safari, Dirk Hartog Island WA 88
Big and Little Sandhills, Moreton Island Qld 67
Big Barge Arts Centre, Cocos (Keeling) Islands 167
Bima Wear, Wurruminyanga, Bathurst Island NT 35
Bishop and Clerk, Maria Island Tas. 193
Blinky Beach, Lord Howe Island NSW 202
Blowholes, The, Christmas Island 94
Blue Lagoon, Moreton Island Qld 67
Blue Lagoon Lodge, Lord Howe Island NSW 201
Blue Pearl Bay, Hayman Island Qld 13, 15
Blue Peter Beach House, Lord Howe Island NSW 201
Blue Room Cafe, Point Lookout, North Stradbroke Island Qld 79
Bluefish Point, Prince of Wales Island Qld 186
Boathouse, The, Currie, King Island Tas. 221
Bobby's Snack Bar, Thursday Island Qld 185
Bob's Bakery, Hamilton Island Qld 45
Bommie Restaurant, Hamilton Island Qld 45

Boon Wurrung/Bunurong People 227
Bounty Bar & Grill, Norfolk Island 206
Bounty Day, Norfolk Island 209
Bowker Beach House, Lord Howe Island NSW 201
Bowling Club, Lord Howe Island NSW 201
Brammo Bay, Dunk Island Qld 122, 123
Bridport Tas. 212
Brisbane/Meanjin Qld 63, 67, 80, 132, 135, 205, 206
Brown Lake/Bummiera, North Stradbroke Island Qld 80
Bruny Baker, Bruny Island Tas. 235
Bruny Boathouse, Alonnah Tas. 235
Bruny Island/Lunawanna-alonnah Tas. 232-7
Bruny Island Berry Farm Tas. 235
Bruny Island Cheese Co. Tas. 235
Bruny Island Chocolate Tas. 235
Bruny Island Premium Wines Tas. 235
Bruny Island Safaris 235
Bruny's House of Whisky, North Bruny Vic. 235
Budget Boat Hire, Mission Beach Qld 122
Bumboras Beach, Norfolk Island 209
Bundaberg Qld 132, 135, 138, 142, 145
Bundaberg Barrel Qld 138
Bundaberg Rum Distillery Qld 138
Burnie Tas. 221
Butchulla People 101
Butterfly Bungalows, Fitzroy Island Qld 151
Butterfly Walk, Magnetic Island Qld 60
Byfield NP and State Forest Qld 178
Bynoe Harbour NT 180

C

Cabn x Cape St Albans, Kangaroo Island SA 112
Cactus Kangaroo Island, Kingscote SA 112
Cafe Nourish, Horseshoe Bay, Magnetic Island Qld 59
Cairns/Gimuy Qld 2, 5, 140, 148, 151, 154, 182, 185, 186
Cairns Aquarium Qld 154
Cairns Esplanade Lagoon Qld 154
Cammeraygal People 217
Cape Barren Island Tas. 210
Cape Bruny Lighthouse, South Bruny Tas. 235
Cape Du Couedic Lighthouse, Kangaroo Island SA 115
Cape Inscription 4WD Adventure Tour, Dirk Hartog Island WA 88
Cape Jervis SA 109, 115
Cape Moreton, Moreton Island Qld 63
Cape Moreton Lighthouse, Moreton Island Qld 67
Cape Queen Elizabeth Walk, Bruny Island Tas. 235
Cape Wickham, King Island Tas. 218
Cape Wickham Golf Links, King Island Tas. 222
Cape Wickham Lighthouse, King Island Tas. 222
Cape Willoughby, Kangaroo Island SA 109
Cape Woolamai, Phillip Island Vic. 228
Cape York Qld 182, 185, 186
Capella Lodge, Lord Howe Island NSW 201
Capricorn Coast Qld 71-5, 174-9
Capricornia Cays NP Qld 145
Captain Cook Lookout, Norfolk Island 209
Cardwell Qld 116, 118, 121
Cardwell Spa Pool, Cardwell Qld 121
Cascade Brewery, Hobart Tas. 236
Cassowary Coast Qld 26-31, 116-23
Castaway, Norfolk Island 206
Castaways, Bulwer, Moreton Island Qld 64
Castle Hill, Townsville Qld 60
Castle Rock, Flinders Island Tas. 214
Cate Cooks, Flinders Island Tas. 213
Catseye Beach, Hamilton Island Qld 43, 46
Ceylon Curry Corner, Nelly Bay, Magnetic Island Qld 59
Champagne Pools, K'gari Qld 106
Champagne Pools, Moreton Island Qld 67
Charles Knife Canyon WA 173
Chase 'n' Thyme's All Corners of the Island Tour, Lord Howe Island NSW 202
Chimere Pearls, Geraldton WA 98
Christmas Island 91-7, 162
Christmas Island Fishing & Adventure 97
Christmas Island NP 91, 94
Christmas Island Orientation Tour 94
Christmas Island Visitor's Centre 97
Churchill Island Vic. 227
Churchill Island Farmers Market Vic. 228
Churchill Island Heritage Farm Vic. 228
CI Apartments, Poon San, Christmas Island 92
CI Bakery, Christmas Island 92
CI Supermarket, Christmas Island 92
Circular Quay, Sydney NSW 217
Clam Bay, Great Keppel Island Qld 72
Cleveland Qld 76
Cloudy Bay, South Bruny Tas. 236
Clubhouse, Hamilton Island Golf Club, Dent Island Qld 46
Cockatoo Island/Wareamah NSW 217
Cockatoo Overboard, Cockatoo Island NSW 217
Coconut Beach, Dunk Island Qld 123
Cocos Club, West Island, Cocos (Keeling) Islands 163
Cocos (Keeling) Islands 92, 158-67
Cocos Islands Adventure Tours 164
Cocos Padang Lodge, Christmas Island 92
Cocos Picnics, Cocos (Keeling) Islands 167
Coffee Lounge, Moreton Island Qld 64
Coles Bay Tas. 195
Convict Prison Tour, Cockatoo Island NSW 217
Conway NP Qld 45
Cook's Look, Lizard Island Qld 6
Coomol, Bedarra Island Qld 31
Coomol Ocean Walk, Bedarra Island Qld 31
Coral Cafe, Lord Howe Island NSW 201
Coral Coast WA 84-9, 98-9
Coral Cove, Hamilton Island Qld 46
Cowes Vic. 228
Crab Claw Island NT 180-1
Crayshack, The, Killecrankie, Flinders Island Tas. 213
Crocodile Island NT 180
crocodiles xix, 33, 140
Crooked Post, The, Lord Howe Island NSW 201
Cruise Whitsundays Qld 43, 157
Cullen Bay NT 180
Currie, King Island Tas. 218, 221
Cylinder Beach, North Stradbroke Island Qld 79

D

Dark Past Tour, Cockatoo Island NSW 217
Darlington, Maria Island Tas. 192
Darlington Probation Station, Maria Island Tas. 189
Darwin/Garramilla NT 33, 34, 36, 180
Darwin Harbour sunset cruise NT 36
Darwin Military Museum NT 36
Day at Dirk tour, A, Dirk Hartog Island WA 87
Deadmans Beach, North Stradbroke Island Qld 79
Deep Creek Conservation Park SA 115
Deeral Qld 140
Degustation Beachside Dining, Lizard Island Qld 5
Denham WA 84, 86, 87, 88
Dent Island Qld 46
Derwent River, Hobart Tas. 236
Devil's Corner Cellar Door, Asplawn Tas. 193, 195
Dingaal Traditional Owners 2
Dining with the Tides, Orpheus Island Qld 21
Dinner Under the Stars, Mackerel Islands WA 171
Direction Island, Cocos (Keeling) Islands 160, 162, 164
Direction Island, Mackerel Islands WA 168
Dirk Hartog Island/Wirruwana WA 84-9
Disappointment Bay, King Island Tas. 222
Discover Stradbroke Qld 79
Discovery Lagoon Campsite, Kangaroo Island SA 112
Discovery Rottnest Island WA 50-3
Djiru People 26, 122
Dolly Beach, Christmas Island 94
'DONGA' Golf Club, Cocos (Keeling) Islands 164
Doorila, Bedarra Island Qld 26, 31
Down the Rabbit Hole, McLaren Vale SA 115
Drakes, Kingscote, Kangaroo Island SA 112
Driftwood Bar & Restaurant, Lord Howe Island NSW 201
Driftwood Bar & Wine Cellar, Lizard Island Qld 5
Dudley Wines, Kangaroo Island SA 112
Dundee's Cafe & Restaurant, Cairns Qld 154
Dune Restaurant, Kingfisher Bay Resort, K'gari Qld 105
Dunk & Lunch, Mission Beach Qld 122
Dunk Island/Connanglebah Qld 122-3
Dunk Island Adventures 122
Dunwich (Goompi), North Stradbroke Island Qld 76, 79, 80
Dwarf Cottage, Flinders Island Tas. 213

E

Early Bird Cafe, Horseshoe Bay, Magnetic Island Qld 59
East Air Qld 5
East Coast Tas. 189-95
East Wallabi Island, Abrolhos Islands WA 98
Eastern Beach, Moreton Island Qld 57
Eat Street Markets, Brisbane Qld 67

Index 239

Echo Hills Cottage, Flinders Island Tas. 213
Eco Abrolhos Cruises, Abrolhos Islands WA 98
Eco Lodge, Dirk Hartog Island WA 86
Eli Creek, K'gari Qld 101, 105, 106
Elysian Luxury Eco Island Retreat, Long Island Qld 25
Emily Bay, Norfolk Island 205, 209
Emu Bay, Kangaroo Island SA 115
Emu Bay Lavender Farm, Kangaroo Island SA 112
Emu Park, Yeppoon Qld 178
Emu Ridge Eucalyptus Distillery, Kangaroo Island SA 115
Encounter Maria Island Tas. 190
Erscotts Hole, Lord Howe Island NSW 202
Ethel Beach, Christmas Island 94
Eurong Bakery, K'gari Qld 105
Exmouth WA 168, 171, 173
Experience Day Tour, Kangaroo Island SA 112

F
False Cape Wines, Kangaroo Island SA 112
Family Islands Qld 29, 30, 122
Family Islands NP Qld 122, 123
Feedive Christmas Island 97
Festival of King Island, Currie Tas. 224
FEVER on Straddie, North Stradbroke Island Qld 79
Fire & Stone, Moreton Island Qld 64
First Point Down, North Stradbroke Island Qld 79
Fishermans Beach, Great Keppel Island Qld 72
Fitzroy Flyer (ferry) Qld 151
Fitzroy Island/Koba Qld 148-55
Fitzroy Island Campground Qld 151
Fitzroy Island NP Qld 148
Fitzroy Island Resort Qld 151, 154
Fitzroy Island Sports Hub Qld 152, 154
Five Acres, Phillip Island Vic. 229
Five Ways, Bedarra Island Qld 31

Fleurieu Peninsula SA 68-9, 115
Flinders Chase NP SA 109, 110, 115
Flinders Island Tas. 210-15
Flinders Island Bakery Tas. 213
Flinders Island Car Rentals Tas. 212
Flinders Island Food Van 7255 Tas. 213
Flinders Wharf, The, Flinders Island Tas. 213
Flying Fish Cove, Christmas Island 94
Footy Grand Final and Art Sale, Bathurst Island NT 36
Forts Walk, Magnetic Island Qld 60
Fossil Cliffs, Maria Island Tas. 193
Fotheringate Beach, Flinders Island Tas. 214
Foundation Day, Norfolk Island 209
Frankie's on Rotto, Rottnest Island WA 53
Frankland Islands Qld 140-1
Frankland Islands Reef Cruises Qld 140, 141
Fraser Coast Qld 101-7
Fraser Island Boat Charters, K'gari Qld 102
Freedom Fast Cats Qld 72
Fremantle WA 49, 50, 55
Freycinet Aqua Taxi Tas. 195
Freycinet NP Tas. 195
Friday Island Qld 182, 185
Fruit Bat Falls, Shelburne Qld 186
Furneaux Distillery, Whitemark, Flinders Island Tas. 214
Furneaux Group of islands Tas. 210, 213
Furneaux Islands Festival, Flinders Island Tas. 214
Furneaux Tavern, Lady Barron, Flinders Island Tas. 214

G
Gab Titui Cultural Centre, Thursday Island Qld 182, 185
Gadigal People 217
Gage Road Freo Brewery, Fremantle WA 55
General Store, Fitzroy Island Qld 152
Geoffrey Bay, Magnetic Island Qld 60
Geordie Bay, Rottnest Island WA 53

Geraldton WA 98
Get Shucked Oyster Farm, Bruny Island Tas. 235
Gheebulum Kunungai (Moreton Island) NP Qld 63
Gippsland Vic. 227-31
Girramay People 116
GKI Sea Way Trail, Great Keppel Island Qld 75
Gladstone Qld 126, 128, 131
Gladstone Fish Market Qld 131
Go Cultural, Rottnest Island WA 55
Gold Coast Qld 132, 135
Golden Bosun, The, Christmas Island 92
Golden Orb Cafe, Norfolk Island 206
Goolwa SA 68, 115
Goompi Trail, North Stradbroke Island Qld 80
Gorge Walk, North Stradbroke Island Qld 79
Grand Mercure Apartments, Magnetic Island Qld 58
Granite Island SA 68-9, 115
Grassy, King Island Tas. 218, 221
Grassy Club, Grassy, King Island Tas. 221
Grassy Harbour, King Island Tas. 224
Great Barrier Reef Qld 2-31, 40-7, 56-61, 71-5, 116-23, 126-57
Great Barrier Reef Marine Park 56, 72, 157
Great Barrier Reef Safaris, Bedarra Island Qld 29, 30
Great Keppel Island/Wop-pa Qld 71-5
Great Keppel Island Hideaway Qld 72
Great Keppel Watersports Qld 75
Great Oyster Bay Tas. 193
Green Fort Lookout, Thursday Island Qld 185
Greta Beach, Christmas Island 94
Grotto, The, Christmas Island 94
Grove Boutique and Cafe, Hayman Island Qld 13
Guided Jet Ski Adventure, Hayman Island Qld 13
Gunggandji People 140, 148
Gutter Bar, Kooringal, Moreton Island Qld 64
Gwandalan Spa, Orpheus Island Qld 21

H
Hamilton & Dune, Kangaroo Island SA 110
Hamilton Island, Whitsundays Qld 9, 25, 40-7
Hamilton Island Airport Qld 10, 43
Hamilton Island Beach Sports Hut Qld 46
Hamilton Island Wildlife Cafe Qld 45
Hamilton Island Wildlife Park Qld 46
Hamilton Island's Journey to the Heart Qld 46
Hammond Island Qld 185
Hanson Bay Wildlife Sanctuary, Kangaroo Island SA 115
Hartog Explorer WA 86
Haven, The (Scraggy Point), Hinchinbrook Island Qld 118
Haven Track, Hinchinbrook Island Qld 121
Hawkings Point, Magnetic Island Qld 60
Hayman Beach House, Hayman Island Qld 10
Hayman Island, Whitsundays Qld 9-15
Hazards Beach Tas. 195
Heart Reef, Whitsundays Qld 25, 46, 157
Hemingway's Brewery, Cairns Qld 154
Hernandia Bay, Bedarra Island Qld 29
Heron Island Qld 126-31
Heron Island Shop, Heron Island Qld 129
Heron Islander Ferry Qld 128
Hervey Bay Qld 101, 102, 105, 106, 132, 135
Hervey Bay Regional Gallery Qld 106
Hideaway Bay, Hamilton Island Qld 46
Hideaway Bar & Bistro, Great Keppel Island Qld 72
High Island Qld 140, 141
Hill Inlet, Whitsunday Island Qld 157
Hinchinbrook Island/ Munamudanamy Qld 21-2, 116-21
Hinchinbrook Island Cruises Qld 118
Hinchinbrook Island NP Qld 119

Hinchinbrook Visitor Information Centre, Ingham Qld 118, 121
Hinkler Hall of Aviation, Bundaberg Qld 138
Hobart Tas. 221, 236
Home Island, Cocos (Keeling) Islands 160, 162, 163, 167
Home Island Tour, Cocos (Keeling) Islands 167
Home of the Manta Ray (Lady Elliot Island) Qld 132-9
Homestead Bay, Dirk Hartog Island WA 87
Homestead Camping Grounds, Dirk Hartog Island WA 86-7
Homestead Restaurant, The, Norfolk Island 205, 206
Honeymoon Bay, Moreton Island Qld 67
Honeymoon Bay Tas. 195
Hook Island Qld 13, 157
Horn Island/Ngurupai Qld 182, 185
Horseshoe Bay, Magnetic Island Qld 58-9
Hotel Bruny, Bruny Island Tas. 235
Hotel Phillip Island, Cowes, Phillip Island Vic. 228
Hotel Rottnest WA 53
House, The, Lizard Island Qld 5
Howard Smith Wharves, Brisbane Qld 80
Hugh's Dale Waterfall, Christmas Island 94
Humpy Island Qld 72
Hundred Acre Hideaway Retreat, Bruny Island Tas. 235
Hundred Acres Reserve, Norfolk Island 209

I
I Am Straddie Arts Trail, North Stradbroke Island Qld 80
I-Spy Semi-Submersible tour, Heron Island Qld 131
IGA supermarket, Penneshaw, Kangaroo Island SA 112
IGA supermarket, Whitemark, Flinders Island Tas. 214
Indian Ocean Experiences 94, 97, 167
Indian Ocean Territories 91-7, 160-7
Inscription, The, Dirk Hartog Island WA 87, 88
Inskip Point Qld 101, 102
Intercontinental Hayman Island Resort Qld 10
Interstate Hotel Bistro, Whitemark, Flinders Island Tas. 213
Island Arts Gallery, Dunwich, North Stradbroke Island Qld 80
Island Beehive, Kangaroo Island SA 115
Island Breeze Motel, Currie, King Island Tas. 221
Island Brunch Cafe, Home Island, Cocos (Keeling) Islands 163
Island Burger, Magnetic Island Qld 59
Island Cafe, The, Granite Island SA 68
Island Eco Trail Walk, Thevenard Island WA 171
Island Explorer Boat, Mackerel Islands WA 171
Island House, Lord Howe Island NSW 201
Island Life Adventures, Dirk Hartog Island WA 87
Island Sustainability Tour, Thevenard Island WA 173
Island Vibe festival, North Stradbroke Island Qld 80
Islander Estate, The, Kangaroo Island SA 112
Isle Hire, Magnetic Island Qld 58
Isola Bar E Cibo, Rottnest Island WA 55
Isola Di Capri, Cowes, Phillip Island Vic. 228

J
Jilamara Arts & Crafts Association, Milikapiti, Melville Island NT 36
Jilamara Fine Art Experience, Milikapiti, Melville Island NT 36
Junior Marine Biologist Program, Fitzroy Island Qld 154
Junior Rangers Program, Heron Island Qld 131

K
Kaiki Walking Trail, Granite Island SA 68
Kangaroo Island SA 109-15
Kangaroo Island Brewery SA 112
Kangaroo Island Seafront Holiday Park SA 112
Kangaroo Island Seafront Hotel SA 112
Kangaroo Island Spirits SA 112
Kangaroo Island Wildlife Park SA 112
Kangaroo Island Wool SA 115
Kaurareg People 182
Kazu Pearls, Friday Island Qld 182, 185
Keppel Bay Islands NP Qld 72
Keppel Dive Qld 72
Keppel Explorer Qld 72
Keppel Konnections Qld 72
Kettering Tas. 232, 235
K'gari Qld 101-7
K'gari Beach Resort Qld 102, 105
K'gari Explorer Tours Qld 105
KI Wilderness Retreat, Kangaroo Island SA 110
Kids Bubblemaker Diving, Fitzroy Island Qld 154
Killecrankie, Flinders Island Tas. 213
Killecrankie Bay, Flinders Island Tas. 214
King Island Tas. 218-25
King Island Airlines Tas./Vic. 218, 221
King Island Bakehouse, Currie Tas. 221
King Island Brewhouse, Pegarah Tas. 222
King Island Butchery, Currie Tas. 221
King Island Car Rentals Tas. 221
King Island Cultural Centre, Currie Tas. 222
King Island Dairy, Loorana Tas. 222
King Island Distillery, Currie Tas. 222
King Island Golf Open Tas. 224
King Island Historical Museum, Currie Tas. 222
King Island Hotel, Currie, King Island Tas. 221
King Island Show Tas. 224
King Island Tours Tas. 222
Kingfisher Bay Ferry Service Qld 102
Kingfisher Bay Resort, K'gari Qld 102, 105, 106
Kings Park, Perth WA 55
Kingscote, Kangaroo Island SA 110, 112
Kingston UNESCO World Heritage Site, Norfolk Island 209
Kite Beach, West Island, Cocos (Keeling) Islands 164
Knife Island NT 180
Koala Conservation Centre, Rhyll, Phillip Island Vic. 228
Koala Park, Selina, Magnetic Island Qld 60
koalas xviii, 56, 60, 79, 115, 227, 228
Kuld Creamery, The Basin, Rottnest Island WA 55
kunanyi/Mount Wellington Tas. 236
Kurramine Boat Hire, Mission Beach Qld 122

L
Labillardiere Peninsula Walk, South Bruny Tas. 235
Lady Barron, Flinders Island Tas. 210, 212, 214
Lady Elliot Island Qld 132-9
Lady Elliot Island Eco Resort Qld 132, 135
Lady Musgrave Experience Qld 142, 145-7
Lady Musgrave HQ Pontoon Qld 142, 145, 147
Lady Musgrave Island Qld 142-7
Lagoon, The, Lady Elliot Island Qld 136
Lagoon Bar, Lady Elliot Island Qld 136
Lagoon Beach, Lord Howe Island NSW 202
Lagoon Deck, Lady Elliot Island Qld 136
Lake McKenzie, K'gari Qld 101, 105
Lake Wabby, K'gari Qld 105
Langford Island Qld 13
Latitude Jewellers, Geraldton WA 98
Launceston Tas. 210, 212, 218, 221
Le C.L.A., Christmas Island 92
Lighthouse, Fitzroy Island Qld 152
Lighthouse, Great Keppel Island Qld 75
Lillies Beach, Flinders Island Tas. 214
Lily Beach, Christmas Island 94
Litchfield NP NT 36
Little Blue Lake Tas. 193
Little Crystal Creek, Townsville Qld 60
Little Porky Beach, King Island Tas. 222

Little Pumpkin Island Qld 178
Little Sahara, Kangaroo Island SA 115
Little Salmon Bay, Rottnest Island WA 55
Lizard Island/Dyiigurra Qld 2-6
Lizard Island Research Station Qld 6
Lizard Island Resort Qld 5
Loaves Bakery, Point Lookout, North Stradbroke Island Qld 79
Lone Pine, Norfolk Island 209
Long Island, Whitsundays Qld 25
Lord Howe Environmental Tours NSW 202
Lord Howe Island NSW 198-203
Lord Howe Island Brewery NSW 201
Lord Howe Island Golf Club NSW 202
Lost Cowe, The, Cowes, Phillip Island Vic. 228
Love Lord Howe, Lord Howe Island NSW 201
Loyalty Beach Campground, Cape York Qld 186
Lucinda Qld 116, 118
Lucky Ho, Christmas Island 92
Luxury Launch transfer, Hayman Island Qld 10

M

Mabel Island Qld 140
McDonald Charter Boats NT 185
McKenzie's On 75, K'gari Qld 105
Mackerel Islands WA 168-73
McLaren Vale SA 115
McRaes Isthmus, Maria Island Tas. 193
Macushla to Cape Richards Track, Hinchinbrook Island Qld 121
Made on Minjerribah, Dunwich, North Stradbroke Island Qld 80
Maggie Comprehensive, Magnetic Island Qld 60
Maggie Discovery Tour with Aquascene, Magnetic Island Qld 60
Maggie Island Bubble Tea, Magnetic Island Qld 59
Magnetic Island/Yunbenun Qld 56-9
Magnetic Island Brewery, Magnetic Island Qld 59
Magnetic Island Ferries Qld 58
Maheno (shipwreck), K'gari Qld 101, 105, 106
Main Beach, North Stradbroke Island Qld 79
Makai Cafe, Thursday Island Qld 185
Malgana People 84
Mamma Roma, Picnic Bay, Magnetic Island Qld 59
Manbarra People 16
Mandingalby Yidinji People 140
Manta Bommie, North Stradbroke Island Qld 79
Manta Lodge, Adder Point, North Stradbroke Island Qld 80
manta rays 132, 146
Maria Island Tas. 189-93
Maria Island Penitentiary Tas. 190-2
Maria Island Tours Tas. 192
Maria Island Walk Tas. 193
Marina Cafe & Bar, Cockatoo Island NSW 217
Marina Tavern, Hamilton Island Qld 45
Marine Conservation Program, Fitzroy Island Qld 154
Marine Discovery Cruise, Moreton Island Qld 67
Marlin Bar, Lizard Island Qld 5
Marlin Bar Tavern, Horseshoe Bay, Magnetic Island Qld 59
Marlin Beachfront Smiths Beach, Phillip Island Vic. 228
Mars Bluff, Bruny Island Tas. 235
Martha Lavinia Beach, King Island Tas. 222
Martin Point, Christmas Island 94
Mata Ray Fraser Island Barge, K'gari Qld 102
Melbourne/Naarm Vic. 210, 212, 218, 221, 227
Melville Island NT 33, 36
Mermaid Cove, Lizard Island Qld 6
Mezz on Rotto, The, Rottnest Island WA 55
MI Rentals, Magnetic Island Qld 58
Mille Mae's Pantry, Penneshaw, Kangaroo Island SA 112
Mindil Beach Sunset Markets, Darwin NT 36
Minjerribah Camping, North Stradbroke Island Qld 79, 80
Mirapool Lagoon, Moreton Island Qld 67
Mission Beach Qld 26, 31, 122
Mission Beach Boat Hire Qld 122
Monkey Mia WA 88
Monkey Point, Great Keppel Island Qld 72
Moreton Bay Fig Trees, Norfolk Island 209
Moreton Island/Mulgumpin Qld 63-7
Moreton Island Adventures Qld 64
Mornington Peninsula Vic. 228
Mount Archer, Rockhampton Qld 75
Mount Gower, Lord Howe Island NSW 198, 202
Mount Killecrankie, Flinders Island Tas. 214
Mount Kootaloo, Dunk Island Qld 123
Mount Lidgbird, Lord Howe Island NSW 198
Mount Maria, Maria Island Tas. 193
Mount Pitt, Norfolk Island 209
Mount Sonder, Townsville Qld 60
Mount Strzelecki, Flinders Island Tas. 214
Mount Tempest, Moreton Island Qld 67
Mountain Seas Lodge, Flinders Island Tas. 213
Muggy Muggy Beach, Dunk Island Qld 123
Mulgrave River Qld 140
Mulgumpin Camping, Moreton Island Qld 64, 67
Mulligan Falls, Hinchinbrook Island Qld 119, 121
Muluwurri Museum, Milikapiti, Melville Island NT 36
Mungalla Station, Ingham Qld 121
Munupi Art, Wurruminyanga, Bathurst Island NT 35
Museum of Underwater Art (MOUA), Townsville Qld 21, 60
Myroo Adventures Qld 122

N

Nation West Aviation WA 98
Nautilus, Killecrankie, Flinders Island Tas. 213
Nautilus Aviation Qld 18
Neck, The, Bruny Island Tas. 236
Ned's Beach, Lord Howe Island NSW 202
Nelly Bay, Magnetic Island Qld 58, 59
Nest, The, Palana, Flinders Island Tas. 214
Ngaro People 157
Ngugi People 63
Ningaloo Aviation WA 171
Ningaloo Reef WA 173
Nobbies Ocean Discovery, Phillip Island Vic. 231
Nomads Magnetic Island Qld 59
Noodles on the Beach, Magnetic Island Qld 59
Norfolk Golf Club, Norfolk Island 209
Norfolk Island 205-9
Norfolk Island Brewing 205, 206
Norfolk Island Fish Fry 206
Norfolk Island Visitors Information Centre 209
Normanby Island Qld 140, 141
North East River, Flinders Island Tas. 213, 214
North Keppel Island Qld 72
North Queensland Island Charters Qld 118
North Stradbroke Island/Minjerribah Qld 76-81
North-West WA 168-73
NRMA Phillip Island Beachfront Holiday Park, Phillip Island Vic. 228
Nudey Beach, Fitzroy Island Qld 152

O

Oasis Mexican Cantina, Point Lookout, North Stradbroke Island Qld 79
Ocean Adventure Phillip Island Vic. 231
Ocean Dunes, Currie, King Island Tas. 222
Ocean Rafting Qld 157
Ocean Reach Brewing, Cowes, Phillip Island Vic. 228
Ocean Villa, Dirk Hartog Island WA 86, 87
Oceanic Gelati, North Stradbroke Island Qld 79
Old Jetty Lookout, Bedarra Island Qld 31
Old Settlement Beach, Lord Howe Island NSW 202
Olive Cafe, Norfolk Island 206

One KI, Kangaroo Island SA 110
One Tree Hill, Hamilton Island Qld 46
Onslow Beach Resort WA 173
Onslow WA 168, 171, 173
Orientation Tour, Norfolk Island 209
Orpheus Island/Goolboddi, Townsville Qld 16–23
Orpheus Island Lodge Qld 19
Orpheus Island NP Qld 16
Orpheus Island Research Station Qld 22
Outdoor Cinema, Poon San, Christmas Island 97
Oyster Bay Tas. 195

P
Pacific Restaurant, Hayman Island Qld 10
packing guide xiv–xv
PADI Dive Courses, Heron Island Qld 129
Painted Cliffs, Maria Island Tas. 193
Pajinka Qld 185, 186
Palana, Flinders Island Tas. 212, 213
Palana Beach, Flinders Island Tas. 214
Palana Beach House, Flinders Island Tas. 214
Palawa People 189, 195
Palm Bungalows, Hamilton Island Qld 43
Palm Cove Qld 6
Palm Island Qld 16
Paluma Range NP Qld 121
Parker Point, Rottnest Island WA 55
Parndana, Kangaroo Island SA 110
Passage Peak Lookout, Hamilton Island Qld 46
Patakijiyali Museum, Wurruminyanga, Bathurst Island NT 34–5
Patriarch Wildlife Sanctuary, Flinders Island Tas. 214
Pavilions of Bedarra, Bedarra Island Qld 30
Pedal & Flipper Hire, Rottnest Island WA 50
Peddells Bus Tour Qld 185
Peddells Ferry Qld 185
Pelorus Island Qld 19
Penguin Discovery Centre, Phillip Island Vic. 231
Penguin Parade, Phillip Island Vic. 231
penguins 68, 224, 227, 231, 236
Penneshaw, Kangaroo Island SA 110
Penneshaw Beach Bar, Kangaroo Island SA 112
Pennicott Wilderness Journeys Tas. 236
Peppers Blue on Blue Resort, Magnetic Island Qld 58
Perth/Boorloo WA 49, 92, 160, 162, 167, 171
Phillip Island, Norfolk Island 209
Phillip Island/Millowl Vic. 227–31
Phillip Island Apartments, Cowes Vic. 228
Phillip Island Brewing Co., Cowes Vic. 228
Phillip Island Chocolate Factory, Newhaven Vic. 228
Phillip Island Grand Prix Circuit Vic. 231
Phillip Island Strawberries, Cowes Vic. 228
Phillip Island Winery, Ventnor Vic. 228
Picnic Bay, Magnetic Island Qld 59
Picnic Bay Hotel, Magnetic Island Qld 59
Picnic Island Tas. 195
Pilbara coast WA 168–73
Pilgrim Adventures, Magnetic Island Qld 60
Pilgrim Sailing, Magnetic Island Qld 60
Pine Trees, Lord Howe Island NSW 201
Pinetree Tours, Norfolk Island 209
Pinky's Beach, Rottnest Island WA 50–3
Pinky's Rottnest Island WA 55
Pinnacle Cliffs, K'gari Qld 106
Pinnacles, The at Cape Woolamai, Phillip Island Vic. 228
Pino's Trattoria, Cowes, Phillip Island Vic. 228
Pisonia Forests, Lady Elliot Island Qld 138
Pizzeria and Gelato Bar, Hamilton Island Qld 45
Point Lookout (Mooloomba), North Stradbroke Island Qld 76, 79
Pool Bar, Fitzroy Island Qld 152
Poon San, Christmas Island 92, 97
Popeyes Takeaway, Hamilton Island Qld 45
Port Douglas Qld 6
Port Elliot SA 68, 115
Port Willunga SA 115
Prawn Shack, North Stradbroke Island Qld 79
Prickly Pear Summer Cantina, Kingscote, Kangaroo Island SA 112
Prince of Wales Island Qld 185
Prinke Eco Store, Norfolk Island 206
Pulu Maraya, Cocos (Keeling) Islands 164
Pumpkin Island Qld 174–9
Pumpkin Xpress (ferry) Qld 177
Puppies Point, Norfolk Island 205
Purple Hen Winery, Rhyll, Phillip Island Vic. 228
Purple Swamphen, The, Whitemark, Flinders Island Tas. 214
Putney Beach, Great Keppel Island Qld 72

Q
QAGOMA, Brisbane Qld 67
Qantas 128, 185, 205, 206
QantasLink 110, 201
qualia, Hamilton Island Qld 43
Quandamooka Country/People 63, 76, 80
quokka xviii, 49, 55
Quokka Coaches Island Explorer, Rottnest Island WA 50, 55

R
Rabbit Island, Lord Howe Island NSW 202
Ratuwati Yinjara (Two Islands) NT 33
Red Cat Adventures Qld 157
red crab migration, Christmas Island xix, 91
Reef Education Centre, Lady Elliot Island Qld 138
Reef View Hotel, Hamilton Island Qld 43
Remarkable Rocks, Kangaroo Island SA 115
Return to 1616 Nature Conservation Program, Dirk Hartog Island WA 87, 88
REX 218, 221
Richardsons Beach Tas. 195
Riedle Bay, Maria Island Tas. 193
Ripples 'N' Tonic, Phillip Island Vic. 229
Rockhampton Qld 75, 177
Rockhampton Zoo Qld 75
Romano's, Hamilton Island Qld 45
Rottnest Air-Taxi WA 50
Rottnest Bakery, Rottnest Island WA 53
Rottnest Express WA 53
Rottnest Island/Wadjemup WA 49–55
Rottnest Island Voluntary Guides WA 55
Round Island Qld 140
Rufus King Seafood, Amity Point, North Stradbroke Island Qld 79
Rumah Baru Jetty, West Island, Cocos (Keeling) Islands 164
Russell Island Qld 140, 141
Rusty's Markets, Cairns Qld 154

S
Sailing Whitsundays Qld 157
Sails, Hamilton Island Qld 45
Sails on Horseshoe, Magnetic Island Qld 59
Salamanca Market, Hobart Tas. 236
Salt Water Murris, Dunwich, North Stradbroke Island Qld 80
Salt Water Restaurant, Lizard Island Qld 5
Saltmakers by the Sea, West Island, Cocos (Keeling) Islands 163
Saltwater, Magnetic Island Qld 59
Saltwater Phillip Island, Newhaven Vic. 228
Salty's Cafe, West Island, Cocos (Keeling) Islands 163
Samphire Rottnest WA 53
San Remo Vic. 231
San Remo Fisherman's Co-op Vic. 231
Sand & Wood, Kingfisher Bay Resort, K'gari Qld 102
Sand Bar & Bistro, The, Kingfisher Bay Resort, K'gari Qld 105

Sandstone to Steel Tour, Cockatoo Island NSW 217
Satellite Island Summer House, Bruny Island Tas. 235
Sault Phillip Island, Phillip Island Vic. 228
Sawyers Beach, Flinders Island Tas. 214
Scally Wags Cafe, Magnetic Island Qld 59
Scenic Discovery Flight, Hayman Island Qld 13
Scout Park, West Island, Cocos (Keeling) Islands 164
Sea Explorer Sundet Cruise, K'gari Qld 106
Sea Kayak Adventures, Hayman Island Qld 13
sea lions/fur seals xviii, 115, 227, 231
Sea Lord Howe, Lord Howe Island NSW 202
Seafront Restaurant, Home Island, Cocos (Keeling) Islands 163
Seal Bay Conservation Park, Kangaroo Island SA 115
Seal Rocks, King Island Tas. 222
Sealevel 21, Amity Point, North Stradbroke Island Qld 79
SeaLink 58, 60, 110, 112, 157, 180
SeaLink Bruny Island 235
SeaLink NT 34, 35
SeaLink Rottnest Island 53
SeaLink South East Queensland 79
Seaview Fish & Chips, Poon San, Christmas Island 92
Second Valley SA 115
Seisia Qld 182, 185
Selina Magnetic Island Qld 59
Sellick's Beach SA 115
Semi-submersible Coral Reef Viewing, Hayman Island Qld 13
Seventy Five Mile Beach, K'gari Qld 102, 103, 105, 106
Shack, The, West Island, Cocos (Keeling) Islands 164
Shark Bay WA 84, 88
Shark Bay Airport WA 86
Shark Bay Marine Park WA 87, 88
Shark Fin Bay, Fitzroy Island Qld 152
Sharp Airlines Tas./Vic. 210, 212, 218, 221

Shearwater Restaurant, Heron Island Qld 127
Shearwater Scenic Villas, Norfolk Island 206
Sheepwash Bay, South Bruny Tas. 235
Shelving Beach, Great Keppel Island Qld 72
Shine Aviation WA 98
Shoal Bay, Maria Island Tas. 193
Shore House, Loorana, King Island Tas. 221
Shute Harbour Qld 25
Signal Point, Lord Howe Island NSW 198
Skydive, Airle Beach Qld 45
SkyRail, Kuranda Qld 6
Somerset Apartments, Lord Howe Island NSW 201
South Bruny NP Tas. 232, 235
South East Head, Hamilton Island Qld 46
South Gorge, North Stradbroke Island Qld 79
South Lookout, Bedarra Island Qld 31
South Macushla, Hinchinbrook Island Qld 118
South Molle Island Qld 157
South Shepherd Bay, Hinchinbrook Island Qld 121
South Zoe Bay, Hinchinbrook Island Qld 118
Southern Great Barrier Reef Qld 126-31, 132-9, 142-7
Southern Ocean Lodge, Kangaroo Island SA 110
Southern Queensland Qld 63-7, 76-81
Spa wumurdaylin, Hamilton Island Qld 46
Spot, The, West Island, Cocos (Keeling) Islands 164
Steep Point WA 84, 86
Stokes Bay, Kangaroo Island SA 115
Store, The, Ventnor, Phillip Island Vic. 228
Straddie Brewing, Dunwich, North Stradbroke Island Qld 79
Straddie Kingfisher Tours, North Stradbroke Island Qld 80
Straddie Woodfire Pizza, Cylinder Beach, North Stradbroke Island Qld 79
Straight Down BBQ, Magnetic Island Qld 59

Strait Experience NT 185, 186
Streets Beach, Brisbane Qld 67
Strzelecki NP, Flinders Island Tas. 214
Sula Servery, Cocos (Keeling) Islands 167
Summit Lookout, Fitzroy Island Qld 152
Sunbus Bus Service, Magnetic Island Qld 58
Sundowner Cruise, Airlie Beach Qld 45
Sunset 4WD Bus Tour, Thevenard Island WA 173
Sunset Bar, Kingfisher Bay Resort, K'gari Qld 105
Sunset Bar & Grill, Lord Howe Island NSW 201
Sunset Cruise, Hayman Island Qld 15
Sunset Lounge, Pumpkin Island Qld 178
Sunset Peak Hike, Hayman Island Qld 15
Swan River Seaplanes WA 50
Swan River wineries WA 55
Sweet Escape Yacht Charters, K'gari Qld 102
Swell Lodge, Christmas Island 92
Sydney NSW 198, 201, 205, 206, 217

T
TAKO, Hamilton Island Qld 45
Tangalooma Island Resort, Moreton Island Qld 63, 64
Tangalooma Island Resort Passenger Ferry Qld 64
Tangalooma Wrecks, Moreton Island Qld 63, 64, 67
Territory Day Park, Christmas Island 94
The Basin, Rottnest Island WA 55
The Blowholes, Christmas Island 94
The Boathouse, Currie, King Island Tas. 221
The Crayshack, Killecrankie, Flinders Island Tas. 213
The Crooked Post, Lord Howe Island NSW 201
The Flinders Wharf, Flinders Island Tas. 213
The Golden Bosun, Christmas Island 92
The Grotto, Christmas Island 94

The Haven (Scraggy Point), Hinchinbrook Island Qld 118
The Homestead Restaurant, Norfolk Island 205, 206
The House, Lizard Island Qld 5
The Inscription, Dirk Hartog Island WA 87, 88
The Island Cafe, Granite Island SA 68
The Islander Estate, Kangaroo Island SA 112
The Koala Park, Selina, Magnetic Island Qld 60
The Lagoon, Lady Elliot Island Qld 136
The Lost Cowe, Cowes, Phillip Island Vic. 228
The Mezz on Rotto, Rottnest Island WA 55
The Neck, Bruny Island Tas. 236
The Nest, Palana, Flinders Island Tas. 214
The Pinnacles at Cape Woolamai, Phillip Island Vic. 228
The Purple Swamphen, Whitemark Flinders Island Tas. 214
The Sand Bar & Bistro, Kingfisher Bay Resort K'gari Qld 105
The Shack, West Island, Cocos (Keeling) Islands 164
The Spot, West Island, Cocos (Keeling) Islands 164
The Store, Ventnor, Phillip Island Vic. 228
The Ville, Townsville Qld 22, 60
The Waterboy Cafe, Cowes, Phillip Island Vic. 228
The Yacht Club, West Island, Cocos (Keeling) Islands 164
Thevenard Island WA 168, 171, 173
Thompson's Store, Lord Howe Island NSW 201
Thomson Bay, Rottnest Island WA 50, 53
Thorsborne Trail, Hinchinbrook Island Qld 116, 119
Thursday Island/Waiben Qld 182, 185
Thursday Island Cemetery Qld 185
Tintoela Homestead & Cottages, Norfolk Island 206
Tiny Palm Coffee Van, Magnetic Island Qld 59

Tiwi By Design, Wurruminyanga, Bathurst Island NT 34
Tiwi Designs, Wurruminyanga, Bathurst Island NT 35
Tiwi Island Retreat, Bathurst Island NT 34, 36
Tiwi Islands NT 33-7
Tiwi Islands Adventures NT 34
Tiwi Islands Day Tour NT 35
Tiwi People 33
Tondoon Botanic Gardens, Gladstone Qld 131
Top End NT 33-7
Top End Hell Pub Crawl NT 180
Torres Hotel, Thursday Island Qld 185
Torres Strait Heritage Museum and Art Gallery, Horn Island Qld 185
Torres Strait Heritage Tours Qld 185
Torres Strait Islands Qld 182-7
Townsville Qld 16, 19, 22, 56, 60
Tracks Tavern, Drumsite, Christmas Island 92
Trannies Beach, West Island, Cocos (Keeling) Islands 164
Triabunna Tas. 189, 190
Tropical North Queensland Qld 2-7, 140-1, 148-55, 182-7
Tropika Restaurant, West Island, Cocos (Keeling) Islands 163
Trouser Point Beach, Flinders Island Tas. 210, 213, 214
Truganini Memorial, The Neck, Bruny Island Tas. 236
Turquoise Bay WA 173
Turtle Bay, Dirk Hartog Island WA 88
Turtle Bay Lookout, Bedarra Island Qld 31
Turtle Beach, Lizard Island Qld 6
Turtle Rehabilitation Centre, Fitzroy Island Qld 152
turtles xviii, 79, 126, 131, 142, 146, 147, 148, 173, 174
Twilight Bay Sunset Cruise, Hervey Bay Qld 106
Twin Falls, Shelburne Qld 186

U
Unavale Vineyard, Flinders Island Tas. 214
Uncle Frankies Cafe, Thursday Island Qld 185
UNESCO World Heritage sites/areas 6, 84, 116, 192, 198, 205, 209, 217
University of Queensland Research Station, Heron Island Qld 131
Upper Settlement Beach, Lord Howe Island NSW 202
Urangan Pier, Hervey Bay Qld 106

V
V/Line Coach Service Vic. 228
Victor Harbor SA 68, 115
View Dining, Currie, King Island Tas. 221
Village Store, K'gari Qld 105
Ville, The, Townsville Qld 22, 60
Virgin Australia 91, 92, 128, 160, 162, 171
Visit Flinders Island Tas. 214
Vivonne Bay, Kangaroo Island SA 109, 110, 115
Vivonne Bay General Store, Kangaroo Island SA 112

W
Waikiki Beach Front at Smiths, Phillip Island Vic. 228
Walkers Lookout, Flinders Island Tas. 214
Wallaman Falls, Cardwell Qld 121
Wallumedegal People 217
Wangal People 217
Wasaga, Horn Island Qld 182
Waterboy Cafe, The, Cowes, Phillip Island Vic. 228
Waterline Restaurant, Yeppoon Qld 178
Wathumba Creek, K'gari Qld 106
Watson's Bay, Lizard Island Qld 6
Waves Apartments, Cowes, Phillip Island Vic. 228
Wedgerock Bay, Bedarra Island Qld 29
Welcome Bay, Fitzroy Island Qld 148, 151
Wellness & Yoga Retret, Lady Mulgrave Island Qld 147
West Island, Cocos (Keeling) Islands 160, 162, 163, 164
West Island Supermarket, Cocos (Keeling) Islands 163
Western KI Caravan Park, Kangaroo Island SA 112
Western Port Ferries Vic. 228
Wet 'N' Dry Adventures, Christmas Island 97
Whadjuk Noongar People 49, 55
Whalebone Brewing, Exmouth WA 173
whales xviii, 67, 68, 76, 79, 106, 147, 173
What's Up Cairns, Dunk Island Qld 123
What's Up Cairns, Fitzroy Island Qld 152
Wheel of Brisbane, Brisbane Qld 67
Wheelhouse Deck, Moreton Island Qld 64
Whitehaven Beach, Whitsunday Island Qld 13, 25, 46, 157
Whitehaven Beach Experience, Whitsundays Qld 13
Whitehaven Indulgence Helicopter Experience, Whitsundays Qld 13
Whitemark, Flinders Island Tas. 212, 213, 214
Whitsunday Apartments, Hamilton Island Qld 43
Whitsunday Coast/Proserpine Airport Qld 43
Whitsunday Island Qld 157
Whitsunday Island NP Qld 157
Whitsundays Jet Ski Tour Qld 13
Whitsundays Qld 9-15, 25, 40-6, 157
Wild Food Farm and Cafe, Rhyll, Phillip Island Vic. 228
Wild Harvest, Grassy, King Island Tas. 221
Wild Hinchinbrook Adventures, Hinchinbrook Island Qld 119
Wildlife Coast Cruises, Phillip Island Vic. 228-31
Wilson Island Qld 12
Wilson's Hire Service, Lord Howe Island NSW 201
Winds of Zenadth Cultural Festival, Thursday Island Qld 186
Wineglass Bay Lookout Tas. 193, 195
Wombat Lodge, Flinders Island Tas. 213
wombats xvii, 189, 190, 210
Wonderland by Night, Norfolk Island 209
Wooli Tavern, Cape Woolamai, Phillip Island Vic. 228
Woppaburra People 71
World War II Darwin Tunnels, Darwin NT 36
Wulgurukaba People 56
Wurruminyanga, Bathurst Island NT 34, 35

Y
Yacht Club, The, West Island, Cocos (Keeling) Islands 164
Yallock-Balluk People 229
Yardie Creek WA 173
Yellow Beach, Flinders Island Tas. 213, 214
Yeppoon Qld 174, 177, 178

Z
Zoe Falls, Hinchinbrook Island Qld 116, 118, 119-21

ACKNOWLEDGEMENTS

The biggest thank you, as always, goes to my husband Thom Shaw. Thank you for believing in me and supporting me, and always figuring out how we can make things work when I suggest huge ideas. Thank you for responding with 'we can do that' when I called you up to tell you I had a great and terrible idea for a second book, when I was even nervous about the magnitude of the idea myself - having just had a baby. Thank you for flying across the country with me countless times, driving us between destinations when we've needed to, carrying a thousand bags for us, and generally just going with the flow on all of this year's adventures. It's been a massive undertaking and I absolutely could not have done any of it without you.

To my daughter, Macey Isla, an island baby in name and spirit. You are such a phenomenal traveller, I am simply so proud of you. From napping on sand islands, to trying any types of food you've been given, exploring and swimming and loving every minute of your life on the islands, you exceeded every expectation we had of travelling with a baby and then a toddler. Your happy little persona made travelling for this book easy, and I will be forever grateful for being able to take you on all these adventures with us.

Thank you to my parents, Frances and Mark Totney, for your endless love and support. Thank you for jumping at the chance to come to any island Thom couldn't make it to. Thank you for days of looking after Macey, so I could write and organise trips. Thank you for travelling with us when we've needed extra hands and even sharing loyalty points with us when we've needed extra flights. Thank you for every little thing you have done to help me make this book a reality, you're the best.

Thank you to each and every reader who purchased this book, and my last, *Ultimate Weekends: Australia*. Being able to make travel writing my job, alongside embarking on the journey of motherhood and being with my daughter every day is a real dream come true, and I wouldn't have been able to continue without everyone who bought a copy of my book. Thank you, from the bottom of my heart.

And thank you to everyone who worked on this book with me to bring it to life. Publisher Melissa Kayser for approving my idea for a second time. My editing team, Alice Barker, Amanda Louey and Megan Cuthbert. And all the people who worked behind the scenes on maps, design and typesetting - Emily Maffei, Andy Warren and Susanne Geppert.

ABOUT THE AUTHOR

Emma Shaw is an Australian travel writer and photographer, based in Melbourne. She spent 12 months island hopping around Australia with her husband Thom and daughter Macey, who was one at the time, exploring and comparing the very best Aussie islands to bring this book to life. When their family isn't island hopping, you can often spot them travelling on the road in their vintage pink caravan.

This is Emma's second book in Hardie Grant Explore's Ultimate series, following *Ultimate Weekends: Australia* (published in 2021), where she shares her travels around Australia, discovering the most beautiful, unique and exciting destinations and experiences that Australia has to offer, perfect for a weekend getaway.

Emma has contributed to publications including Holidays with Kids, Caravan & Camping with Kids and Caravanning Australia, and is also a member of the Australian Society of Travel Writers.

You can find more of her and her family's adventures on socials @exploreshaw and on her travel blog exploreshaw.com.

Above Huge thank you to my Mum and Dad *Opposite* Emma, Thom and Macey on Heron Island *Overleaf* Main Beach on North Stradbroke Island/Minjerribah

Published in 2024 by Hardie Grant Explore,
an imprint of Hardie Grant Publishing

Hardie Grant Explore (Melbourne)
Wurundjeri Country
Building 1, 658 Church Street
Richmond, Victoria 3121

Hardie Grant Explore (Sydney)
Gadigal Country
Level 7, 45 Jones Street
Ultimo, NSW 2007

www.hardiegrant.com/au/explore

All rights reserved. No part of this publication may be reproduced, stored in a retrieval system or transmitted in any form by any means, electronic, mechanical, photocopying, recording or otherwise, without the prior written permission of the publishers and copyright holders.

The moral rights of the author have been asserted.

Copyright text and photography © Emma Shaw 2024
Copyright concept, maps and design © Hardie Grant Publishing 2024

The maps in this publication incorporate data © Commonwealth of Australia (Geoscience Australia), 2006. Geoscience Australia has not evaluated the data as altered and incorporated within this publication, and therefore gives no warranty regarding accuracy, completeness, currency or suitability for any particular purpose.

Made with Natural Earth. Free vector and raster map data @ naturalearthdata.com.

Image credits: All images © Emma Shaw & Thomas Shaw except pp. 24, 25: Elysian Retreat; pp. 116–118, 121: Katie Purling/Tourism and Events Queensland; p. 120: Jack Schmidt/Tourism Tropical North Queensland; p. 184 (top): Tourism Tropical North Queensland; p. 187: Tourism Tropical North Queensland; pp. 188, 192: Ashley Dobson; p. 190: Stu Gibson/Tourism Tasmania; p. 193: Jamie Douros & Camille Helm/Tourism Tasmania, p. 194: Picnic Island; p. 216 (top): Daniel Tran/Destination NSW, (bottom): Rob Mulally/Cockatoo Island Harbour Trust; pp. 234 (top left), 236: Adam Gibson/Tourism Tasmania; p. 234 (top right): Rob Burnett/Tourism Tasmania; p. 237: Tourism Australia.

 A catalogue record for this book is available from the National Library of Australia

Hardie Grant acknowledges the Traditional Owners of the Country on which we work, the Wurundjeri People of the Kulin Nation and the Gadigal People of the Eora Nation, and recognises their continuing connection to the land, waters and culture. We pay our respects to their Elders past and present.

For all relevant publications, Hardie Grant Explore commissions a First Nations consultant to review relevant content and provide feedback to ensure suitable language and information is included in the final book. Hardie Grant Explore also includes traditional place names and acknowledges Traditional Owners, where possible, in both the text and mapping for their publications.

Traditional place names are included in *palawa kani*, the language of Tasmanian Aboriginal People, with thanks to the Tasmanian Aboriginal Centre.

Ultimate Island Escapes: Australia

ISBN 9781741178821

10 9 8 7 6 5 4 3 2 1

Project editor Amanda Louey
Editor Alice Barker
Proofreader Jenny Varghese
First Nations consultant Jamil Tye, Yorta Yorta
Cartographer Emily Maffei
Design Andy Warren
Typesetting Susanne Geppert
Index Max McMaster
Production manager Simone Wall

Colour reproduction by Megan Ellis and Splitting Image Colour Studio

Printed and bound in China by LEO Paper Products LTD.

 The paper this book is printed on is certified against the Forest Stewardship Council® Standards and other sources. FSC® promotes environmentally responsible, socially beneficial and economically viable management of the world's forests.

Disclaimer: While every care is taken to ensure the accuracy of the data within this product, the owners of the data (including the state, territory and Commonwealth governments of Australia) do not make any representations or warranties about its accuracy, reliability, completeness or suitability for any particular purpose and, to the extent permitted by law, the owners of the data disclaim all responsibility and all liability (including without limitation, liability in negligence) for all expenses, losses, damages (including indirect or consequential damages) and costs which might be incurred as a result of the data being inaccurate or incomplete in any way and for any reason.

Publisher's Disclaimers: The publisher cannot accept responsibility for any errors or omissions. The representation on the maps of any road or track is not necessarily evidence of public right of way. The publisher cannot be held responsible for any injury, loss or damage incurred during travel. It is vital to research any proposed trip thoroughly and seek the advice of relevant state and travel organisations before you leave.

Publisher's Note: Every effort has been made to ensure that the information in this book is accurate at the time of going to press. The publisher welcomes information and suggestions for correction or improvement.